# MODERNISM

## INTRODUCTIONS TO BRITISH LITERATURE AND CULTURE SERIES

*Medieval Literature and Culture*
Andrew Galloway

*Renaissance Literature and Culture*
Lisa Hopkins and Matthew Steggle

*Seventeenth-Century Literature and Culture*
Jim Daems

*Eighteenth-Century Literature and Culture*
Paul Goring

*Victorian Literature and Culture*
Maureen Moran

*Romanticism*
Sharon Ruston

# MODERNISM

*Leigh Wilson*

continuum

**Continuum**

The Tower Building
11 York Road
London SE1 7NX
www.continuumbooks.com

80 Maiden Lane, Suite 704
New York
NY 10038

© Leigh Wilson 2007

First published 2007

All rights reserved. No part of this publication may be reproduced or transmitted in any form or by any means, electronic or mechanical, including photocopying, recording, or any information storage or retrieval system, without prior permission in writing from the publishers.

Leigh Wilson has asserted her right under the Copyright, Designs and Patents Act, 1988, to be identified as Author of this work.

**British Library Cataloguing-in-Publication Data**
A catalogue record for this book is available from the British Library.

ISBN: HB: 978-08264-8560-1
     PB: 978-08264-8561-8

**Library of Congress Cataloging-in-Publication Data**
A catalog record for this book is available from the Library of Congress.

Typeset by YHT Ltd, London

# Contents

# Acknowledgements

'Oread' by H. D. (Hilda Doolittle), from *Collected Poems, 1912–1944*, © 1982 by The Estate of Hilda Doolittle. Reprinted by permission of New Directions Publishing Corp. (US and Canada) and Carcanet Press (UK and Commonwealth).

Excerpts from 'The Second Coming' by W. B. Yeats, reprinted by permission of A. P. Watt on behalf of Michael B. Yeats.

Excerpts from 'Zong Toomb Toomb' by F. T. Marinetti, from *Selected Poems and Related Prose*, selected by Luce Marinetti, Elizabeth R. Napier and Barbara R. Studholme (trans.), © 2002 by Luce Marinetti. Reprinted by permission of Yale University Press.

Excerpts from 'Song of the Bowman Shu' by Ezra Pound, from *Personae*, © 1926 by Ezra Pound. Reprinted by permission of New Directions Publishing Corp. (US and Canada) and Faber and Faber Ltd (UK and Commonwealth).

For Toby, Henry and George

# Introduction

When you put a novel away without having finished it, when you walk past a painting, glancing only long enough to know you don't want to look, or when you come out of a film perplexed and irritated, what is it that those works have failed to give you? Perhaps the characters in the novel have failed to come to life or to provoke your sympathy, perhaps the painting has not made it clear enough what it is a painting *of*, or perhaps the film has lacked a plot and action that make you want to keep watching. Although, of course, your perception of the work's failure may be quite valid – it might just be bad – these criticisms reveal too what we expect from a novel, from a painting, from a film. They suggest that we look for characters we can know and sympathize with, a plot that will pull us along and resolve satisfactorily at the end, and subject matter that will be comprehensible and interesting. In other words, we expect art to conform to the conventions of realism. In expecting this, we are still in some ways very like our fellow readers and viewers from the beginning of the twentieth century. When, like them, we come to modernist works, to T. S. Eliot's *The Waste Land* (1922), to James Joyce's *Ulysses* (1922), to a painting by Pablo Picasso or a film by Jean Cocteau, we can be bored or irritated, or suspicious that the artist is having a joke and that it may be at our expense. We can suspect too, again like many early twentieth-century readers and viewers, that what we are reading or viewing finally lacks talent or artistry.

Why read these books or look at these paintings, then, if to do so seems to bring us the opposite of what we expect from art – not pleasure but pain, not satisfaction but irritation, or even offence? And yet we know that these names – Joyce, Eliot, Picasso – are revered as 'great' artists, giants of twentieth-century culture. How can these two things fit together? Should we just assume that 'great art' is to be revered, rather than understood and enjoyed?

This guide to literary modernism acknowledges the crucial nature of these questions – indeed many of them were asked and struggled with by modernist artists themselves. Through the course of this book we will look at those aspects of late nineteenth- and early twentieth-century culture which formed and shaped modernism, at the forms and shapes modernism took, and at the ways modernist works have been read and understood by literary critics over the last 100 years. In doing so, we will be considering the very questions set out above, and using a number of methods – contextual, formal and theoretical – to suggest why these questions arose, and how writers responded to them.

Of course, these questions cannot be fully answered. Modernist writers asked these questions themselves because, as we shall see in the following chapters, they perceived that the familiar world, the world of Victorian certainties and comfortable Edwardian optimism, was disappearing. In its place, a more changeable, more chaotic, faster world was emerging. Whether modernist writers saw this as something to be welcomed, or as a terrible disaster, they shared a belief that these developments required a change in the way novels, poetry and plays were written and constructed. Previous forms which did attempt to provide answers, to resolve things neatly, were rejected, and replaced by more open, less certain forms.

What has just been said rather assumes that the term 'modernism' itself is an unproblematic description for certain techniques, practices and artists. However, in Anglo-American literary studies, the term was not really used in this way until the 1960s. Since then, not only *what* modernism is, but *when* it was has been a matter of persistent debate for literary critics. While there is a general consensus that the 1920s sees the rise and climax of modernism, this guide focuses in the main on the period 1900–39. This begins rather earlier than some periodizations of modernism, as we look at modernism's precursors and influences, and Chapter 1 gives a view of the cultural and social world from 1900 which produced it. The period covered extends to 1939 in acknowledgement of the significant works produced by modernism during this troubled decade. It is an acknowledgement too that the end of the Second World War saw a profound change toward experimental writing in the British context, and younger writers attempted to shake off the modernist legacy. The exception to this focus is in the area of drama, where innovation in the form only really began to be felt in the British context in the 1950s.

We have dealt briefly with the *when* of modernism, but what about the *who* of modernism? The term modernism has come to cover a vast range of works and practices, in music, architecture, dance, painting and sculpture, as well as in writing. The focus of this book is Anglo-American literary modernism – that is, innovative prose, poetry and drama produced by British writers or by foreign writers writing in English and sometimes based in Britain. However, the fact that a good proportion of these writers originated elsewhere – in the US in the case of Pound and Eliot, in Ireland in the case of Joyce – is an indication of the international nature of modernism and the problems associated with such categorizations. In acknowledgement of this, we will also look at aspects of European modernism, and see how it influenced and intersected with Anglo-American modernism. Indeed, one of modernism's distinguishing features is the way it crossed many conventional boundaries, including boundaries of nation, but also of discipline. So, while our focus is literary, we will also be considering modernism in the other arts, particularly the visual arts, and exploring the mutual influence between them.

As suggested above, historical periodization is always debatable, but the issue has remained alive because the *when* of modernism has significant implications for the *what.* For Virginia Woolf the moment of change occurred 'in or about' December 1910 (Woolf 1986: 113). That month contained both the death of Edward VII, and therefore the end of the Edwardian age and the beginning of the new Georgian, and the opening of the Post-Impressionist Exhibition in London by Roger Fry, artist, critic and central figure in the Bloomsbury Group. The show introduced artworks by Paul Cézanne, Paul Gauguin and Vincent Van Gogh, and provoked a mixture of shocked recoil and guffawing laughter in the majority of viewers. For Woolf, though, the radical approach of these painters to perspective, colour, brushwork and composition offered a productive model for her own writing, for the way the present in all its complexity could be adequately represented in art. Such connections have been made by a number of critics, but none of this is explicitly mentioned by Woolf in her essay. What she does describe, however, is also an important indication of the crucial link between *when* and *what.*

> The Victorian cook lived like a leviathan in the lower depths, formidable, silent, obscure, inscrutable; the Georgian cook is a creature of sunshine and fresh air; in and out of the drawing-room, now to borrow the *Daily Herald*, now to ask advice about a hat. (Ibid.)

For Woolf, this moment of change is figured as a change in human relations which opens up possibilities, which brings light, air and connection where previously there had been darkness, stagnation and estrangement. And for her, too, this change is signalled both in the kind of books that were written – the essay as a whole is a defence of new kinds of writing, that of Joyce, Eliot and of Woolf herself – and in the way we read (ibid.: 127–8).

If we move from Woolf to some of the other canonical figures of Anglo-American literary modernism, however, it is possible to see how the question of *when* and *what* can be quite differently inflected. For Ezra Pound, T. S. Eliot and the artist and writer Percy Wyndham Lewis, the crucial moment of change and the formal innovations required by it can be seen as coming later, and in less optimistic circumstances. Although all had produced innovative work before the beginning of the First World War, the publication of the first issue of Lewis's journal *Blast* a week before the assassination of Archduke Ferdinand in Sarajevo, and the huge importance given by critics of the time and subsequently to Eliot's *The Waste Land* (1922), construe the war as *the* determinant of change. The destructive effect of the war on these writers is then read back into their earlier work, and so there too pessimism, violence and loss are seen as the hallmark. *Blast* was published as the journal of Vorticism, an artistic movement founded and named by Wyndham Lewis and Pound. Its first issue (there were only two, the second in July 1915) shocked the public with its brash colour, layout and typography as much as its content. The content – essays, poetry, visual art – set out the Vorticist agenda and its language eschewed the good manners of Edwardian prose; it is direct, aggressive and often violent. It seems presciently to make itself one with the carnage that was to follow. Later, Vorticist artist Henri Gaudier-Brzeska exclaimed in his 'Vortex Gaudier-Brzeska (Written From the Trenches)', published in the second issue of *Blast* in 1915: 'THIS WAR IS A GREAT REMEDY' (Gaudier-Brzeska 2003: 166).

Clearly, if we view the cataclysmic destruction of the war as the central engine of modernism, in contrast to the 'sunshine and fresh air' of Woolf's December 1910, a very different sense of *what* modernism is will arise. Does the rejection of familiar unifying conventions – character, plot, linear chronology, traditional verse forms – in the work of all the modernists suggest the resulting fragmentation is mimetic of a collapsing world, and indeed a celebration of this collapse? Or does it rather suggest that through the fragmentation other possibilities, more real, more human than those they replace, are being allowed to come into being? Of course, the comparison discussed above is purposefully stark – the war had a profound effect on Woolf's writing too. Jacob, the protagonist of her first modernist novel, *Jacob's Room* (1922), is killed during the war. But the questions raised by it are crucial in beginning to grasp the complexities of modernism as a period, as a literary practice and as a critical tool.

As you begin to read and think about modernist writing, the purpose of this guide is to aid that reading through contextual information, a clear setting out of the complexities of who, what and when, and a sense of the crucial place of modernist writing in the discipline we all practise – studying literature. It is hoped too that the guide will begin the process of transforming the oppositions with which this introduction opened – that in your reading pain may become pleasure, and boredom or irritation, delight.

## HOW TO USE THIS BOOK

This book has been written in such a way that it is not necessary to read it straight through, beginning at the beginning and reading through to the end. Each main section can be read on its own, and should be coherent and useful in its own right. In a book of this size, though, it is impossible to explore within each section all the implications of a particular topic, or all the connections

it may have with related areas. Because of this, comprehensive cross-references have been used to direct you
to other areas of the book where a subject has been dealt
with in more detail, or where more information has
been given.

You will find that often, when a work is referred to and
then quoted from, two very different dates are given over
the course of a few lines. This may look strange at first,
but follows a generally used citation system. On the first
mention of a text, the date of first publication is given,
and then any quotation from or paraphrase of it is
referenced using the date of and page numbers from
the particular edition I have used (the Harvard system of
referencing).

Both the Chronology and Glossary contain extensive
information, not all of which has been covered in the
main part of the book. This has been done in order to
broaden the amount of information available, and
extensive cross-referencing has been used between the
Glossary and the main parts of the book in order to
indicate useful connections.

At various points, I have referred to artworks –
paintings and sculpture – which have interesting relations with literary modernism, or whose innovations
usefully illuminate some aspect of it. Websites where
reproductions of these works can be found are listed in
Further Reading and Resources.

# 1

## Historical, Cultural and Intellectual Context

Arts and culture
Philosophy and religion
Politics and economics
Developments in science and technology

The sections which follow take a somewhat different approach from attempts to contextualize, say, nineteenth-century writing. This is because the range of experimental writing which has come to be grouped under the category 'modernism' had as one of its explicit purposes a revolution in the ways that relations between literary texts and the world in which they were produced were understood. Modernists wanted to create art which intersected with the world in new, strange and disturbing ways. Indeed, they wanted their work to profoundly rethink what the world is and how human beings experience it. While Dickens, for example, or George Eliot, took issue with many aspects of the society of which they were a part, and incorporated these criticisms into their novels, this was done from a position of being part of that society. Modernist writers, on the other hand, often saw themselves as estranged from their world, a sense which for many of them led to actual exile or alienation from the societies in which they had grown up. In the following sections, instead of providing a detailed historical background as such, therefore, I have focused on a number of key areas which were influential themselves in remaking the world in radical ways. I have used these with key texts to show how the society of the late nineteenth and early twentieth centuries shaped modernist works, and how these works themselves fed into the debates and anxieties of the period.

## ARTS AND CULTURE

At the beginning of the twentieth century, numerous things – for example, changes in social organization, new technologies, changes in publishing practices – contributed to a changing sense of the meaning of culture, and a changing relation between writing and the world. In this section I will focus on some of the key implications of this, and attempt to explain why these changes contributed to the writing practices known as modernism. The first two subsections contain a broad discussion of changing understandings of the term 'culture'. I will then go on to chart some of the specific areas where this had significant effects – in the role of the writer, in censorship, in the relation between the literary work and its readers, and in general understandings of the function of language.

### The idea of culture

The complex cultural networks which produced modernism had their roots in the Industrial Revolution, which began over a century earlier. Urbanization, vast movements of people, increasing reliance on machinery, unprecedented poverty and unprecedented wealth all appeared to be changing human relations, and many commentators saw the effects as almost entirely destructive. Indeed, throughout the nineteenth century, politicians, churchmen, writers and critics lamented these effects on society. The old order was losing its grip, and what was taking its place seemed less a new order, more a new chaos.

The Victorian poet and critic Matthew Arnold (1822–88) shared this sense that society was fragmenting and breaking down, but what marks his contribution as particularly significant in any consideration of arts and culture is his proposed remedy. For Arnold, it was not religion, a revitalized aristocracy or philanthropy that would save the nation, it was a shared set of *cultural* values to be found pre-eminently in a revitalized literary criticism and a living poetry. In *Culture and Anarchy* (1869), Arnold argues that right order (which he called 'the will of God') would only be restored through the operations of culture:

> Now, then, is the moment for culture to be of service, culture which believes in making reason and the will of God prevail, believes in perfection, is the study and pursuit of perfection, and is no longer debarred ... from getting acceptance for its ideals, simply because they are new. (Arnold 1982: 206–7)

While many commentators articulated their disquiet that different groups in society no longer held core beliefs in common, what they were really seeing was a loss of authority in those groups in society who had previously held power. The power of the aristocracy and the Church had gradually waned throughout the century; and at the same time, and just as gradually, the newly formed working class had developed its own values, confidence and culture. While Arnold reviles the aristocracy as much as the working class in *Culture and Anarchy*, and indeed saves his most damning words for the middle classes, what his proposition for a new cultural consensus based on 'the pursuit of sweetness and light' (ibid.: 225) masks is a continued reliance on an elite – this time cultural rather than social or political.

## Writing and 'mass culture'

Much Anglo-American modernism inherits from Arnold the belief that 'culture' in general, and literature in particular, provides a store of values that are unifying in the face of cultural dislocation. However, for most modernist writers the power of these values had become fragile, if it had not disappeared altogether. Between Arnold's essay and the turn of the century, modernity produced not just fragmentation but what we might call 'massification'. The power of any kind of elite, cultural or otherwise, was perceived as being swamped by the increasing power of 'the masses' (see Mass democracy and the modernist response, p. 42).

By the time of the third Reform Act in 1884, the suffrage was open to the majority of men, and voting in local elections was open to some women. While the move towards mass democracy developed a sense of authority and confidence among the newly enfranchised, cultural changes fed them with a new diet of entertainment and information. The first mass-market newspaper, the *Daily Mail*, began publication in 1896. Priced at a halfpenny, the paper was generally affordable, and its enormous circulation was guaranteed by this, as well as by its accessible style. In book publishing too the trend was towards 'massification'. In the final decades of the nineteenth century, the three-volume novel, the staple form for the publication of fiction for much of the century, was losing its economic viability. It was replaced by the single volume, with a cover price within the means of a larger number of people. This change contributed to a polarization of the novel – between the 'serious' and the popular – which fed into the modernist claims for the novel as poetic and artful. The relations between 'serious' novels and the rest in the fin de siècle is a complex and interesting one (see Daly 1999 and Ardis 2002). What is clear, though, is that the period produced a new way of thinking about novels, a way of thinking that began to see mass taste as a credible gauge of success. The term 'bestseller' was coined in the 1890s, and the term was quickly taken up in the industry to generate publicity. Although the term could apply to any book that sold in large numbers, almost immediately it suggested a certain sort of content. As Peter Keating suggests, '[t]he true best-seller was read and bought by the "quarter-educated"' (Keating 1991: 440). While such novels often focused on the uncertain and fragmentary state of contemporary life, in response they asserted moral confidence, a faith in absolute values and a sureness over a sense of shared assumptions (ibid.: 442–5). It is exactly this certainty of shared values that Arnold and other critics desired, but for most, the 'bestseller' cemented its relation with the reader through the wrong values.

It wasn't just from other kinds of writing that many modernist writers saw a threat to both society and art. Cinema was one of the most significant contributions to the development of mass culture during the period. From its beginnings in the mid-1890s until the years just before the First World War, films were shown first in music halls, and then in fairgrounds, both locations associated with the urban working class, and seen by the other classes as vulgar and cheap. The subjects of early films matched their locations, dominated as they were by music hall turns and scenes from everyday life. Later, once the possibility for showing longer films was developed and the form came to be dominated by fictional narratives, the conventions and subject matter of melodrama dominated, again a form looked down on by the educated.

Some theorists of modernism, both at the time and more recently, have seen film as an archetypally modernist medium, however. Its use of cutting and montage produces 'shocks' in the viewer in the same way that modernist art or writing disturbs and unsettles (Benjamin 1992: 215; Williams 1989: 9). A number of modernist writers had close links with the development of cinema – James Joyce (1882–1941) worked briefly as the manager of the first cinema in Dublin, and H. D. (1886–1961), Dorothy Richardson (1873–1957) and Gertrude Stein (1874–1946) wrote for the first journal of film criticism and theory, *Close Up*, in the late 1920s and early 1930s. Nevertheless, many Anglo-American modernists had an ambiguous if not overtly hostile relation to film. Its associations in terms of class, and its sentimentality and accessibility, led to a deep suspicion of it. For them, the cinema demanded passivity and created false emotion; its mechanical nature could lead only to degraded effects (Lawrence 1998c: 172; Eliot 2005a: 165).

Writers who were alive to the challenge of *mass* culture to an Arnoldian idea of *culture* began to rethink the role and identity of the writer. If the production and consumption of writing had changed so much, what did this mean for the identity of the writer? In the next two sections, we will focus on two crucial debates which shaped literary modernism and which centre on the identity and function of the writer. Implicit in these debates are many of the questions, issues and problems which dominated the arts during the period.

## The role of the writer: the artist vs the professional

Changes in publishing and in the nation's reading habits at the end of the nineteenth century in many ways improved working conditions for writers, and made it more likely that a living wage could be earned from writing. The Society of Authors was set up in 1883 and campaigned on behalf of its members, and increasingly authors employed literary agents to handle the financial and business side of their work. Rather than writers needing to be well off already in order to write, writing became a profession from which money could be earned. In a few cases, such as that of Arnold Bennett

(1867–1931), a lot of money was earned, and writing really for the first time had the capacity to make a person very rich. More generally, the professionalization of writing went along with an admission that writers were the most important element in the production of books. This was enshrined in the Copyright Act of 1911 in Britain, which for the first time admitted in law that such rights should belong to the creators and not the publishers of books.

However, for many writers, these new structures and institutions were not unproblematically good news for writing. While they, along with new developments in travel and communication, did widen audiences, and create an explosion in the number of publishing houses, journals and magazines, many writers worried about relations between writing and the marketplace. For many of the experimental and innovative writers of the early twentieth century, these new trappings of writing as a profession damaged writing and, therefore, damaged writers. For in the end, they argued, the professional writer was utterly dependent on his or her audience. If profit was the final line for most publishers and magazine editors, then the demands of the audience were paramount. Success became measured in currency, and writing took on the task of flattery. If the Romantics had seen the poet as 'unofficial legislator', as priest, as conscience, as teacher, then it seemed as if the early twentieth century was constructing the writer as entertainer. While the professionalization of writing promised to improve the financial status of writers, to stop them starving in garrets, it threatened to take away their authority and freedom.

In the second half of the nineteenth century, these questions of audience and institutions, of experimentation and success, had been made flesh in developments in painting, particularly in France. Artists like Édouard Manet (1832–83), the Impressionists, and later Paul Cézanne (1839–1906) challenged the art establishment and the general public on questions of subject matter, composition and technique. Their paintings gave priority to individual perception and to the possibilities of the medium of paint. Traditional painting, they believed, was concerned with copying the world, and pretending that it wasn't painting. But painting shouldn't be secondary to the world. It should draw attention to its 'paintedness' by making its own worlds according to its own laws.

This championing of art as a special sphere, related to the world but not to be dictated to by it, had enormous influence on young British artists in the early years of the twentieth century, but also on practitioners in other areas. In particular, some writers began to make similar claims for their work, and this had consequences not just for how many writers saw themselves, but for the sort of work they produced. This is particularly clear, for example, in the debate between novelists Henry James (1843–1916) and H. G. Wells (1866–1946) about the function of the novel (see Edel and Ray 1958).

It has been argued by the critic David Trotter that, despite their protestations, far from setting themselves against the professionalization of writing, Anglo-American modernists' will to experiment and innovation was a move towards it (Trotter 2001). The professionalization of an activity is achieved through the construction of boundaries, and the exclusion of some and the inclusion of others. Henry James's claim for the novel as art, which was taken up by his younger admirers such as Ezra Pound (1885–1972) and Ford Madox Ford (1873–1939), can be seen as professional boundary-making by another name. James wrote that:

> It is art that *makes* life, makes interest, makes importance for our consideration and application of things, and I know of no substitute whatever for the force and beauty of its process. (Edel and Ray 1958: 267; emphasis in original)

If the novel is such a serious business, these writers insist, then only a few can be admitted as 'real' writers. However, whether we see modernist writers as reacting against the professionalization of writing, or as taking up the exclusionary dynamic of the professions, it is clear that modernist conceptions of the writer's role and of form have a complex relation to the developing mass culture (see Rainey 1998).

## Readers, obscenity and censorship

Along with its relation to the products and strategies of mass culture, literary writing's other significant relationship is with its reader. Virginia Woolf's (1882–1941) essays 'Modern Novels' (1919) (republished as 'Modern Fiction' in 1925) and 'Mr Bennett and Mrs Brown' (1924) have been seen as significant by many critics for their attempts to rethink the ways writing represents reality, indeed to reimagine the nature of reality itself. However, in a good portion of the latter essay, what she concentrates on is the way this rethinking by 'Georgian' writers – her term for those experimental writers working after the accession of George V in 1910 – affects the relation between writers and readers: 'At the present moment we are suffering, not from decay, but from having no code of manners which writers and readers accept as a prelude to the more exciting intercourse of friendship' (Woolf 1986: 125).

Woolf's main examples of this breakdown are the work of T. S. Eliot (1888–1965) and James Joyce (1882–1941). Eliot's poetry, she says, flouts the existing code of manners between poetry and its readership by refusing to provide the reader with the means of orientation – regular rhythm and rhyme, single and coherent voice, and so on. Joyce, on the other hand, flouts the 'politenesses of society' by including the obscene. Woolf figures this in her essay as the 'calculated indecency of a desperate man who feels that in order to breathe he must break the windows' (ibid.: 126). Obscenity and obscurity are the two constituents of the 'breaking and falling, crashing and destruction' (ibid.: 125) enacted for Woolf by Georgian writing.

Writing and art generally during the Victorian period worked through a tacit sympathy between writer or artist and reader or viewer. In the main, works were structured to ease communication between the two, and more than that to demonstrate that, at bottom, the beliefs and values of the two were the same. Even those novels which wished to change the reader's mind about something – say about the Poor Laws in Dickens's *Oliver Twist* – based their challenge on a fundamental identity between the values of the writer and those of the reader. Modernists were not the first to challenge this sympathy. During the last two or three decades of the nineteenth century there was an increasing sense among the general reading public, and the critics who spoke for them, that writers were threatening this cosy relation. One of the most explosive threats to this relation was the challenge by writers and artists to accepted notions of the obscene.

Changing practices and attitudes around obscenity and censorship at the turn of the century did not follow a straight developmental line from repression to increasing openness. Throughout the period covered by this book, legally, writing was subject to the strictures of the Obscene Publications Act (1857). The act was most notable for its extreme vagueness in defining obscenity, and it contained no possible defence that could justify particular passages by the overall artistic or educational purpose of the work. However, censorship at the turn of the century was less a matter of draconian enforcement of the act by police and state, and more an atmosphere created by the piecemeal activities of campaigning groups and the enormous power of the circulating libraries.

A loosening of prohibitions in the early 1890s, influenced in part by the popular enthusiasm for Thomas

Hardy's (1840–1928) *Tess of the d'Urbervilles* (1891), was reversed by reactions to Oscar Wilde's (1854–1900) trials for sodomy and the publication of Hardy's *Jude the Obscure*, both in 1895. The trial and the novel shocked by making public previously hidden areas of life. Wilde and Hardy refused the supposed function of the writer as keeper of the nation's morals, and indeed both wished to rethink the nature of morality itself. Hardy presented 'distasteful' material without comment in *Jude*, and Wilde's life challenged assumptions about 'normal' relations between the sexes and between classes. However, Wilde's fate following the trial, and his time in Reading gaol, and Hardy's repudiation of the novel following the reception of *Jude* make clear the dangers of such challenges to moral orthodoxies.

The early twentieth century saw a surge in attempts to censor novels and to create a public panic. A number of campaigning groups wished to persuade the government to police printed material more vigorously, and to instil in the public a sense that the very security of the nation was under threat. While the power of such campaigning was limited, it did foster an atmosphere in which publishers and printers lacked the confidence to 'publish and be damned'. It was this that created the difficulties for, for example, James Joyce in his attempts from 1905 to find a publisher for *Dubliners* (1914), and for D. H. Lawrence (1885–1930) in his similar struggles with *Sons and Lovers* (1913), *The Rainbow* (1915) and *Women in Love* (1921).

After the First World War, the power of the private circulating libraries had dwindled as book prices continued to fall and the number of public libraries grew. Also, and crucially for modernist writers, the years around the First World War saw an increase in the number of 'little magazines' and journals with tiny circulations (see The 'little magazines', p. 118), and of small independent presses. These were often funded by wealthy patrons, and so were under no pressure to make a profit. Instead of needing to appeal to as wide an audience as possible for financial reasons, they were directed toward a small and 'discriminating' audience, and the books and magazines were often sold entirely by subscription. So, although the Obscene Publications Act remained in place, these methods of publication remained largely outside the sphere of influence of the circulating libraries, and their narrow audience appeal kept them mostly clear of attention from the campaigning groups. When James Joyce's *Ulysses* (1922) was first published in Paris, it was banned in Britain under the Obscene Publications Act. However, by this time sections of the novel had already been published in 'little magazines', *The Egoist* in Britain and *The Little Review* in the US. Significantly, the legal ban did not stop copies of the book moving across the Channel, but it did have the effect of raising the value of the novel both financially and aesthetically (see Rainey 1998: Chapter 2).

## The 'difficulty' of art

Woolf's most famous statement in 'Mr Bennett and Mrs Brown' is that 'in or about December, 1910, human character changed' (Woolf 1986: 113). As suggested in the introduction, many critics have seen in this an implicit reference to Roger Fry's (1866–1934) first Post-Impressionist Exhibition (Goldman 2004: 42–5). Many viewers believed that the works of art on show had flouted some 'code of manners', one that stated that artists should make it as easy as possible for audiences to understand their works, to see themselves and their lives directly reflected in them, and to derive from them a straightforward pleasure.

Anglo-American modernist writers insist that, not only was the truth about the world sometimes tellable only through the 'obscene', but that it could never be told directly, in a cosy chat between writer and reader.

Direct telling evaporated the truth. The most important truth about the world may well be the extreme difficulty with which any truth can be grasped. In the prose of Joseph Conrad (1857–1924) we can see how this lack of directness, of distinct and clear perception, characterizes imagery, character and plot. In *Heart of Darkness* (1902), Marlow's narration of his journey up the Congo is framed by an anonymous narrator whose interjections undermine the status of the former as a simple retelling of the truth. Whereas the Victorian narrator was omniscient, Marlow's inability to see clearly is constantly at issue. As he first approaches the coast of Africa, his vision of the land is indistinct and watery (Conrad 1998: 150).

His sense of the meaning of his story, and therefore the sense of his listeners and the reader, is troubled, illusive and impressionistic.

> Do you see the story? Do you see anything? It seems to me I am trying to tell you a dream – making a vain attempt, because no relation of a dream can convey the dream-sensation ... No, it is impossible; it is impossible to convey the life-sensation of any given epoch of one's existence ... It is impossible. We live, as we dream – alone ... (Ibid.: 172)

Despite Woolf's assertion that Conrad's nationality made him useless as a model for the Georgians (Woolf 1986: 118), modernists did see Conrad as an important influence specifically for the way he wrote, not just *about* obscurity, but obscurely. T. S. Eliot used a line from *Heart of Darkness* as the epigraph to 'The Hollow Men' (1925) and in the opening section of *The Waste Land* (1922), a voice alludes to the title of Conrad's novella, but Eliot takes the sense of obscurity further. It is not just darkness that inhibits knowledge, but light too (Eliot 1985: 64).

As Woolf suggests in 'Mr Bennett and Mrs Brown', the modernist uses of obscenity and obscurity drove a wedge between modernist writers and their works and the bulk of the reading public. This was in order to challenge assumptions about the relations between writers and readers, and more fundamental assumptions about the nature of the world and our ability to perceive it. However, this may imply that modernist writers wanted to show the general reader these things in order to persuade them and thereby win them over, but this was not unproblematically the case. While Henry James was mystified and troubled by the failure of his books to sell, for some later writers the alienation of the general public was not so much an unintended consequence as a deliberate aim. Woolf's essay ends with a call for sympathetic tolerance from the reader in the hope that one day a new code of manners would lead to 'the more exciting intercourse of friendship' (1986: 125), but for some modernists, their very sense of themselves as artists meant a rejection of any mass readership. In the preface to his *Fantasia of the Unconscious* (1922), D. H. Lawrence, no stranger to charges of obscenity, makes his rejection explicit:

> The generality of readers had better just leave it alone. The generality of critics likewise. I really don't want to convince anybody. It is quite in opposition to my whole nature. I don't intend my books for the generality of readers. I count it a mistake of our mistaken democracy, that every man who can read print is allowed to believe that he can read all that is printed. I count it a misfortune that serious books are exposed in the public market, like slaves exposed naked for sale. (Lawrence 1960: 53)

## The problem of language

Obscenity and obscurity changed the nature of the relation between writers and readers partly because both challenged the idea that literature was important primarily because it offered up something of value 'behind' the words, and that the words were mere channels through which this 'behind' could be seen. Implicit in the sympathy assumed between writers and their readers in the nineteenth century was the idea that their mutual accord existed not in spite of but *because* of a shared language; a language which was able to fully convey meaning, to transfer ideas from writer to reader directly and without difficulty. However, not the least of the consequences of the breakdown of social consensus or social power discussed above was a fading of the sense that the language was held in common. In 1930, in opening his essay, *Mass Civilization and Minority Culture*, decrying the effects of mass democracy and the breakdown in cultural authority for their impact on literary values, the critic F. R. Leavis (1895–1978) laments that he cannot even depend on his readers sharing his sense of the word 'culture'. His essay is in many ways a reworking of Arnold's *Culture and Anarchy*, but, writes Leavis, at least Arnold could rely on a shared understanding of key words and phrases.

> For Matthew Arnold it was in some ways less difficult ... Today one must face problems of definition and formulation where Arnold could pass lightly on. When, for example, having started by saying that culture has always been in minority keeping, I am asked what I mean by 'culture'...
> (Leavis 2000: 169–70)

In the 60 years between Arnold's and Leavis's essays, those forces creating a mass culture had combined to so dissipate and divide society that there were no longer the supposed incontrovertible sources of authority to which all agreed to subject themselves. In a society where one person's 'culture' could easily be another's barbarism, and no final authority exists to judge between them, language becomes less a channel of communication and more a battlefield.

Many young writers, even those outside of the

category of modernism, believed in response to this that the novel, poetry and drama needed to develop new forms, and new ways of speaking. Modernist writers went further. If language could no longer communicate directly and without breakdown, then writing was not just achieved via the struggle with language, but came to be *about* it.

## PHILOSOPHY AND RELIGION

This section suggests some of the ways that thinking about the world at the most fundamental levels took shape at the turn of the nineteenth and twentieth centuries. It begins with an overview of the crisis of traditional religious faith in the nineteenth century, and then goes on to look at some of the alternative visions of the world and humanity which both challenged and replaced it. In these sections I have focused on three of the most influential thinkers – three who in different ways had much influence on and connections with modernist writing – Friedrich Nietzsche, Sigmund Freud and Henri Bergson.

### The loss of faith

By the second half of the nineteenth century, the possibility that an intelligent, educated person could retain an orthodox Christian faith had been stretched very thin. Science had established criteria for attaining knowledge about the world based on evidence produced by repeatable experiments, and these criteria percolated through to other areas of human life beyond the scientific (see Science, technology and the construction of modernity, p. 55). Increasingly, it was difficult for 'truth' to be claimed outside scientific methods. Evolutionary theory, textual criticism of the Bible and comparative religious studies had combined to make the claims for the truth of Christianity fall far short of the standards demanded by science. This intellectual crisis was augmented by social and political changes. The rise of parliamentary democracy and the reorganization of society in response to the Industrial Revolution had eroded some of the legal and political authority of the Church of England, causing internal shifts and struggles.

Many middle-class Victorians did retain their Christian beliefs, despite all this. For those earnest Victorians who did renounce their faith, however, the prospect of a universe completely devoid of the meaning and order given to it by Christianity was intensely troubling. Their loss of faith did not lead to a meaningless and nihilistic universe. Christian values and meaning were replaced with others – Love, Duty, Honour, for example – which maintained, and indeed in many ways replicated, the worldview of bourgeois Christianity.

Nineteenth-century philosophers tended to follow this pattern of confrontation with a godless universe only to finally recoup some order, pattern and meaning through a priori assumptions or unacknowledged volte faces. Even Arthur Schopenhauer (1788–1860), the first philosopher to be openly atheist, retained a belief in metaphysics and finally urged a position that shared much with Eastern mysticism in its rejection of the world. However, Schopenhauer's primary contribution to philosophy was his concept of the primacy of the 'Will'. For him, the 'Will' is distinguished from the idea of volition, and means rather a force or energy which propels things below or beyond consciousness. It is in this that Schopenhauer is so important in terms of his influence on the thinkers and philosophers who created the intellectual coordinates of the early twentieth century. At the centre of the thinking of Friedrich Nietzsche (1844–1900), Sigmund Freud (1856–1939) and Henri Bergson (1859–1941) was a version of Schopenhauer's Will. For each of them, human beings were not in the end governed or controlled by their intellect or their reason, let alone by the Christian God, but by a force beyond the individual's rational knowledge and control. While each of these thinkers defined and valued this force differently, what is clear is that the period saw a loss of faith, not only in God, but also in the human being of the Enlightenment, whose reason would guarantee progress and morality.

## Friedrich Nietzsche and the 'transvaluation of all values'

Friedrich Nietzsche was the first philosopher in the Western tradition to reject metaphysics completely and explicitly. This tradition had, since Socrates, assumed as an *a priori* or first principle the existence of a realm beyond the material as perceived through human consciousness. This realm, while unreachable, determined the world of appearances. It was *the* reality, over which was laid the secondary reality of the world of things. However, Nietzsche's famous statement that 'God is dead' (Nietzsche 2001: 120) was an assertion not just of the end of the Christian God, but of any forces, powers or realities thought to be beyond the world of material nature and human culture. Unlike other philosophers and thinkers of the nineteenth century, then, a loss of faith for Nietzsche could not mean maintenance of a Christian worldview or a Christian ethics in all but name. As he writes in *Twilight of the Idols* (1889), one of his last books:

> When one gives up the Christian belief one thereby deprives oneself of the *right* to Christian morality. For the latter is absolutely *not* self-evident ... Christianity is a system, a consistently thought out and *complete* view of things. If one breaks out of it a fundamental idea, the belief in God, one thereby breaks the whole thing to pieces: one has nothing

of any consequence left in one's hands. (Nietzsche 1988: 69–70)

Nietzsche believed that the continuation of Christian morality beyond the death of God was responsible for much of the cultural sickness he saw in European society. Christianity, he argued, made human beings meek and passive. Its doctrine of original sin, its focus on love and pity, and its God who willingly submitted to the most ignominious of deaths had sapped the will of European culture, resulting in its decadence and inauthenticity.

It is not just Christianity, however, against which Nietzsche launches his critique. He also sees in Western philosophy throughout its history a seam of destruction and wrong thinking. His most vehement critique in this regard is directed at Socrates for his supposed belief in the primacy of reason. In his first published work, *The Birth of Tragedy* (1872), Nietzsche outlines his criticism, seeing Socratic rationality as having destroyed non-intellectual forces:

> In this quite abnormal character, instinctive wisdom appears only to *hinder* conscious knowledge at certain points. While in all productive people instinct is the power of creativity and affirmation, and consciousness assumes a critical and dissuasive role, in Socrates instinct becomes the critic, consciousness the creator – a monstrosity *per defectum!* (Nietzsche 1993: 66; emphasis in original)

Nietzsche's position, with regard to philosophy, Christianity, and indeed all the dominant ideological systems of European culture, led to his call for what he termed in *Twilight of the Idols* the 'transvaluation of all values'. Human culture, and human beings themselves, needed to be remade from the foundations. The contemporary world was for Nietzsche one of degradation, falsity and sickness. Like most critics of the period, Nietzsche had his golden age – the pre-Socratic Greece of Aeschylus and Sophocles – but unlike most, he was under no illusions about the possibilities of its revival in the present. However, this did not mean that he championed valuelessness or nihilism. On the contrary, he wanted to construct new values that celebrated human beings unbowed and untwisted by the dogmas of Christianity and rationalism. But Nietzsche's problem was how to construct new values when all that exists is rejected as rotten and dying, and when any idea of the metaphysical is dismissed as dangerous and deluded. How can the new be born when all that exists from which it can be born is the decadent old?

Where Nietzsche does attempt to outline these new values and what they should affirm – in the figure of the *Übermensch* or 'Superman', in his theories of art, his concept of the will, or in his general and rather nebulous positive value of 'Life' – the immense struggle to define them outside of what already exists fractures and fragments his thinking, leading to contradiction and paradox, and often making it difficult to understand exactly what he means. In this, Nietzsche is an exemplary modern. His work is drenched with the terrible sense of being either too late or too early. The great, clear, simple, noble cultures have passed and are no longer possible, and Nietzsche often refers to himself or his work as 'untimely'. The resulting sense of utter alienation in the present warps the very language that is his only tool for constructing anything better.

Nietzsche's writing style through his productive life acted out his criticisms, his values, and above all the immense struggle of his thought. His dominant and most characteristic style is the short, aphoristic essay which neither shows the reasoning that led to it, nor makes visible its connection with the other short, aphoristic essays around it. His writing requires hard work on the part of the reader, who has to fill in these gaps, yet in its commitment and rage it is exhilarating, far more so than more conventional philosophical writing. Indeed, Nietzsche's style, and his work generally, in some ways have far more in common with modernist writers of poetry or prose fiction than with contemporary philosophers, and it is no wonder then that he was so influential on a great many of these. Many Anglo-American modernist writers were aware of Nietzsche's work from the late nineteenth century on, either in the original German, via the first multi-volume English translations (1896–1913), or through a number of journals and pamphlets which promoted his thought, most notably A. R. Orage's *New Age*, to which a number of modernist writers contributed.

W. B. Yeats (1865–1939), D. H. Lawrence, T. E. Hulme (1883–1917) and James Joyce were all influenced by Nietzsche to some degree. In July 1904, James Joyce signed a postcard to a friend 'James Overman', light-heartedly aligning himself in his youth and ambition with Nietzsche's '*Übermensch*'. Recent critics have seen his influence even in writers, such as Ezra Pound, who expressedly rejected him (Lindberg 1987). Certainly it seems that a number of modernist writers shared Nietzsche's attitudes to European civilization, and had their ideas confirmed rather than formed by reading him. While it is true that the versions of his thought assimilated by these writers sometimes bore only a strange resemblance to his actual thought, it is also true that some of the less savoury aspects of these writers' opinions chime very strongly with Nietzsche's. In particular, the loathing for mass democracy of Yeats, Lawrence and Percy Wyndham Lewis (1882–1957), and their desire for strong, powerful leadership not dependent on the will of the people, attracted them in varying degrees to fascism between the two world wars.

Nietzsche has been charged by some with responsibility for the origins of fascism in Europe. His belief that very few people would have the will and courage to recreate themselves, to scrutinize their lives so that nothing second-hand remains, and to claim power unapologetically, does seem to resemble the leader worship of 1930s Germany, and to justify the elimination of those deemed 'weak'. Both Hitler and Mussolini used him to claim intellectual legitimacy for their ideas. However, there is much in Nietzsche – and by far the most important part – which is anathema to fascism, not least his hatred for the state.

## Sigmund Freud and the unconscious

As with Nietzsche, the influence of Sigmund Freud was sometimes direct, but, again like Nietzsche, his thinking did not just influence specific individuals in the early twentieth century, it contributed to the very construction of the period, and indeed of the whole century. Freud's thought shares a number of common origins with Nietzsche's and, as did Nietzsche, Freud took from these a particular understanding of the will as crucial to the construction of the human. However, Freud's 'will' was not something that could be utilized by an individual; it was outside of consciousness, unknowable and alien to what is conventionally understood to be the 'self'. It was through this concept of the 'unconscious' that Freud, more than any other thinker, articulated the period's faltering faith in rationality. In his work, the Enlightenment human being, dignified by and made capable of morality and progress through the possession of reason, gave way to a human being whose thoughts, behaviour, relationships and greatest achievements are the result of destructive forces of which they have no knowledge and over which no control. For Freud, this constituted the 'third blow' to human vanity, the first being the establishment of the heliocentric universe associated with Copernicus, and the second being the establishment of evolution by Charles Darwin (1809–82) and others. While these two undermined humanity's claims to be 'lords of creation', psychoanalysis dealt the more wounding blow as it 'seeks to prove to the ego that it is not master even in its own house, but must content itself with scanty information of what is going on unconsciously in its mind' (Freud [1917] 1963: 285).

The concept of the 'unconscious' was not invented by Freud. Since Leibniz's *New Essays on Human Understanding*, written in the late seventeenth century, the idea of unconscious mental processes had been important in German philosophy and psychology, and writers and artists from the Romantics on paid attention to them. In particular, the late nineteenth century saw the rapid expansion of the discipline of experimental psychology, and the development of ideas on that part of human life beyond, below, or above consciousness in the work of, among others, William James and Pierre Janet. However, in a number of ways Freud's work was revolutionary, and for reasons which many found disturbing. Freud was the first to suggest a systematic theory for investigating the mind, and consequently the first to map out a dynamic model of it. He suggested that the conscious and unconscious parts of the mind interacted with one another, and that this suggested a very different model of the human than that assumed by either Enlightenment thinking or Christian doctrine.

For Freud, the different parts of the mind are in a constant state of conflict. He developed a number of models for the psychic processes during his life, but the one with which most people are familiar, the topographical model, suggests the mind is divided into the id, the ego and the superego, and all human beings are the result, not of an individual and unique soul, nor a dominant rationality, but of conflict between these three. As Freud figures the relation in *The Ego and the Id* (1923), 'in its [the ego's] relation to the id it is like a man on horseback, who has to hold in check the superior strength of the horse' (Freud 1961: 25).

The id is Freud's term for the unconscious and unknowable desires which derive their energy from bodily instincts and are utterly unaffected by the demands of reality, of morality or of social rules. The urgent and sometimes irrational demands of the human baby, demands which convulse the body and will only stop when sated, do not cease to exist as the individual matures, but remain, still powerful and turbulent. As the ego – that part of the self in direct contact with external reality, dominated by reason – develops, these desires are repressed. Very often destructive, utterly selfish, and fundamentally sexual, they are incompatible with external reality and 'civilization'. However, repression does not stop them, but rather energizes them, and they are forced to obtain their ends by indirect means. It is these indirect means that produced the many and various symptoms which Freud believed presented themselves in his consulting room during his long life. But, as he began to suggest in some of his earliest works of psychoanalysis, *The Interpretation of Dreams* (1900), *The Psychopathology of Everyday Life* (1901) and *Jokes and Their Relation to the Unconscious* (1905), the effects of repression on unconscious wishes and desires produces not just neurotic symptoms but those things previously seen as most nobly or uniquely human. Art, literature, the bond between parents and children, dreams, jokes, work, ambition, love, religion – are all the result of these conflicts and struggles; indeed the traces of the struggle shape and define them. So, for Freud, religion is 'the universal obsessional neurosis of humanity; like the obsessional neurosis of children, it arose ... out of the relation to the father' (Freud [1927] 1964: 43); Hamlet is hysterical (Freud [1900] 1953: 367); and romantic love is a symptom of problems in psychical development (Freud [1912] 1957).

As with Nietzsche, the relationship between Freud's ideas and Anglo-American modernism is complex and various. Modernism has been seen as both cause and effect of psychoanalysis. Aside from the issue of influence, though, psychoanalysis and modernism do seem to share central concerns, as Kylie Valentine has argued: 'the aesthetic practices and thematic concerns critically important to modernism – decentring of the subject, crises in narratives of the self, biological and scientific knowledges, classicism, sexuality, embodiment – are also those of psychoanalysis' (Valentine 2003: 31).

Although there are areas in European modernism where Freud's influence is direct and acknowledged, for example in Surrealism (see The European avant-gardes, p. 112), in Anglo-American modernism there is a more general tendency to deny Freud's influence, or vehemently disagree with his ideas, while writing about worlds inflected by his discoveries and in a language which acts out his claims. For some writers, such as May Sinclair (1863–1946), this paradoxical relation is acknowledged through a partial acceptance of him; for a few, such as H. D., the influence of Freud on her personal life is publicly celebrated (H. D. 1985). For most, however, Freud's ideas are too reductive, and when used as an explicit framework produce poor art. In this, though, psychoanalysis exists within a paradox common to modernity and to many modernist writers themselves. In its methodology and its alignment of itself with science, psychoanalysis demonstrates a commitment to the rational, but its conclusions uncover the predominance of the irrational in human life.

However, for others at the beginning of the Freudian century, it was the irrationality uncovered by psychoanalysis which dominated, either suggesting the possibility of liberation from the shackles of bourgeois morality, or a source of deep pessimism at human destruction and selfishness. For D. H. Lawrence, in *Psychoanalysis and the Unconscious* (1921), the problem with psychoanalysis was that it was not 'irrational' enough. While he praises Freud for going beyond consciousness, for exploring that which for Lawrence is the most essential aspect of the human being, the unconscious, psychoanalysis confuses the original contents of

the unconscious with the products of secondary intellectual deduction. It is for this reason that psychoanalysis finds an unconscious full of 'Nothing but a huge
slimy serpent of sex, and heaps of excrement, and a
myriad repulsive little horrors spawned between sex and
excrement' (Lawrence 1960: 5). Opposed to this 'sack of
horrors' (ibid.: 9) is Lawrence's notion of the 'pristine
unconscious'. Free from ideas and intellect, it is 'the
spontaneous life-motive in every organism' (ibid.: 13),
the source of creativity and 'Life'. Not only is this
unconscious warped by intellectual interference, it is
'unanalysable, undefinable, inconceivable. It cannot be
conceived, it can only be experienced, in every single
instance' (ibid.: 15).

## Henri Bergson and the rescue of humanity

The American critic Lionel Trilling (1905–75) suggested
in his 1955 essay on Freud that central to modernity was
a yearning for a place 'beyond' or away from the 'reach
of culture' (Trilling 1955: 93). Lawrence's opposition to
Freud is that Freud does not go far enough 'beyond'
culture. Lawrence's yearning is common to a number of
modernist writers, the desire for a realm beyond the
change, chance and decay to which the human world is
subject. The 'beyond culture' of conventional religious
belief was no longer available, and, while influential, the
radical anti-metaphysics of Nietzsche did not satisfy
everyone. Other philosophers shaping thinking in the
early twentieth century did share with Nietzsche a sense
of the non-intellectual as valuable, but were less pessimistic about its possibilities within modernity because
they offer versions of this 'beyond culture'.

Among these the most influential with both fellow
philosophers, and more generally with writers and the
educated public, was the Anglo-French philosopher,
Henri Bergson. Bergson lectured in London during
1911; these lectures generated huge interest, and his

ideas spread widely among writers and intellectuals. A number of his works were published in English translations in the years before the First World War, and in the years 1909 to 1911 over 200 articles appeared on Bergson and his ideas in English books, newspapers, journals and magazines (Gillies 2003: 97).

As suggested by Mary Ann Gillies, at the heart of Bergson's attraction was his identification of exactly the 'blows' to humanity described by Freud, and crucially his attempts to rescue humanity from such degradation. For example, in *L'Evolution Créatrice* (1907; translated into English in 1911 as *Creative Evolution*), his best-known work, Bergson tries to reconcile Darwin's theory with the idea that some force exists at the heart of the universe, ordering, patterning and giving meaning. While Bergson valued the methods and discoveries of science, and was extremely knowledgeable about them, he maintained that there were significant aspects of human experience which could not be accounted for or explained by a rationalistic science. Unlike Freud's unconscious, these aspects were seen as positive, as existing outside time and history.

In his philosophy, and in his conception of human beings, Bergson gave central place to 'intuition'. Bergson's intuition was not in opposition to the intellect; it was capable of gaining knowledge, and was an 'instinct that has become disinterested, self-conscious, capable of reflecting upon its object and of enlarging it indefinitely' (Bergson 1911a: 186). However, unlike the intellect, what intuition was crucially able to apprehend was 'duration', a concept at the heart of Bergson's philosophy and greatly influential on modernist writing.

Bergson distinguished between time as 'duration' – as the indivisible, continuous flow experienced only by the individual – and time as divisible, quantitative and studied by science, the 'public' time of the external world. According to Bergson the latter spatializes time; that is, it divides it, names it, regularizes it, makes it into a quantity. While Bergson acknowledges this is necessary in order to analyse and explain, he privileged duration as that which indicated most truthfully the nature of existence. In duration, time is quality not quantity. While external measures might tell us that time moves regularly – it cannot speed up or slow down – the individual's experience says otherwise.

In duration, the past and the present are not distinguished (that would be to see them as spatial entities), but form a whole, and so memory plays a crucial role in Bergson's philosophy.

> Pure duration [*durée*] is the form which the succession of our conscious states assumes when our ego lets itself *live*, when it refrains from separating its present state from its former state ... [I]n recalling these states, it does not set them alongside another, but forms both the past and the present states into an organic whole, as happens when we recall the notes of a tune, melting, so to speak, into one another. (Bergson 1913a: 100; emphasis in original)

For Bergson, memory is a way of suggesting relation between the material and the 'spiritual', a relationship denied by public, spatialized time. In the foreword to *Matter and Memory,* he writes that '[t]his book affirms the reality of spirit and the reality of matter, and tries to determine the relation of the one to the other by the study of a definite example, memory' (Bergson 1911b: xi). Memory is the bridge between impressions experienced during the flux of duration and the recollection which makes them usable. Bergson distinguishes two types of memory: voluntary and involuntary. The former is cerebral and can be activated by the will; the latter is spontaneous and cannot be called up by an effort of will. Again, although both are necessary, involuntary memory is privileged by Bergson, and it is the representation of this sense of memory in the work of a number of Anglo-American modernists, and most famously in the novel *À*

*la récherche du temps perdu* (1913–27) by the French writer
Marcel Proust (1871–1922), that indicates the influence
of Bergson on writing (see Imagism, p. 101). Indeed,
Bergson himself acknowledged the possibilities of the
novel for representing the individual's complex and
nuanced experience.

> Now, if some bold novelist, tearing aside the cleverly woven
> curtain of our conventional ego, shows us under this
> appearance of logic [in language] a fundamental absurdity,
> under the juxtaposition of simple states an infinite per-
> meation of a thousand impressions which have already
> ceased to exist the instant they are named, we commend him
> for having known us better than we know ourselves. (1913a:
> 133)

In *Mrs Dalloway* (1925), Virginia Woolf presents us with
characters who each show very different proportions of
duration and clock time in their lives. Septimus Smith,
by the end, has retreated wholly into his internal world;
Dr Bradshaw's name indicates clearly his privileging
of clock time, as 'Bradshaw' was the name of the first
official train timetable.

However, the attempt in modernist writing to elaborate Bergson's ideas reaches a paradox inherent in but
acknowledged by his philosophy. Duration can only be
represented in retrospect, and that very retrospective
recreation interrupts, divides and fragments flow and
continuity. Writing must spatialize. While *Mrs Dalloway*
purports to be a record of impressions of past and present existing in a continuous flow, a narrative cannot be
present to the reader in one moment, undifferentiated
and undivided. Narrative is enmeshed with before and
after, with cause and effect. Moreover, a record must
have a recorder who selects and prioritizes. Woolf's
narrator is not the God-like narrator of the nineteenth-
century novel, directing and interfering, but it could be
argued that the modernist narrator's 'absence' is

tendentious in this respect. Such a narrative pretends it is not mediated when actually it is. Bergson, however, recognized that, while true living occurred within duration, all human beings must have a relationship with the external world, and that this makes necessary the spatializing of 'clock time'.

## Spiritualism, mysticism and the occult

The popularity of Bergson's ideas before the First World War stemmed in part from his attempt to value lived human experience and resist its perceived reduction by science and rationality. In working towards this, Bergson's influences and interests included spiritualism, psychical research – the method developed in the late nineteenth century using scientific methods to investigate the claims of spiritualism – and Eastern mysticism. In this too his work chimed with the intellectual climate of pre-war Britain.

Spiritualism had been popular since its importation from the US in the 1840s, but the late nineteenth century saw a resurgence of interest, particularly in trance states, automatic writing and speaking and clairvoyance (see Oppenheim 1985; Luckhurst 2002). The Society for Psychical Research was founded in Britain in 1882 for the investigation of such phenomena, and in the early twentieth century Bergson was a President and Freud a corresponding member. The work of the Society, while mocked by some, nevertheless became an important and widely recognized cultural icon, and many well-known writers and intellectuals were members.

Interest in the writings and teachings of Eastern religions – Buddhism and Hinduism in particular – grew with new translations and with the visit to Britain in 1912 of the Indian writer, Rabindranath Tagore (1861–1941). Again, this interest had its roots in the nineteenth century, but certainly the immediate pre-war period saw it increase, and Evelyn Underhill's (1875–1941) work

*Mysticism* (1911), a comprehensive study of both Western and Eastern mysticism, and a claim for the mystical experience as belonging to '[t]he most highly developed branches of the human family' (Underhill 1995: 3), had gone into 14 editions by 1942.

While such interests can seem incongruous amid the 'disenchantments' of modernity – the rationalizing effect of science and technology – they rather constitute another aspect of modernity. The losses of faith discussed above included a loss of faith in rationality, and one of the consequences of this was the creation of 'other worlds' which, while acting out this loss, at the same time offered the security of alternative kinds of order and meaning.

Anglo-American modernism can often seem to deride such interests as low brow and credulous. In T. S. Eliot's *The Waste Land* (1922), Madame Sosostris, 'famous clairvoyante', clearly comes off badly in comparison with the sages and mystics of the past. However, modernist writers and their work are in fact drenched in the atmosphere and yearnings of 'other worldly' imaginings. For writers such as W. B. Yeats and Ezra Pound, the mythic, circular time of the occult offered a way out of what they saw as the doomed linearity of Western history (see Williams 2002). Yeats's mystical work *A Vision* (1925) reveals the workings of the universe which, Yeats claimed in later editions, had been passed to him through the automatic writing of his wife, Georgie. In the novel *Armed with Madness* (1928), by Mary Butts (1890–1937), the modern world represented by a group of young friends is blown apart by a violence released when they believe they are in possession of the Holy Grail. More generally, the modernist short story is strongly associated with the haunted, the uncanny and the supernatural (see Gilbert 2004).

With the developments in science and technology (see p. 54), in politics (see Politics and economics, below) and in philosophy (see above), the loss of secure foundations meant that a sense of familiarity with the world which is necessarily our home was becoming less and less credible. The home made uncanny, made threatening and dangerous, is of course the central trope of a gothic tradition which seems to have little in common with modernism. However, modernist experiment breaks down formal convention in order to question our sense of reality, our sense that we know and understand the world. It is no surprise, then, that the creation of such fissures should release a multitude of peculiarly modern ghosts (see Smith and Wallace 2001).

## POLITICS AND ECONOMICS

The first decades of the twentieth century contained a number of political and economic cataclysmic events which transformed the social and cultural worlds of Europe. I begin with the First World War, which historians now see as in many ways beginning the 'short' twentieth century (Hobsbawm 1994), and certainly the event which most obviously shaped the modernism of the 1920s. I then go back to the period before the war to map out more general social and political changes from 1900 and through the interwar years, in particular the achievement of mass democracy and the changing role of the state, before looking at the ideological clashes of the 1930s between fascism and communism.

### The First World War (1914–18)

Without doubt, the central political event of the early twentieth century, and the central event for Anglo-American modernism, was the First World War. Many historians speak of the 'long nineteenth century' because the Europe of that century remained essentially intact until 1914. This world was destroyed by the First

World War. Although the completeness of the destruction was not obvious until well after the war was over, even at its beginning it was clear that the conflict would reshape the world.

Through the nineteenth century it had been assumed that the major European countries represented 'civilization', and that the attributes of civilization precluded an outbreak of violence and destruction at its heart. As suggested by the historian Eric Hobsbawm, 'This civilization was capitalist in its economy; liberal in its legal and constitutional structure; bourgeois in the image of its characteristic hegemonic class; glorying in the advance of science, knowledge and education, material and moral progress; and profoundly convinced of the centrality of Europe' (1994: 6). Not only did the war destroy the belief that such bases for society could maintain stability and peace, but it also undermined faith in these bases per se.

Up until 1914 there had been no major war for a century; those wars that had involved major powers lasted only a matter of months; and since 1871 there had been 'no wars in Europe at all in which the armies of major powers crossed any hostile frontier' (ibid.: 22–3). Previous wars meant loss of face, loss of trade, loss of influence, and the loss of relatively small numbers of servicemen; the Great War of 1914–18 led to 9 million deaths among the combative nations, of which approximately 750,000 were British (Winter 2003: 75). It saw the destruction of three empires – the Ottoman, the Austro-Hungarian and the Russian – and was at its close the bloodiest war in history. Beyond this, millions of people were left wounded, disabled, displaced, traumatized, grieving. Although the idea of an actual 'lost generation' – which immediately after the war and since has so dominated cultural memory – has been challenged by some recent historians (DeGroot 1996: 271–5), the trauma of loss is *the* legacy of the war. As Jay Winter suggests, '[a]mong the major combatants, it is not an exaggeration to suggest that every family was in mourning; most for a relative – a father, a son, a brother, a husband – others for a friend, a colleague, a lover, a companion' (Winter 1998: 2). As well as this, what was lost was at a most fundamental level a sense of 'at homeness' in the world. For those who experienced the war, the world had become an alien place.

Among the accounts, literary and otherwise, of those who had fought in the war and those who experienced it on the home front, the most common claim is that the events of the war were beyond comprehension. The usual ways of seeing the world became lies. The novelist, poet and essayist Ford Madox Ford came back from the front unable to see the world as most non-combatants did:

> You may say that everyone who had taken physical part in the war was then mad. No one could have come through that shattering experience and still view life and mankind with any normal vision ... it had been revealed to you that beneath Ordered Life was stretched the abyss of Chaos. (Ford 1933: 48–9)

For combatants the war was most commonly hell, but a hell that stretched previous conceptions or images of hell. The war stretched to breaking point language, imagination, the codes and assumptions which dictated how the very surface of the world was perceived as can be seen so clearly in the fragmented, shattered First World War paintings of the British artist Paul Nash (1889–1946).

In some situations the wrench of the war seemed to open up possibilities rather than destroying them. It has been argued, for example, that for women the war presented unprecedented freedoms and possibilities (Gilbert and Gubar 1988: 260). However, a number of critics have questioned this as too simplistic (Ouditt 1994: 8). Even where such possibilities are clear, the sense of trauma and loss which accompanies them is clearer. Helen Zenna Smith's (1896–1985) novel, *Not So Quiet* ... (1930), is based on a diary kept by a woman who had served as an ambulance driver in France. Written in the first person, it is a grimly realistic account of the lives of the women ambulance drivers; but such is the strange horror of their 'reality', the novel uses the elliptical, staccato style of modernist prose. Early on, one character, Tosh, decides to cut off her hair as it is infested with lice. The other women with whom she shares her room, including the narrator, are torn between horror and envy at this symbolic act of liberation and freedom, but also of loss (Smith 1988: 13ff.). It is indeed the sense of violence forced on Tosh's body through the circumstances of war that most lingers, and this is echoed later when Tosh's ambulance is bombed and she is killed, 'her head hanging childishly on one side' (ibid.: 159). The narrator's sister, Trix, doing war work in France, experiences the sexual freedoms made possible through the war, but becomes pregnant and has to go through an illegal abortion, after which she 'is miserably thin and white, and there are lines about her mouth that are not good to see in a girl of nineteen' (ibid.: 212). The new ways of living and new ways of writing forced on women by the war were possibilities born of trauma, and as such could not be experienced unproblematically as gain.

## Mass democracy and the modernist response

The effects of the First World War reached into virtually every aspect of life, from the wearing of wristwatches to significant developments in plastic surgery. However, the great underlying shifts which most profoundly affected British society for the rest of the century were the establishment of mass democracy and the increasingly interventionist role of the state. While undoubtedly the war made such changes irreversible, events and debates before the war had already begun to strain and shift the country's sense of itself in this regard.

Britain at the end of the nineteenth century was already a nation in which the vast majority of people lived in urban areas (78 per cent by 1901) and where technology had already begun to shape the lives of the majority; but in a number of ways, the country in 1900 did retain some traditional structures and assumptions. The most important sources of wealth were still land, banking and commerce (Pugh 1999: 17), and the most powerful groups in the country were still in agreement over a basically liberal vision of society – the freedom of the individual was paramount and the principles of free trade were contestable only in a crisis. It is these areas that events led many to experience the pre-war period too as one of conflict, tension and far-reaching change. While nineteenth-century liberalism had at its heart the primacy of the freedom of the individual, from the 1870s on, a number of groups (women, workers, Irish nationalists) began to ask who this free individual might be. Their campaigns made very clear the limits of traditional liberal 'freedom' for marginalized groups, and began to demand more clearly a move from subjection to the claims of full subjectivity.

By the beginning of the twentieth century, most men over the age of 21 had been granted the right to vote in general elections, although a sizeable number were still excluded. All women remained excluded, and the period saw the acceleration of the 'votes for women' campaign with the founding of the Women's Social and Political Union (WSPU) by Emmeline Pankhurst and her family in 1903. The period from the founding of the WSPU until the outbreak of war saw the transformation of the campaign from one willing to work within constitutional boundaries and through the institutions of existing political parties to a campaign committed to militancy, and the concomitant rise of public awareness and press coverage.

While the WSPU was by no means the whole of the women's suffrage campaign, the Union was significant in its instigation of protest and campaigning tactics which went beyond those previously used, and challenged not only the constitutional proprieties of the state, but also more generally conventional understandings of what kind of behaviour was proper to women, and more particularly to 'ladies'. Recent historians have suggested that suffragette militancy in fact delayed the franchise (Pugh 2002a), but it is clear that such conflicts deeply challenged cherished notions of femininity, masculinity and the proper relation between men and women. From the autumn of 1905 until the outbreak of the war, the WSPU campaign came to include the policy of 'interrupting' meetings, chalking slogans on pavements, hunger strikes, the committing of 'technical assaults' in order to get arrested, stone throwing, pouring acid into post boxes, the cutting of telegraph wires and setting fire to empty houses. Opponents of the campaign justified the harsh treatment of suffragettes, including manhandling, imprisonment and later the forced feeding of women on hunger strike in prison, on the grounds that the women had initiated a breaking of traditional conventions of behaviour between men and women.

While these challenges were at their most acute in the militants' campaign, non-militant feminists, and those who continued to campaign for the vote using non-militant means, also questioned conventional understandings of women's character and role. The non-militant suffrage groups had come together under the National Union of Women's Suffrage Societies in the 1880s, and during the pre-war years they held hundreds of public meetings, and saw a large increase in their memberships. In the summer of 1913, the NUWSS organized a huge pilgrimage. Processions from all over the country converged on London at the end of July, and a mass rally was held in Hyde Park.

A number of women associated with modernism campaigned for the vote, many of them, such as novelists May Sinclair and Violet Hunt (1866–1942), belonging to the Women Writers Suffrage League. However, challenges to orthodox sexual politics from modernists tended to be more usually outside the strict boundaries of campaigns for the vote. The complex relations between modernist writing and the politics of gender before the war can be traced in the history of the weekly periodical founded in 1911 by Dora Marsden as *The Freewoman.* Marsden had previously worked for the WSPU, but where the suffragette organization was militant and its aims were limited to securing the vote, Mardsen created a paper that was radical and that saw feminism as speaking to the foundational principles of society. In it feminist politics were linked with challenges to conventional sexuality, the mistreatment of workers, and the discussion of wages for motherhood. Women's subjection was not crucially in being excluded from the vote, but in their traditional roles as daughter, wife, mother and low-paid worker. Unlike either the WSPU or the NUWSS, *The Freewoman* linked women's oppression to capitalism.

By the end of 1912, however, the paper's publisher had gone bankrupt and W. H. Smith stopped distributing it due to its radical content. It was relaunched in 1913 as *The New Freewoman* with financial support from readers, including May Sinclair, Amy Lowell (1874–1925), Dorothy Shakespear (1886–1973), H. D. and Dorothy Richardson. By this time, Marsden was moving further away from her roots in the suffrage movement, and the paper shifted its focus from feminism to 'individualism' more generally. At the same time, Ezra Pound persuaded Marsden to include literary material, for which he would act as editor. Towards the end of 1913 poetry appeared by Pound himself, H. D., Amy Lowell, William Carlos Williams (1883–1963), the Imagist poet F. S. Flint (1885–1960) and Ford Madox Ford. Through

1914 the paper became a space for the publication of experimental writing, firstly Imagism, then later the work of T. S. Eliot and James Joyce. By the end of this year Marsden had changed the paper's name to *The Egoist* (see The 'little magazines', p. 118). She retired in 1914 and the editorship was taken up by Harriet Shaw Weaver. From this point, *The Egoist* became a purely literary journal. The modern, experimental writer, rather than the 'freewoman', became the standard for the individual who claims autonomy and freedom, and lives according to their own standards and beliefs. This movement of the journal from a radical politics of inclusion to one that was implicitly and sometimes explicitly elitist encompasses the broad and complex field of modernist politics (see The interwar years, p. 49).

If a number of modernist writers championed a radical individualism, this position was shaped not just by aesthetics, but also as a reaction against the tangible changes in the political makeup of Britain. By the 1920s, democracy had opened out to include, not just women, but working-class men previously excluded from the suffrage. As Arthur Marwick argues, Britain in 1914 was not a democracy: 'the franchise was not based on any universalist principle, but on certain property or residential qualifications, with the result that two-fifths of all men, apart from all women, did not have the vote; some men had several votes' (Marwick 1991: 29). The Representation of the People Act passed in February 1918 gave the vote to almost all men and to women over 30 who were, or were married to, local government voters. This Act increased the electorate from the pre-war figure of between 7 and 8 million to 13 million men and over 8 million women. For the first time the majority of the electorate were working class. The Equal Franchise Act of 1928 enfranchised men and women on an equal footing and increased the electorate to nearly 29 million; for the first time the majority of voters (52.7 per cent) were women.

## The changing role of the state

Throughout the period of this book, various changes in political parties and institutions began to change the makeup of those who actually held power. The Parliament Act (1911), brought in by the Liberal government, not only curtailed the power of the House of Lords in vetoing legislation, but also introduced a salary for MPs. The authority of the aristocracy was challenged and undermined, and for the first time those without independent wealth could stand for election and take their seats in the House of Commons. Other legislation in the pre-war period changed the rules governing the funding of political parties, as a result making it possible for the unions to set up a political party to represent working-class people, to finance candidates in elections, and to fund a national network of local parties. The Labour Party was founded in 1906, and returned 29 MPs in the election of that year. Its presence was further established when a number of ministerial positions were held by Labour MPs in the wartime coalitions. By the early 1920s, following the expansion of the electorate in 1918, the Labour Party could command enough support to supplant the Liberal Party as the second party, and the first Labour government was formed in 1924. While Labour MPs on the whole came from the lower middle classes, rather than the working class, still the emergence of the party in the first two decades of the century represented a significant change at the heart of the country's ruling elite.

This shift in the personnel running the state was accompanied during this period by a shift in assumptions about the role of the state. Nineteenth-century liberalism had at its heart a horror of government intervention in anything beyond its traditional areas of interest – the constitution, the law, the Church and foreign policy – and by the end of the century this had become the consensus at the heart of both the main

political parties. However, the new century brought a
panic provoked by the poor health revealed by the
rejection of thousands of men who volunteered for the
Boer War. The end of the war in 1902 saw not only a
challenge to British imperial might, but also anxiety
about the state of the nation more generally. As it was
increasingly admitted that poverty and ill health had
causes in economic forces beyond the control of the
individual, so too the responsibility of the government
for the welfare of its people began to be acknowledged.

This growing sense went hand in hand with the
expansions in democracy discussed above. The newly
elected representatives of the working class began to
demand government action, but also representatives of
the traditional elite saw the taking up of such responsibilities as a way of avoiding more radical demands or
even revolution. Early reforms by the Liberal government of 1906 concentrated on children – the provision
of free school meals, of medical inspection in schools,
the compulsory registration of births, and a Children's
Act of 1908. Unlike earlier welfare provision, the Liberal
reforms acknowledged the recipient as a full citizen
rather than treating them as a criminal. Under earlier
poor law legislation, for example, the recipients of help
lost their franchise. The Liberal government removed
such penalties. In his first budget as Chancellor of the
Exchequer in 1908, David Lloyd George introduced a
scheme for old age pensions, and in his 'People's budget' of 1909 went further in recreating the relations
between the state and its people. The budget

> established the principle that taxation ought to be related to
> capacity to pay. This was reflected both in the system of
> graduation and in the shift from indirect taxes on con-
> sumption, which were largely paid by the poor, to direct
> taxes on income and wealth. ... Much of the extra revenue
> was now spent on social welfare ... Thus the effect of this
> combination of social and taxation policies was

unquestionably to redistribute the nation's income from rich to poor, albeit very slightly. (Pugh 1999: 135)

The demands of war increased intervention, with the government assuming control of the railways and the coalfields, managing food distribution and controlling levels of rent. While much of this was reversed at the end of the war, in a number of areas, in particular health and social welfare, the pre-war changes and the experience of the First World War itself initiated a governmental role which peaked in the establishment of the welfare state by the 1945 Labour government.

## The interwar years: communism and fascism

Overall, the pre-war Liberal reforms and the changes brought about by the war, from changes in industrial relations to new maternity provision, enmeshed working-class people more and more firmly into the operations of the state. While this was certainly viewed with suspicion by some working-class people, it was viewed with horror by some writers and artists. Modernism as an artistic practice has at its heart a particularly high valuation of the aesthetic, of artworks, and for many modernists this was inherently linked to the values of tradition and leisure encapsulated by a strong aristocracy. Not only did these changes lessen the power of the aristocracy, they gave power to the working classes and, crucially, transformed the state from one concerned with tradition and the heritage of the past to one concerned with bureaucracy and financial efficiency. More generally, many in Europe reacted to the upheaval of the Communist Revolution in Russia in 1917, and to the conflict produced by the difficult economic situation throughout the interwar years, by moving towards a right-wing politics that seemed to promise strength and stability.

In 'Sailing to Byzantium' (1928) by W. B. Yeats, the

speaker leaves the contemporary world for that of Byzantium where the possibility of a perfect artistry exists which can create outside the troubling effects of history (see Glossary: myth). For Yeats, the lower class that *is* valued is that of the peasant artisan, close to the land, living in harmony with their 'betters', and the carriers of valuable knowledge, spiritual and creative. This reactionary rejection of the contemporary for a temporally or culturally distant society – Byzantium for Yeats, medieval Provence or China or Japan for Pound – where it is believed that aesthetic values are stable and the artist is valued by those in power is characteristic of a number of Anglo-American modernists. It is this that most obviously attracted some of these writers to fascism, as it seemed, at least initially, to offer a return to such values. Among the works of modernist writers which are most explicitly sympathetic to extreme right-wing politics are Percy Wyndham Lewis's *Hitler* (1931), T. S. Eliot's *After Strange Gods* (1934) and Ezra's Pound's *Jefferson and/or Mussolini* (1935). Pound's radio broadcasts from Italy (1941–43) are perhaps the most notorious instance of this, and led to charges of treason against him at the end of the Second World War.

In the 1930s, it became clear that the context for these anxieties and instabilities in Britain was not so much an expanding democracy and a strong labour movement galvanized by rising unemployment and attempts to recover from the war, but a worldwide situation where economic depression produced by the Wall Street Crash in 1929 and the tumultuous political effects of the war were producing extreme ideological conflict. While this was more marked in other European countries, in Britain the 1930s was still experienced as a decade of increasing political and economic crisis. Unemployment continued to rise (it never fell below 1 million during the interwar years), and in the first half of the decade, the National Government, formed in 1931 in response to the economic crisis following the Crash, seemed to have little idea how to remedy the situation, and this led many on both left and right to despair of parliament. More generally the sense of crisis both was an effect of and generated a sense that British fortunes could not be isolated from what Hobsbawm has called an 'international ideological civil war' (Hobsbawm 1994: 144).

While Mussolini had come to power in Italy in 1922, and, as suggested above, right-wing reaction to the Russian Revolution in 1917 and workers' movements more generally was a feature of Europe in the 1920s, fascism became a significant presence in world history only after Hitler became Chancellor in Germany in 1933. In Britain, the most 'successful' fascist grouping was Oswald Mosley's British Union of Fascists. While the BUF was never a dominant force in British politics, it did produce reactions, positive and negative, which were significant over and above its actual political power. The strength of these can be seen in the violence associated with the BUF, particularly during its rally at Olympia in 1934 and most famously during the battle of Cable Street in 1936. While its membership was probably never huge, its ideas influenced a good many very influential people, including some in the Conservative Party. During a debate in the House of Commons in 1934 praise was given to 'the thousands of young men who have joined the Blackshirt Movement. They are among the best elements in this country' (Pugh 2002b: 232). The appeal of strong leadership, order, an agenda which promised to revitalize British industry and refocus British power on the empire appealed to many, from land-owning aristocrats to impoverished industrial workers.

In Britain, membership of the Communist Party, while also never huge, increased dramatically during the decade, from 2,500 in 1930 to 18,000 in 1938. While evidence of Stalin's murderous activities in the USSR was difficult to deny, what maintained support for the Soviet Union among the people and governments of liberal democratic nations was its trenchant opposition to fascism. Fascism presented such a strong 'common enemy' that it managed to unify, however briefly and problematically, countries and political positions which otherwise would have little in common. While to many in the 1930s, Germany may have seemed a stable country with just a few distasteful attributes, for many intellectuals it was clear early on that the regime wished to overturn those very things which had come to constitute 'civilization'. Mass democracy, the rights of the individual, equality before the law, the state as protector rather than aggressor, the value of 'disinterested' knowledge – Nazi hostility to these became clear as Jewish and left-wing intellectuals left Germany during the 1930s, and the regime began to burn books and ban artworks. For these reasons, many artists and intellectuals became some of the first to oppose Hitler and his government.

## The Spanish Civil War (1936–39)

In Europe, one strategy that did seem to have some localized, although often short-term, success in resisting fascism was the creation of 'popular fronts' – the uniting of the various factions which made up the centre and left. Popular front governments dominated France in the 1930s, and it was the electoral success of a popular front government in Spain which led to the Spanish Civil War (1936–39) which in turn became the focus of the 'international ideological civil war' in the second half of the decade. In response to the election of the government, the right in Spain, led by the generals, staged a military coup to overturn it. Although the coup was not wholly successful, the ferment led to the civil war. Both sides, the popular front government and the generals, looked for external support. While the response of ordinary people in Europe was immediate and very strong, the response of the non-fascist governments was less so. British government policy was one of non-intervention, as nominally was that of France and the USSR, although even the appearance of non-intervention was quickly abandoned by the latter. The support for the Republican cause in Spain by the USSR did much to raise the Soviets' prestige during the period; the USSR was the only government to help the legitimate government of Spain.

However, thousands of ordinary people did lend support. The International Brigades were founded to give military aid to the Republicans, and over 40,000 foreigners from over 50 nations fought in these. In particular, many writers and intellectuals either joined the Brigades or contributed to the cause in other ways. In Britain, a number of the most important younger poets of the 1930s – including W. H. Auden (1907–73), Stephen Spender (1909–95) and John Cornford (1915–36) – spent time in Spain, fighting, driving ambulances, writing propaganda. John Cornford died there aged 21. For writers politicized by the situation in the 1930s, Spain seemed to offer a clear and unambiguous platform from which to oppose fascism and unite in a vital cause (see Poetry, p. 69).

The lack of organization on the Republican side, and the infighting which wracked the various factions on the left, so memorably represented in George Orwell's (1903–50) *Homage to Catalonia* (1938), and the lack of support from other governments, meant that a victory went to the Generals, and Spain in 1939 entered a long period of isolation. It was nominally neutral during the Second World War. The Civil War produced much important writing and art, though, not least because, for the moment of the war, it seemed as if art could have an impact on and change the world.

The conflicts that were played out in Spain during the Civil War were of course writ large across the world following the outbreak of the Second World War in 1939. In many ways, the changes that had been forced on Britain during the First World War – changes in relation between classes, between men and women, and between the individual and the state – were sealed and made permanent by the Second. The landslide victory of the Labour Party in the General Election of June 1945 makes this clear. While the Conservative Winston Churchill was revered by most as a great wartime leader, the majority of people in the country wanted something new for peacetime. The Labour Party formed only their third government, and their first majority government. The new government's programme of nationalization and their creation of a welfare state changed the way millions of people lived. It changed too perceptions on questions of authority, class privilege and social and cultural entitlement.

By 1945, a number of the central figures of Anglo-American modernism – Lawrence, Joyce and Woolf – were dead. Following the war, many younger British writers rejected the formal innovations of modernism in part because of their associations with the now discredited political and class affiliations of the writers. As the horror of the Holocaust became clear, and as Britain was reshaped through the reforms of the Labour government, the political consensus of the country began to move from rigid class boundaries and an acceptance of privilege and elitism towards, on the surface at least, a more meritocratic and democratic society.

## DEVELOPMENTS IN SCIENCE AND TECHNOLOGY

This section begins by looking at the role of science in the creation of modernity (see Glossary: modernity), and at the way that developments in scientific thought have affected the wider society. It then goes on to focus on one of the most important scientific discoveries of the early twentieth century, Albert Einstein's theory of relativity. The period saw many significant changes in scientific thinking and practice, but Einstein's theory was unique in the way it became famous beyond the world of science, as well as fundamentally changing scientific thinking and the way our perception of the world was understood. We then look at technology, mapping the role of technology during the period before looking at a particular use of technological thinking, Frederick Taylor's (1856–1915) *Principles of Scientific Management*, and the changing understandings of the human body it reveals.

## Science, technology and the construction of modernity

When we speak of 'modernity', we mean the events, forces, practices and innovations which, from the late eighteenth century onwards, created the world, and the worldview, of the West. While many things before this date can be seen in retrospect as contributing to the construction of modernity – for example, Gutenburg's invention of the printing press in 1450 – two broad changes by the late eighteenth century instigated major shifts in the way the world was understood and in the tools through which it was managed and experienced.

First, while individuals since ancient times had been practising 'science' in the sense of trying to understand and explain the natural world, conclusions were not based on repeated experimentation, and natural phenomena were explained rather through deductive reasoning, that is reasoning based on existing beliefs and traditions. The great scientific revolution which changed this and was initiated by, among others, Galileo (1564–1642), René Descartes (1596–1650) and Isaac Newton (1643–1727) in the seventeenth century, claimed that nature was nothing but matter which should be investigated through experimentation, through logical induction, rather than existing beliefs. In 1687 Newton published his laws of motion of material objects, providing the basis for the mechanical view of the universe that dominated science for the next two centuries. If all the laws which determined the natural world could one day be established, then not only were the operations of nature fixed and predictable, but human knowledge was capable of a complete understanding of the world. Nature was neither capricious nor mysterious, but was itself systematic, was a machine.

The second of these two shifts, the Industrial Revolution, which began in the eighteenth century, was a complex of new inventions and practices which depended on the shifts in thinking described above. Changes in manufacturing practices radically changed the economy of Britain, the first country to industrialize, and this in turn changed the whole texture and fabric of society, from demographics to diet, from architecture to political power, from conceptions of time to conceptions of humanness.

The Industrial Revolution and its effects constructed modernity. To take one example, the explosion in population experienced at this time, and the movement of large numbers of people from rural to urban areas to work in the new 'manufactories', eventually forced governments to begin to take on responsibilities for the well-being of their citizens through the provision of sanitation, housing and, eventually, education and medical care. In order to provide these things, governments needed to know who and where the population of the country was. Beginning with the first population census in 1801, and via hundreds of surveys and reports throughout the nineteenth century, the state mapped its population. The consequences of this were not just more housing and better drains, however; these efforts fundamentally remade the relation between the individual and the state. If the state knew who you were and where you lived, it could insist on your paying taxes, could monitor the way you treated your children, and make sure you did nothing detrimental to its own interests. The complex and binding relation of mutual duties and responsibilities between state and citizen with which we are so familiar was created during this period. Indeed, not the least of the changes brought about by the Industrial Revolution was people's sense that the time they lived in was 'modern', so our sense of our modernness paradoxically places us within the long history of modernity.

While the changes that constructed modernity can be seen as far more significant than any that followed *within* modernity, nevertheless by the end of the nineteenth century changes in scientific thinking and technological innovation were such that they began to undermine the confidence in human ability and the sense of social and political progress produced through the changes out-lined in the previous section. It is responses to these shifts in particular that we can see informing and fis-suring the work of literary modernism.

For example, the rediscovery of work on the laws of inheritance by Gregor Mendel (1822–84), lost for over three decades, created the science of genetics at the beginning of the twentieth century, and in so doing shifted nineteenth-century understandings of evolution. While studies in genetics provided a more solid basis for theories of evolution, they also suggested that change over generations, rather than being continuous, was in fact discontinuous, and proceeded in mutations or 'jumps'. Indeed, geneticists argued that it was only through mutation that real change could occur. Given the social and political uses to which Darwin's theories had been put during the second half of the nineteenth century, such assertions seemed to undermine liberal ideas of non-violent social progress and of the extent to which evolutionary change could be controlled and directed.

It was in physics, though, that new theories and dis-coveries were among the most radical in science at the turn of the nineteenth and twentieth centuries. Experimentation in the area of electricity had led to the discovery of X-rays by Wilhelm Röntgen (1845–1923) in the late 1890s and the discovery of radioactivity by Henri Becquerel (1852–1908) in 1896. Both of these, and the discoveries which followed from them, profoundly affected ideas of vision, of hierarchies of surface and depth, of the substantiality of the human body, and the nature of the material world. More radical still, Max Planck's (1858–1947) quantum theory of 1900 was a fundamental challenge to classical physics. While it was less generally well known than the theories of relativity of Albert Einstein (1879–1955), it was the most important innovation in physics during the period. It established a new system of physics and suggested a worldview which, contrary to Newtonian physics, seemed to deny the possibility of a complete understanding of reality. Einstein was one of the first to see the implications of Planck's theories, using them in his special theory of relativity (1905). Einstein revolutionized and went on to popularize scientific thinking, and in so doing became the most famous scientist in the world. His special and general theories of relativity (1916), as they were known in the English-speaking world, created the foundation upon which the twentieth century's picture of the physical world was based. If the eighteenth century saw the first scientific revolution, Einstein's work in the early twentieth century initiated the second.

## Albert Einstein and the second scientific revolution

From Aristotle onwards, thinkers and scientists had inferred the existence of something called 'ether', a transparent substance which permeated the whole universe. The scientists of the scientific revolution in the seventeenth century revived the idea. If the mechanistic view says that the universe consists of matter and motion, then matter must move *through* something. If the mechanistic view were correct, then a mechanistic ether had to exist. The establishment of the wave theory of light in the early nineteenth century again seemed to necessitate the existence of ether. In order for the theory of light waves to conform to the laws of mechanics, the waves had to be carried by matter, and that matter was believed to be the ether. The work of the physicists Michael Faraday (1791–1867) and James Clerk Maxwell (1831–79) on electromagnetic forces suggested that light was part of the electromagnetic spectrum, and this changed the focus of physics from forces acting on matter at a distance to investigating how forces themselves moved through space. Again, ether seemed to fill the literal and conceptual gaps, and between the work of Faraday and then Maxwell and the end of the century, an enormous amount of work was done to try to measure and define a 'luminiferous' (light-bearing) ether which was strong enough to support waves of light, and flexible enough to allow the movement of the largest of material bodies, such as planets. The problem was that, despite the efforts of such greats of nineteenth-century science as Lord Kelvin (1824–1907) and Maxwell himself, no physicist had been able to detect ether, or to measure its effects.

By the end of the century, the new equations explaining and detailing the forces of electromagnetism, light in particular, still demanded a resolution with Newton's mechanical worldview. This central problem of physics fired the young Einstein. He began the thinking that led to his theories by asking questions about how electromagnetic forces move through space, and whether the existence of 'ether' was a necessary supposition. His special theory of relativity, first published as 'On the Electrodynamics of Moving Bodies' in 1905, attempted to answer these questions by making two fundamental, although seemingly contradictory, assumptions. First, Einstein took Galileo's principle of relativity – that steady motion is only detectable with reference to an outside point, that is there is no such thing as absolute rest, everything is moving in relation to something else – to apply to electrodynamics (that is, the movement of light) as well as mechanical motion. Second, he took the speed of light as finite (it is always c. 186,000 miles per second, or c. 300,000 kilometres per second, regardless of the motion of its source or its receiver). These two assumptions appeared to be contradictory – the first suggests the speed of light should be relative, the second asserts that it is absolute – until Einstein realized the implications of this for assumptions about time. If the speed of light is absolute, then two observers at different distances from the source will see it, or the images of the objects from which it bounces, at different times. What is relative is not the speed of light but the time it takes to reach each observer. Speed is distance divided by time; so if the speed of light is absolute, and distance between observers is variable, then time has to be variable too in order to make the equation work. In other words, if the speed of light is absolute, then, contrary to the assumptions of Newtonian physics, space and time cannot be. And if they are not absolutes, then ether is not needed to understand how light moves. As Einstein stated in the second paragraph of his paper: the 'introduction of a "light ether" will prove to be superfluous, inasmuch as the view to be developed here will not require a "space at absolute rest" endowed with special properties' (quoted in Panek 2005: 30–1).

Einstein's general theory (1916), which described gravity as a distortion of space rather than a mechanical force which travels through the ether, was confirmed towards the end of 1919 by measurements of a total eclipse of the sun by English astronomer, Arthur Eddington (1882–1944). This confirmation was widely reported in the newspapers, and Eddington became an enthusiastic popularizer and disseminator of 'relativity' in newspapers and journals and in his *Space, Time and Gravitation* (1920). Einstein himself was happy to explain his theories beyond the scientific community, publishing *Relativity: The Special and the General Theory* in 1920 for a lay audience. The next decade saw a spate of books attempting to explain relativity, including the British philosopher Bertrand Russell's (1872–1970) *ABC of Relativity* (1925). In 1921 Einstein was awarded the Nobel Prize, and from then on, he became very famous, known around the world as *the* modern scientist. As Tim Armstrong suggests, Einstein's impact was not just *on* modernism, but also *as* a modernist.

> Einstein *is* a modernist in his background (*fin de siècle* Vienna), in his models (trains moving across time zones), and in the way he was represented (the genius-iconoclast).
> (Armstrong 2005: 115; emphasis in original)

Despite the popularizing efforts, however, many, perhaps most, people did not have a clear, or indeed accurate, idea of Einstein's theories, or of the significance of their implications. Einstein's theories did not say that 'everything is relative'. While they showed that some things are, the crux was that a single fixed law describes all relations between any two systems. Nevertheless, the most widely reported aspect of Einstein's work – that the phenomena of the physical world as experienced by human beings do not have absolute value, that all perception of reality is, rather, relative – had an enormous impact. Further, Einstein's work asserted that what needed to be considered was not just matter and motion, but the medium by which any observer perceives them – that is, light. What was crucial was an entity that was a tiny part of a spectrum that was mostly invisible, that according to the laws of classical physics was neither matter nor motion, that seemed indeed without substance. This seeming proof of the ephemerality of reality led to all sorts of conclusions with which Einstein certainly would have had no truck.

The fact that not many could understand Einstein's theories, coupled with the sense that his work had fundamentally shifted conceptions of the universe, began to suggest to people that the most important truths of the world were no longer directly comprehensible. Contrary to the mechanistic view of the universe, where scientists and lay people alike could at least *see* the operations of physical laws, the new physics, astronomy and cosmology initiated by Einstein's findings were beyond the perception and indeed conceptualization of the vast majority of human minds.

## Technology and the speed of modernity

Einstein's discoveries suggested the brilliance of which a human mind was capable, and revived a kind of wonder about the natural world, but they also suggested to many that human perception was partial, untrustworthy, and sometimes just wrong. Technological developments during the period, while celebrated for improving living conditions and medical knowledge, for example, similarly began to remake humanity in difficult and problematic ways. 'Technology' refers to the ways in which scientific discoveries are put into practice and made useful to human society. The scientific ideas discussed above are very abstract, and it took some time for their revolutionary implications to become clear to a wider society. However, by the beginning of the twentieth century, the practical, or technological, implications of many scientific discoveries had already begun to change fundamentally the way people lived and, crucially, the way they thought about what it meant to be human.

The economic boom of the late nineteenth century had led to an explosion in technological innovation and invention. New methods of transport (in particular the car and the aeroplane), research into the application of electricity to industry, and the mass production of consumables from clothes to paper to food changed the very texture of the world in industrialized countries. In particular, innovations in communications technology – the telephone (1870s) and then the radio (1896) –

remade understandings of presence, absence, time, and the boundaries between individuals (see Thurschwell 2001; Luckhurst 2002; Kern 2003).

Some modernist artists and writers, particularly in Europe, championed this new world, and saw their own experiment as an extension of its dynamism. For example, the French painter Robert Delaunay (1885–1941) was fascinated by the Eiffel Tower and celebrated it over and over again in paintings such as *The City of Paris* (1912), *Eiffel Tower* (1911) and *Sun, Tower, Airplane* (1913). The tower had been built in 1889, the tallest structure of its time. Its use in 1913 to send the first time signal around the world – effectively standardizing time – further secured it as a symbol of the speed, efficiency and rationalizing effects of modernity. However, for many, and for many Anglo-American modernists, the way such innovations reshaped understandings of, in particular, the human body and human identity, was cause for disquiet rather than celebration.

## Technology and the 'scientizing' of the body

All technology, from a sharpened piece of flint to the most sophisticated telescope able to see far into space, augments the human body. Technology extends and refines the possibilities of the five senses: spectacles and the microscope extend sight; the telephone and the stethoscope extend hearing, and so on. Technology enables human actions to be faster and more precise. This augmentation was very often greeted with excitement and enthusiasm, but a sense that the human body is somehow unfit for the modern world has always been a feature of modernity. If the augmentation offered by technology was increasingly necessary for humans to live in the modern world, then surely this meant that the human body itself was terribly lacking, was simply not enough. By the beginning of the twentieth century this sense of anxiety and crisis around technology focused on the reduction of the body to being merely a part of a mechanized and systematized process, rather than its own complete self.

The mechanization of the human body had been of concern since the beginning of the Industrial Revolution. The Romantic idea of the self was in part a reaction to this, and criticism of industrial and economic processes which treated human beings as machines fuelled many of the most influential essays of the early nineteenth-century critic Thomas Carlyle (1795–1881). While industrial method dominated both the enthusiasms and concerns of the first half of the century, by the later nineteenth century, the methodologies of science had become dominant. It was the language and practices of science that had come to dominate all attempts at understanding and organization, including those directed at human beings themselves. Of course, if we want to understand, for example, how human beings reproduce, then anatomy and chemistry do seem obvious places to go for an answer. However, the scientizing of the human body began to go far beyond the biological or the medical. More than this, while each new innovation provoked anxiety that bodies would somehow be harmed by it – bicycles would harm the reproductive organs of women; driving at speed in cars would harm the major organs of everyone – far more fundamental shifts in conceptions of the human body and of human identity were occurring through new ways of regulating and disciplining the body. Crucially, these disciplinary practices were made legitimate and credible by drawing on the language and methodologies of science. Human activities previously understood as occupying the spheres of the family, the domestic, the traditional, were 'technologized' by the application of science.

In his 1911 work, *The Principles of Scientific Management*, the American Frederick Taylor wrote that his methods could apply 'with equal force to all social activities: to the management of our homes; the management of our

farms; the management of the business of our trades-
men, large and small; of our churches, our philan-
thropic institutions, our universities; and our
governmental departments' (Taylor 1911: 8). Taylor had
begun his career in the 1870s as a foreman in the steel
industry, and through observing the work practices of
his peers developed his principles which aimed to
eliminate waste and increase productivity through the
'scientific' systematization of each job and the 'scientific' training of every worker. To instigate scientific
management, every movement and task of each worker
was scrutinized and timed; the optimum time for the
completion of each task was calculated, and the worker
was drilled in the movements and actions necessary to
achieve this. While most of Taylor's examples focus on
manual work, as the quotation above suggests, he saw his
principles as relevant to all areas of human life, and
indeed as necessary to promoting harmony (ibid.: 12).
By 1911, Taylor had been practising and disseminating
his ideas for 30 years; the publication of his *Principles*
introduced them more widely.

Taylor's ideas rest on the assumption, not just that
human beings can be thought of as machines whose
movements can be efficient, ordered and precisely
repeated, but crucially that without scientific management the body is wasteful, chaotic and ignorant. The
'true science' (ibid.: 8) of his principles is therefore the
only way of acquiring knowledge about any particular
action, and management by an initiated elite is necessary to regulate bodies incapable of self-regulation:

> in almost all of the mechanic arts the science which under-
> lies each act of each workman is so great and amounts to so
> much that the workman who is best suited to actually doing
> the work is incapable of fully understanding this science,
> without the guidance and help of those who are working
> with him or over him, either through lack of education or
> through insufficient mental capacity. (Ibid.: 15)

However, more than doubting the capacities of individual workers, Taylor asserts that the knowledge of workers, based on their familiarity with the traditions of their trade or craft, is not useful to industry without the disciplining and regulation which he sees as scientific:

> The managers assume ... the burden of gathering together all of the traditional knowledge which in the past has been possessed by the workmen and then of classifying, tabulating, and reducing this knowledge to rules, laws, and formulae which are immensely helpful to the workmen in doing their daily work ... The development of a science ... involves the establishment of many rules, laws, and formulae, which replace the judgment of the individual workman, and which can only be effectively used after having been systematically recorded, indexed, etc. (Ibid.: 21–2)

For Taylor, work becomes a 'task' to be codified, and to which the worker needs to be subjected. This subjection involves the gradual evisceration of everything unnecessary to the efficient completion of the task – the body beyond the task is implicitly redefined as waste.

Such notions of waste and efficiency can also be seen in the 'science' of eugenics in the late nineteenth and early twentieth centuries. Eugenicists believed that humanity could be improved through the management and organization of reproduction. They wanted healthy, 'superior' types to be encouraged to reproduce and 'inferior', degenerate types to desist. 'Waste' – the sick, the criminal, the less intelligent – could be eliminated through the application of demographics (see Bradshaw 2003: 34–55; Armstrong 2005: 74–8). Although since the Second World War eugenicist ideas have been most closely associated with Nazi atrocities, in the first half of the century they were widely accepted by many on both the right and the left of the political spectrum. A number of Anglo-American modernists – including D. H.

Lawrence, W. B. Yeats and Virginia Woolf – also espoused them to varying degrees (see Childs 2001).

Changes in concepts of organization in the years around the turn of the nineteenth and twentieth centuries began to shift ideas of the operation of physical laws, the nature of reality, the relations between human beings, and indeed the very definition of the human itself. Unsurprisingly, in the arts, works by artists alive to the modern world reflected these changes, discussed them, and used their awareness of the modern to mark them as different from the work of previous generations. Ezra Pound and the Imagists, for example, distinguished their poetics from those of previous writers through strictures about the elimination of useless words and poetic conventions (see Imagism, p. 101). The Imagist poem was to be rigorously efficient. Indeed, in her introduction to the first of Pound's poems to appear in the journal *The New Freewoman* in 1913, the novelist and critic Rebecca West (1892–1983) suggests that as Taylor wanted 'to introduce scientific management into industry so the *imagistes* want to discover the most puissant way of whirling the scattered star dust of words into a new star of passion' (quoted in Clark 1996: 125).

However, for some artists, the scientizing and technologizing of culture was profoundly disturbing. While artists such as Pound and Eliot may have used the language of science and technology to talk about their experiments, the standardization of culture through the application of technological processes was perceived by them and others as a threat to crucial aesthetic values. Critiques of Taylorism and the rhetoric of efficiency it spawned focused on the lavatory – the place where the cyclical time of the body resists the imposed linearity of the Taylorist model and where waste is most insistently present. In Charlie Chaplin's film comedy, *Modern Times* (1936), Chaplin plays a factory worker whose trip to the lavatory, and other bodily intrusions such as sneezing and itching, wreaks havoc with his ability to be efficient and productive on the production line. Laughter, too, can be seen as one of the body's 'waste products', unproductive, unsystematic and excessive. It is significant that in those artistic practices that most fundamentally resisted the technologization of life – for example, in the European avant-garde movement known as Dada (see The European avant-gardes, p. 112) – the humorous, the childish and the trivial are a central feature.

# 2

## Modernist Literature

Major genres
Movement and literary groups

## MAJOR GENRES

### Poetry

When we first come to read modernist poetry – whether it be an Imagist poem by Ezra Pound (see Imagism, p. 101), or his later *Hugh Selwyn Mauberley* (1920), T. S. Eliot's 'Love Song of J. Alfred Prufrock' (1917) or *The Waste Land* (1922), or Gertrude Stein's *Tender Buttons* (1914) – our most likely reaction is to close the book irritated, offended, and to ask, why does it need to be it so difficult? That it *is* difficult we can usually see from the very pattern of the words on the page. Lines do not always cohere into recognizable sentences, sections stand apart from each other, refusing to display their connection, single words hang, fragmented, foreign languages, many unfamiliar, pepper the page. Indeed, it may not look like poetry at all. Often what we read is not spoken by one person, the 'voice' of the poem; it seems to be spoken by many voices or by none.

But why? These difficulties are not the result of our failure as readers; they are an acknowledgement of what is distinctive about the poetry that is grouped together as modernist; they are a result of its very terms of composition, and of its poetic origins.

An important influence on those poets who constructed a self-consciously modern poetic at the beginning of the twentieth century was the French Symbolist movement of the previous century. Symbolist poetry rejected the public voice of the poet, and spoke instead of an intensely private world. The focus of the poetry was on moments and experiences, often involving contact with the world of alcoholism, crime and sexual perversion, which transfigured ordinary life and propelled the individual into a transcendent spiritual realm. Crucial here was the symbol, which fixed in an almost mystical way the intense, private experience and made it available, however ambiguously and obscurely, to the reader. In working towards this aim of the precise evocation of intense experience, Symbolist poetry began to move towards *vers libre* (free verse) (see Glossary: free verse).

Although Symbolist poetry was very influential on Anglo-American modernist poetry, the latter was in many ways created through Ezra Pound's critique of Symbolism. Certainly, by 1914, in his essay on Vorticism, Pound explicitly set his poetics against those of the Symbolists. Before this, in his collaborations with Yeats, H. D. and Eliot, Pound set out to create a poetry in which '[t]here must be no book words, no periphrases, no inversions' (Pound 1971: 48–9), and in so doing he acted as midwife to a modernist poetics. Against the dream-like state of the Symbolist poem, shaped by the poet's subjective experience, its imagery watery and vague, its technique 'mushy' (Pound 1916: 97), Pound wanted poetry which showed '[o]bjectivity and again objectivity' (Pound 1971: 49).

However, modernist poets did take from Symbolism a commitment to the autonomy of art as opposed to what they saw as the didacticism and moral urging of Victorian poets such as Alfred, Lord Tennyson (1809–92). For modernists, the first responsibility of poetry was an aesthetic one, to tell the truth in the most appropriate verbal forms. In their refusal to provide comforting illusions, modernist poets also shared with Symbolists a sense of estrangement from the general reader. However, while for the Symbolist poet this estrangement was at bottom caused by the fine sensibility of the poet, for modernists such a focus on the poet was a problem. Their focus was on the precision of the *poem* (see Glossary: classicism).

It is in Imagist poetry (or *Imagiste*, as it was known at its beginning) that we see both the working out of the rejection of Symbolism, and the reason for the 'difficulty' at the heart of modernist poetry (see Imagism, p. 101). Imagism begins modernist poetry, not least in its challenge to conventional expectations, and a reconception of what should be demanded formally from poetry is, of course, inseparable from a sense of its relation to the world, and its sense of what that world is like (see The 'difficulty' of art, p. 19, and The problem of language, p. 21).

In the poetry of the central Anglo-American poets – Yeats, Eliot and Pound – this sense is dominated by a focus on the relationship of the present to the past. This concern takes in the relation of the poet, of poetry and of society to the past. For each of these poets, modernism wasn't a rejection of the past per se, it was a rejection of the immediate past (see The interwar years, p. 49). Yeats's use of Irish history and legend and Pound's use of troubadour poetry and translations of ancient Chinese poetry gave them narratives, forms and languages with which, paradoxically, they could renew the poetics of the present. So, for Pound, Chinese poetry provided a model of simplicity and directness which cut through the dead conventions of European poetry. In his translation the 'Song of the Bowmen of Shu' (1915), the dominance of monosyllabic words, the use of the present tense, and the simple, communal voice produces a powerful emotional effect despite the subject of the poem being culturally and temporally distant.

Here we are, picking the first fern-shoots
And saying: When shall we get back to our country?
...
The enemy is swift, we must be careful.
When we set out, the willows were drooping with spring,
We come back in the snow,
We go slowly, we are hungry and thirsty,
Our mind is full of sorrow, who will know of our grief?
(Pound 2005: 44, ll. 1–2, 20–4)

This sense of the present at odds with the values to be found in the past often leads in modernist poetry to intimations of apocalypse. In order to explain the terrible lack and confusion of the present, a number of modernist poets developed ideas of history which saw it as circular rather than linear, so that those moments of value and coherence in the past may one day return (see Glossary: myth) (Williams 2002). For it to return, the present age must end. Nevertheless, an apocalypse was treated with an ambiguous mixture of welcome and terror – the end would mean the end of those things in European culture which were valuable and desirable too. These concerns are evident in Yeats's poetry after his collection *Responsibilities* (1914). As documented in his prose work *A Vision* (1925), Yeats had the most fully worked out historical system, and it both structures and provides imagery for many of his poems, most famously 'The Second Coming' (1920).

The darkness drops again; but now I know
That twenty centuries of stony sleep
Were vexed to nightmare by a rocking cradle,
And what rough beast, its hour come round at last,
Slouches towards Bethlehem to be born? (Yeats 1990: 211)

The major Anglo-American modernist poets saw themselves and their poetry as radically out of step with their time. The politics, culture and economics of the present were sources of melancholy and foreboding. Most problematically for poets, the 'futility and anarchy' (Eliot 2005b: 167) of the present had infected language, their very tool, and it was too late to find it easy to say exactly what they meant, to communicate straightforwardly with the reader. To wrest any truth and order from a degraded language – in T. S. Eliot's words '[t]o purify the dialect of the tribe' (Eliot 1985: 218) – meant then a huge struggle, a struggle that necessitated the use of other, unfamiliar languages, past forms, and sentences which stopped the reader from passing easily from line to line. The 'difficulty' of modernist poetry is both an acting out of the difficulty of the present – torn from the values of the past, chaotic, and destructive – and a revisioning which would bring some kind of redemption.

At the same time, though, there exists in modernist poetry a severe scepticism – sometimes accepting, sometimes melancholy – about poetry's function in the world, about its capacity to intervene. This scepticism increased following the First World War. Before, it was possible, as in the 1914 issue of *Blast*, for example, to celebrate the capacity of avant-garde art to purge and destroy in order to renew (see Vorticism, p. 107). After the destruction of the war, however, this capacity seemed less welcome, and in any case the consequences of the huge destructive power of the modern state – using bureaucracy and the mass mobilization of people and machines – mocked any claims for poetry's agency.

Nevertheless, it is also the case that, following the war, a number of modernist poets began their longer works, poems which clearly (though not always directly) addressed the contemporary world via the broad historical view of the epic form. While pre-war experiments in poetry, centred on Imagism, championed a poetics of limit and restraint, by the middle of the war Pound was suggesting that a long Imagist poem was a possibility (Pound 1916: 109).

In these most important poems of the high modernist

period, the poets consider the central questions of the contemporary world – the rise of democracy, the threat to Europe from violence and disorder, the question of what values the modern world can live by. However, they all – Pound's *Cantos* (1917–69), Eliot's *The Waste Land* (1922) and *Four Quartets* (1935–42), William Carlos Williams's *Spring and All* (1923) and *Paterson* (1946–58) – do this without a linear narrative to give coherence or a vehicle for progress. So, in the *Cantos*, Pound attempted, in the words of his friend Yeats,

> to achieve a work as characteristic of the art of our time as the paintings of Cézanne ... as *Ulysses* and its dream association of words and images, a poem in which there is nothing that can be taken out and reasoned over, nothing that is not a part of the poem itself. (Yeats 2005b: 370–1)

The poetic achievements of modernism paradoxically depend on ambitious claims for poetry coupled with a sense of its marginalization in the world. During the pressing political climate of the 1930s, this difficult position led to a further withdrawal from the world seen in Eliot's *Four Quartets*, or a more explicit attraction to right-wing politics (see The interwar years, p. 49).

The next generation of innovative poets – W. H. Auden, Stephen Spender, Louis MacNeice (1907–63) – had a complex relation to their modernist predecessors (Hynes 1979). In contrast to the latter, for at least part of that decade, all were committed to left-wing political activity and vision, but they display far more restraint in their poetry, and claim far less for poetry's role in the world, while at the same time attempting to communicate with a wider audience.

## The novel

In his 1923 essay, '*Ulysses*, Order and Myth', T. S. Eliot, in commenting on James Joyce's work of the previous year, suggests that the novel as a distinct genre ended with the French novelist Gustave Flaubert (1821–80) and the Anglo-American novelist Henry James (1843–1916). Eliot does not justify this assertion, but uses it to go on to see *Ulysses* as the first of a new genre, one employing the 'mythical method' to remake the form for the post-war world (Eliot 2005b). The sense that the novel needed to be renewed and transformed is *the* unifying element of modernist fiction; writers as different as Virginia Woolf, D. H. Lawrence and Ford Madox Ford self-consciously worked on stretching the limits of the form. Woolf acknowledges this in her attempt to find a new word for it in a diary entry during the writing of *To The Lighthouse* (1927) (Woolf 1982: 34).

In the middle of the nineteenth century, Flaubert had challenged the dominant form of the novel by asserting that the genre, as much as poetry, demanded a rigorous method and style. For him, the nineteenth-century novel was an unruly, untidy monster, only held together by an overbearing and sentimental moralizing. But, argued Flaubert, the novelist had a responsibility to order his work, to transform the material of life into art. Central to his rethinking of the novelistic method was a new approach to the narrator. In *Madame Bovary* (1857), Flaubert's narrator attempts to take an impartial rather than moralistic approach to the action of the novel. The narrative is unfolded through the consciousness of the central character or characters without comment, while at the same time these characters are themselves open to ironic scrutiny.

This approach to the writing of prose fiction was taken up by other European writers such as the Russian novelist and short story writer Ivan Turgenev (1818–83). In terms of the novel in English, Henry James was the pre-eminent follower of Flaubert's lead. In his work, the role of the narrator is transformed from an interferring, hectoring guide into a kind of director or stage manager who arranges things without comment. In his late period works, such as *The Wings of the Dove* (1902) and *The Golden Bowl* (1904), subtle use is made of dialogue in order to display the tiniest nuances of personality and relation, and in the narrative itself sophisticated changes in perspective happen sentence by sentence, almost clause by clause.

Of course, the novel did not end, but Eliot's assertion that the novel ended with Flaubert and James acknowledged the extent to which their approach and theories stretched the form beyond recognition. However, by the beginning of the twentieth century, mainstream English novels, even the most serious and literary, remained untouched by Flaubertian and Jamesian innovations. It is those novelists who critiqued the mainstream novel, and attempted to continue the work of Flaubert and James, who have been retrospectively categorized as modernist. What these writers desired was that the novel be allowed to address the complex and ambiguous realities of the time; that it should accurately reflect these realities as *experienced*, and this was seen as being at odds with the ways previous novels had envisioned it, Christianity had taught it, or convention said it *should* be. What their works demonstrate is that in so doing, the form of the novel had to be transformed.

Three of the most important of these 'realities' can be categorized as follows: individual perception and the mobility of the self; the importance of sex; and irrationality and ambiguity. These categories overlap, but looking at each in turn suggests *why* modernist writers believed the novel had to change.

The innovations in the European visual arts in the late nineteenth and early twentieth centuries had a profound effect on Anglo-American modernist novelists. In their Cubist works, for example, Pablo Picasso (1881–1973) and Georges Braque (1882–1963) undid the convention in Western art for one-point perspective and painted objects flattened and multifaceted, as if seen from multiple positions. While this was certainly partly in order to make visible the particular properties of paint as a medium, rather than concentrating on copying the world, it also asserted the plurality and malleability of vision. We do not all see the world alike, but our vision is shaped by our own individual histories, memories and desires. More than this, perception is mobile – it shifts and changes and cannot be represented by the fixed mimetic image.

This fluidity of perception was also being systematically explored by philosophers and in the new discipline of experimental psychology during the period. Thinkers such as William James (1842–1910) (Henry James's brother), Henri Bergson, and Sigmund Freud, while different in many respects, all stressed the self as in flux rather than as rigidly fixed (see Philosophy and religion, p. 23). For Freud in particular, this flux was conceived as conflict. Not only was the self not fixed, but it was also constantly subject to contradictory aims and desires which led to struggle and tension. Hence, modernist novelists keen to represent truthfully what they saw as the experience of the individual drew on European art, experimental psychology and philosophy. To a certain extent, Henry James's prose, as it wove together a number of different and sometimes jarring perspectives, had already provided a model for this. However, James's aim was to achieve an overall unity and organicism in his work, despite the attention given to such plurality. For many of the younger novelists, this coherence became itself problematic, almost as much a lie as the omniscient narrator's God-like position.

In *Ulysses* (1922), the most iconic modernist novel in English, James Joyce abandons the cohering voice of even the least interfering narrator. In the early books, the characters' thoughts, memories and associative meanderings give the narrative a fragmented texture (see Glossary: stream of consciousness). The narrator limits their intervention to the description of action. Later books, such as Book 15, 'Circe', seem even more disjointed and obscure, having the qualities and distortions of a dream. The novel does have an ordering principle, though one that is of a different kind to that of the traditional novel. This alternative order was revealed by Joyce's friend Stuart Gilbert in *James Joyce's Ulysses* (1930). Gilbert's work contains charts showing how each book in *Ulysses* is cohered around an organ, art, colour, symbol, and style, and the links between Joyce's novel and Homer's epic poem *The Odyssey* are made explicit.

For a number of late Victorian and Edwardian novelists, sex was central. For the later novels of Thomas Hardy, for the 'New Woman' novelists, for H. G. Wells, the problems of contemporary sexual mores, particularly the way in which the sexual double standard constrained and hurt women, shaped their work (see Miller 1994). However, sex during this period, where it featured at all, was always a problem. It destroyed lives through its incompatibility with the social and behavioural demands of 'civilization'. For the most progressive of novelists, such as the New Woman writers, the resolution of such problems was still most often renunciation or death.

While for modernist novelists, too, sex was in conflict with the conventional demands of the time, its disruptive effects were seized as positive and, significantly, these effects were allowed to disrupt the shape of their prose. In Ford Madox Ford's *The Good Soldier* (1915), the tardy realization of the force of sexual desire by the first-person narrator, John Dowell, upends all his assumptions and certainties. As the powerful sexual desires of his own wife, Florence, and of Edward Ashburnham are revealed to Dowell, not only is he no longer able to tell the 'good' person from the 'bad', but his ability to tell a story in the correct order, to pattern and to judge, is lost: 'I have, I am aware, told this story in a very rambling way so that it may be difficult for anyone to find their path through what may be a sort of maze' (Ford 1996: 161).

The novelist who made the most use of the disruptive and exuberant possibilities of sex was D. H. Lawrence. It is true that Lawrence's novels are not as formally innovative as those of other modernists and he does not eschew the interventional narrative voice. Nevertheless, Lawrence's sense of the force of sexual desire shaping individuals and challenging the destructive and, for him, deathly demands of society led him to create a new way of thinking about character in his novels, in particular in *The Rainbow* (1915), *Women in Love* (1921) and *Lady Chatterley's Lover* (1928).

Lawrence's aim as a novelist was to present a completely new way of living, to remake and redeem human life, and for him the novel was *the* place to do this because it worked through the representation of changing emotions rather than through fixed abstractions. The most essential part of emotional life was the sexual, connected, as it was for Lawrence, with a true sense of the past, of nature and of the spiritual. For him, life consisted in achieving 'a pure relationship' (Lawrence 1998b: 174) between ourselves and all that is not ourselves. Morality consisted in the fragile balance of any relation, so for Lawrence a true sexual relation, made up of the most complex and various set of emotions, is the most moral, the most pure thing. Further, as with Joyce, although to quite different ends, Lawrence's focus on sex reasserts the body, challenging the conventional Western privileging of the mind and intellect.

For some modernist writers, including Joyce and Lawrence, the new place of sex within the novel led to censorship, both direct and indirect (see Readers, obscenity and censorship, p. 16). While conventional society saw the sexual content of these novels as degraded and depraved, for the modernist novelist sex functioned as perhaps the most radical sign of the third 'reality' which was transforming the novel: irrationality and ambiguity.

The forms of the novel dominant in the nineteenth

century – a linear, chronological narrative, with a trust-worthy omniscient narrator who directs the reader, characters whose motives can be explained, and a resolved ending – suggested a world in which people are primarily understandable and reasonable. From the last decades of the nineteenth century a number of things had begun to challenge the idea that human beings were creatures of reason. In philosophy, Nietzsche railed against the undervaluing of the irrational, and saw it as the most creative and affirmative part of the human being. In the developing discipline of psychology, numerous writers began to see that which was beyond the conscious as crucial in the makeup of the self (see Philosophy and religion, p. 23). Modernist novelists began to create novelistic worlds in which the irrational and the unexplained dominated, and portray characters that were mysterious and inexplicable, to themselves and to the reader (see Glossary: stream of consciousness). In Joseph Conrad's novella *Heart of Darkness* (1902), the narrator, Marlow, can hardly communicate the story of his trip up the Congo, so beyond usual expectations were his experiences (Conrad 1998: 172–3). In Djuna Barnes's (1892–1982) *Nightwood* (1937), the baroque detail of the writing points to the difficulty of representation, and the unstable representation of marginalized characters brings to centre stage that which Western culture had previously repressed.

## Drama

Far less has been written on modernism in the theatre than modernism in poetry or the novel, and what critical work there is tends to use a different terminology and periodization. In studies of the theatre, the boundaries between the terms 'modern' and 'modernism' are less defined than in critical writing on the other genres (Innes 2003), and overall innovation in the Anglo-American theatre happened much later than in the novel or poetry. This section focuses on the origins of innovative theatre in Europe in the late nineteenth century, and the engagement of later modernist writers, both Anglo-American and European, with the form, rather than attempting a comprehensive study of modern theatre.

Despite the differences, all modernist writers attempted to reconstruct the relationship between author, work of art and audience, and nowhere is this more true than in the theatre. Unlike the novel, and poetry in its published form, drama depends upon the physical presence of an audience in order to fully exist. The audience's response constitutes a direct and active role in the unfolding of the play. The precariousness of this relation is both made very clear and tested to the limits by all types of modernist theatre; as Miss La Trobe laments in Virginia Woolf's *Between the Acts* (1941): 'Audiences were the devil. O to write a play without an audience ...' (Woolf 1992: 111).

Modernist theatre has its origins in the revolutions in theatrical practice centred in Paris in the 1880s. Two strong trends were created at this time – symbolism and naturalism – and they were taken up by a number of new, small independent theatres, in particular Aurélien-Marie Lugné-Poë's Théâtre de l'Oeuvre (estab. 1893) and André Antoine's Théâtre Libre (estab. 1887).

Naturalism in the theatre had at its head in the late nineteenth century the French novelist Émile Zola (1840–1902). His principles were first set out in the preface to his stage adaptation of *Thérèse Raquin* (1873). He wanted to abolish all existing conventions in the theatre, and to create plays that were an exact 'fragment of life' rather than a fancy or an escape from life. To do this he urged a change in the conventions of acting, more verisimilitude in scenery and staging, and costumes that suited the character rather than flattering the actor. Zola's ideas were very influential and were taken up by young playwrights and directors.

Symbolist theatre – seen particularly in the plays of French playwright Maurice Maeterlinck (1862–1949) – eschewed previous theatrical concentration on the surface of life and instead attempted to create dramas of internal action and psychological power. Symbolist theatre had at its heart a desire to create a link to what it saw as the most important part of human reality – that which was beyond the material, the observable or the rational. It used suggestion and ambiguity to represent multiple levels of reality, and was often lyrical and dream-like.

The complex relation between these two elements in the creation of modernist theatre can be seen in the work of one of the most important of its progenitors, the Norwegian Henrik Ibsen (1828–1906). Indeed, it is in the combining of elements of naturalism with symbolism and poetic vision in his later, most celebrated work that Ibsen creates the possibilities for a truly modern drama. In its honest exploration of contemporary life, Ibsen's later work caused scandal in his native Scandinavia and throughout Europe. In particular, *Ghosts* (1881) provoked critical outrage. The play deals with the disturbing effects of heredity – the 'ghosts' of the title – and the way in which the consequences of corruption and hypocrisy continue through the generations. Set in an upper-middle-class household in contemporary Norway, the play openly discusses adultery, incest and syphilis, not as barely mentionable problems of the poor but as direct consequences of bourgeois Christian morality, especially its repressive and prohibitive sexual mores. At the same time, *Ghosts* constructs a poetic and symbolic vision which powerfully portrays psychological conflict, particularly that of its central character, Mrs Alving.

Despite Ibsen's great influence on many writers, such as the Anglo-Irish playwright George Bernard Shaw (1856–1950), neither his example, nor that of the Parisian independent theatres, did much to change the institutions of theatre in Britain. Although there were attempts to set up small independent theatres, such as the Independent Theatre Society (1891), these had little impact, and censorship via the office of the Lord Chamberlain remained prohibitive for serious drama in particular. This may go some way to account for the absence of really significant dramatists among the central Anglo-American modernists. The main exception to this is Yeats. His dramatic theory and practice reveal the difficulty of audience for experimental dramatists in the British Isles.

Yeats was one of the main forces in the creation of the Irish Literary Theatre in Dublin in the 1890s. This became the Irish National Theatre Company in 1902, and it found its eventual home at the Abbey Theatre in 1904. The theatre's raison d'être was the creation of a space for the exploration and celebration of Irish cultural, historical and political identity. For Yeats this offered a chance for a truly popular (rather than populist) theatre, uniting contemporary Ireland with its distant past.

However, Yeats's commitment to a politically engaged theatre waned through the years of controversy associated with the Abbey Theatre, and he felt the need for new ways of writing and performing. Through his friendship with Ezra Pound, Yeats was introduced to Japanese Noh theatre. Originating in the fourteenth century, Noh (meaning 'accomplishment') was a court drama, played before nobles and comprising ritual dance by a small group of masked actors, accompanied by music and a chorus. Here Yeats found a model for a new kind of theatre that would provide a way of representing the world beyond the material for a select audience of what he believed to be the aesthetic aristocracy. His first play inspired by Noh was *At the Hawk's Well* (1917), first performed in front of an invited audience in 1916. The play combines the forms of Noh theatre – using masks, minimal scenery and props, ritual gestures and movements, and lyrical language, and reducing the distance between players and audience – with the mythology of the Irish heroic age to explore history and eternity, the different pulls of corporeal human life and immortality.

While Yeats was finding in Noh theatre a solution to his problems as a dramatist (Yeats 2005a: 364), in Europe too the bases of the relation between performance and audience were being challenged. Dada emerged as an avant-garde practice in Zurich during the war, and spread to the major cultural centres of Europe, Berlin and Paris, and then on to New York. Although not strictly theatre, performance was central to Dada. Hugo Ball's (1886–1927) Cabaret Voltaire in Zurich provided a stage for performance art which set out to shock, challenge and confuse its audience. Surrealism, Dada's successor among the European avant-gardes, also produced a theatre which challenged audience expectations. Although André Breton (1896–1966) abandoned the form in the late 1920s, believing it to be irredeemably bourgeois, Surrealism produced some important theatrical experiments, eschewing the logical for the marvellous and the strange in an attempt to connect with the hidden, irrational places of the self, as in Louis Aragon's (1897–1982) *The Mirror-Wardrobe One Fine Evening* (1924) and Antonin Artaud's (1896–1948) *Jet of Blood* (1927) (see The European avant-gardes, p. 112).

Expressionism, the first modernist theatrical movement to make a major impact in the twentieth century, developed in Germany just before the First World War and originated in the visual arts. It focused on individual perception rather than the object-focus of impressionism. In its representation of the isolation and alienation of the individual in the modern world, it shattered conventional ideas of beauty in its use of power, violence, madness and death. Expressionist theatre was influenced by psychoanalysis, the non-realist plays of Swedish playwright August Strindberg (1849–1912) and

Maeterlinck, and the idea of socialist revolution. It attempted to represent the centrality of subjective perceptions of reality by using abstract and declamatory speech, elliptical plots, distorted movement, and a non-realist mise-en-scène.

Expressionism was an important early influence on the work of the German Marxist playwright and director Bertolt Brecht (1898–1956), as in his work *Baal* (1918). He went on to create what he called 'epic theatre'. Through use of images, words and music, Brecht attempted to stimulate the intellect of the audience by representing the everyday as strange and unexpected. In this way he hoped to encourage social awareness and rational thought. In particular, Brecht challenged the notion that the theatre represented universal values. In plays such as *Mother Courage and her Children* (1941) and *The Caucasian Chalk Circle* (1955), Brecht wanted to represent specific, historical values and situations that would make audience complacency impossible and generate a commitment to change.

Although expressionism did influence some Anglo-American modernists from the end of the First World War, Britain in the 1930s saw both a return to the dominance of realism and the increasing challenge of the cinema, now 'the talkies'. While T. S. Eliot continued to experiment with non-realist, ritualized drama, and with dialogue in verse, for example in *Sweeney Agonistes* (1926/27) and in the historical drama, *Murder in the Cathedral* (1935), the next important wave of drama did not arrive until the 1950s, and it is not until then that a truly modern theatre really began to dominate in Britain, in the work, for example, of Harold Pinter (b. 1930), and to enjoy wider dissemination.

The possibilities for this theatre were created by the work of the Theatre of the Absurd, originating in Paris after the Second World War. Dramatists such as Samuel Beckett (1906–89), Jean Genet (1910–86) and Eugène Ionesco (1909–94) share a lack of conventional plot and characterization and a sense of the subjective isolation of individuals in an indifferent universe, indeed a sense of the absurdity of human life. Their plays use elements of music hall, farce, the circus and *commedia dell'arte*. Dialogue is often sparse, repetitious and clichéd, symptomatic of a disintegrating language (see The problem of language, p. 21).

Certainly a sense of the failure of language and black humour dominate Beckett's second play, *Waiting for Godot* (written 1948/49; first performed in Britain in 1955). This play has come to be considered by many as the most significant of the twentieth century. Its apocalyptic mise-en-scène and the repetitive, static conversation and concerns of its two central characters, Vladimir and Estragon, while waiting for Godot who never arrives, combine to produce an effect on audiences of bafflement, dis-ease and disturbance.

Beckett's dramatic work following *Waiting for Godot* continued to challenge realist conventions both of the theatre and of human identity. His plays are fascinated by the restriction and limitation of human beings, often portraying this literally, as in *Endgame* (first performed 1957), where two characters spend the play in rubbish bins, and *Happy Days* (first performed and published 1961), in which the female protagonist is buried up to her waist in sand in the first act, and up to her neck in the second.

Absurdist plays identify and challenge many of the conventions, moral, conceptual and theatrical, identified by the earliest experimenters such as Ibsen. In the Theatre of the Absurd, however, any notion that an alternative exists, that new ways of living can be found and authenticated, is rejected.

## The short story

The term 'short story' was first used with its modern meaning in 1884 by an American critic, Brander Matthews, in a periodical article. His theory of the form was later elaborated in his *The Philosophy of the Short Story* in 1901. Between these two dates, the modern short story was born in Britain. In the early twentieth century it was taken up by many of the central Anglo-American modernist writers, and has come to be seen by some critics as the 'quintessentially modernist form' (Head 1992: xi). Indeed, both *Ulysses* (1922) and *Mrs Dalloway* (1925) began as short stories, and Dominic Head has suggested that, rather than the short story being a kind of lesser novel, the modernist novel is in fact indebted to the short story for its characteristic forms and techniques (1992: 6). The length of the short story, rather than narrowing down possibilities, provided the modernist writer with a fitting form to represent the fragmentation, fleetingness and unsatisfied yearning which they saw as characteristic of modernity.

The 'tale' had been an important and popular form in nineteenth-century writing. The magazines and periodicals which flourished from the middle of the century onwards published hundreds of short pieces of prose fiction, very often depicting strange, mysterious or supernatural subjects. At the same time, the tale was a dominant form for American writers of the period such as Edgar Allan Poe (1809–49) and Nathaniel Hawthorne (1804–64). Poe's review of Hawthorne's *Twice-Told Tales* in 1842 contains his famous and influential definition of the form: 'In the whole composition there should be no word written, of which the tendency, direct or indirect, is not to the one preestablished design' (Poe 1994: 61). These innovations in the 'tale' filtered into British writing in several ways – Poe's influence via Charles Baudelaire (1821–67) (who translated his works into French) and then the Symbolists, and Hawthorne's via

Henry James. Indeed, James called his short stories, written in the main between the 1860s and the 1880s, 'tales' in the tradition of Poe and Hawthorne, but brought to the tale a focus on pattern, symbolism and suggestiveness which form the heart of the later modernist short story.

Two European writers of short prose also reshaped the form radically. The French writer Guy de Maupassant (1850–93) published around 300 short stories in the 1880s and 1890s. His stories brought together the realism of Gustave Flaubert with dramatic plotting, and often an atmosphere of the strange or marvellous. At the turn of the century, the short prose of the Russian writer Anton Chekhov (1860–1904) was beginning to be read in Britain and the US. Although Chekhov died in 1904, his influence and renown really began with the translation of a number of his stories in 1914 and 1915.

While the innovations of both Maupassant and Chekhov contributed to the possibilities of the modernist short story, establishing the form as realist, ironic, concerned with the experience of the modern, it is Chekhov who has been seen as the most important precursor to the short stories of James Joyce, Virginia Woolf and, in particular, Katherine Mansfield (1888–1923). Though he did sometimes write stories based around plot, suspense, or a neat solution, Chekhov's best and most influential short stories are focused not on narrative interest but on mood, atmosphere and psychological state. The language is spare and without decoration, and character suggested rather than drawn in detail. In these stories, extreme experiences and feelings are inexpressible in and frustrated by a drab and banal world of boredom, meanness and isolation. As the narrator of the story 'Gooseberries' (1898) laments: 'what is terrible in life goes on somewhere behind the scenes' (Chekhov 1977: 381). While characters cannot fully express these things, Chekhov's stories reveal the 'terrible' within scenes of ordinary life without preaching or direct comment, but in such a way that the reader is clearly supposed to be provoked and disturbed.

James Joyce insisted that he had not read Chekhov before writing the stories that went to make up *Dubliners* (1914), written between 1904 and 1907, but critics at the time and since have seen them as Chekhovian in mood and technique. Like Chekhov's best short stories, they depict a world of boredom, banality and frustrated hopes (even when the hopes themselves are ordinary and inconsequential). Joyce's characters are lower middle class, often ignorant or self-deluded, and live lives marred by poverty, disappointment and religion. What links the stories most strongly to Chekhov, though, is their narrative technique. With minimal plotting, the distanced narrative voice, while eschewing direct comment and intervention, speaks instead through the characters' own voices. So, in the opening of the most famous of Joyce's stories, 'The Dead' – 'Lily, the caretaker's daughter was literally run off her feet' the cliché is Lily's, not Joyce's (Joyce 1975: 173). This technique, free indirect style (see Glossary: free indirect style), while creating an ironic distance between the narrator and reader, and the characters – a distance in which we can see their delusions and weaknesses – also creates sympathy.

Katherine Mansfield wrote only short stories, and among them are some of the best and most influential of the form. Three books of short stories were published during her short life, *In a German Pension* (1911), *Bliss* (1920) and *The Garden Party* (1922). As with Joyce, her stories use free indirect style, but take it further to produce ambiguity and conflict of the self. In 'The Prelude' (1916), the unspoken sexual tensions which shape the family are partially acknowledged by Linda as she considers her husband while she walks in the garden with her own mother:

> Yes, yes, it was true. Linda snatched her hand from her mother's arm. For all her love and respect and admiration

she hated him ... There were all her feelings for him, sharp and defined, one as true as the other. And there was this other, this hatred, just as real as the rest ...

How absurd life was – it was laughable, simply laughable. (Mansfield 1962: 55–6)

This ambiguity regarding the self in the modernist short story is most clearly seen in that moment which has come to define the form, the epiphany (see Glossary: epiphany). While the epiphanic moment has been seen as creating and cohering the subject through a fusing of emotional, sensual and intellectual knowledge, in both Joyce's and Mansfield's short stories the moment of revelation illuminates a character to themselves, but often what it illuminates is confusion, complexity and uncertainty. At the end of Mansfield's 'Bliss' (1920), the significance of Bertha's relations with her friend Pearl – which have been one of the origins of her bliss during the day – is revealed to be quite other than what she imagines. This revelation is no resolution for Bertha, though, as she cries in the final lines of the story: 'Oh, what is going to happen now?' (Mansfield 1962: 110).

The importance of the short story in the modernist representation of modernity can be seen in contemporaries' comparison of the form to the new technology of film. In the introduction to her anthology *The Faber Book of Modern Stories* (1937), Elizabeth Bowen, one of the outstanding practitioners of the form, argues that

[t]he cinema, itself busy with a technique, is of the same generation [as the short story]; in the last 30 years the two arts have been accelerating together. They have affinities – neither is sponsored by tradition; both are, accordingly, free; both, still, are self-conscious, show a self-imposed discipline and regard for form. (Bowen 1937: 7)

As film – both modernist and otherwise – saw as its subject the very modernity which had created it, so the short story in its brevity, intensity and ironic candour was a fleeting glimpse of the modern. Paradoxically, though, many modernist short story writers chose to revise and remake one of the staple subjects of the traditional 'tale'. The stories of Woolf, Lawrence and May Sinclair often contain elements of the uncanny and the strange. These stories transform the conventions of the ghost story to disturb the materialist and rationalist assumptions of modern life or to suggest the potentially liberating strangenesses of modernity.

## The essay

While modernist innovation in writing can be most clearly seen in poetry and prose fiction, the essay form also was subject to innovation and experimentation during the first decades of the twentieth century.

During the nineteenth century, a number of writers established a strong essay tradition in Britain. Thomas Carlyle, Matthew Arnold and John Ruskin (1819–1900) had throughout the century written striking and powerful essays, using the form as a kind of secular sermon with which to challenge and provoke their readers about the effects of industrialization. By the beginning of the twentieth century, though, the essay had become a very popular form of entertainment, filling the pages of the many magazines and periodicals that proliferated during the Edwardian period. Writers such as G. K. Chesterton (1874–1936) and Hilaire Belloc (1870–1953) wrote essays of 'elegant whimsy' (Baldick 2004: 254), informal in tone, privileging a decorative style and focusing on the amusing oddities of life. It was exactly such a use of the form that modernists rejected. Disliking what they saw as both the censoriousness of the Victorians and the dilettantism of Edwardian 'belles-lettres', modernists recreated the essay for their own purposes.

One of the things that marked modernist essays as distinctive was the attention paid to the practice of writing itself and to literary criticism. In this, as in so much, Henry James was an important precursor and model. In his essay 'The Younger Generation' (1914), James begins by saying that the state of the contemporary novel paralleled the state of contemporary criticism. For James, writing fiction and writing criticism were part of the same thing. The crucial aspects of writing fiction – detachment, a concentration on form, and a belief in the novel as art – led to a necessary self-awareness on the part of the writer. This in turn made a self-conscious exploration of the practice of fiction writing, both the writer's own and that of other writers, an obvious occupation (James 1914).

During the first three decades of the century a number of small magazines and journals began which were devoted to such an awareness of the practice of writing (see The 'little magazines', p. 118). Ford Madox Ford's *English Review* and the later *Transatlantic Review, The Egoist, The Dial* and Eliot's *Criterion*, as well as the more mainstream *Times Literary Supplement* and *The Athenaeum*, provided space for prose non-fiction devoted to analysing and explaining recent experimentation. A number of the most important collections of literary critical essays by modernist writers brought together those first published in these magazines, or first given as lectures to small audiences. Many of the essays in Eliot's *The Sacred Wood* (1920) and *The Use of Poetry and the Use of Criticism* (1933) and Virginia Woolf's two volumes of *The Common Reader* (1925/32) had such origins.

Eliot and Woolf, along with D. H. Lawrence, were three of the most original practitioners of the modernist essay. In very different ways, their essays on literary criticism and other subjects came to dominate views about modernist aesthetics, both at the time and since.

In 'Tradition and the Individual Talent' (1919), and in other essays in the early 1920s, Eliot launched what Baldick has called 'a revolution in literary taste' (2004: 256). Eliot's fundamental argument in these essays – the assertion of the need for a detached and rigorous literary criticism – is emphasized at the beginning of 'Tradition':

> criticism is as inevitable as breathing, and ... we should be none the worse for articulating what passes in our minds when we read a book and feel an emotion about it, for criticizing our own minds in their work of criticism. (Eliot 1975b: 37)

In 'The Metaphysical Poets' (1921), Eliot applies this to a rethinking of English poetry, critiquing Milton, Dryden, Shelley and Tennyson because, unlike the metaphysicals, their poetry suffers from the split between intellect and feeling (Eliot 1975c). Eliot's judgements here overturned conventional thinking about English poetry, and were immensely influential on F. R. Leavis and, through him, on school and university curricula (see Modernism and contemporary criticism 1818–39, p. 126).

While the subject of Eliot's essays challenged aesthetic judgements, the style brought to the form a detachment completely at odds with the familiar chattiness of the Edwardian essay. The lofty coolness of the Eliotic voice acted out his sense that the previous tenets of criticism were too subjective and amorphous. Indeed, even Rebecca West, in an essay which challenges Eliot's authority as a critic, admits that before him 'English criticism was at its low ebb ... it was purely arbitrary and impressionist' (West 2005: 713). In Eliot's essays on culture more generally, and in particular in those on popular culture, what the tone acts out is his profound disgust with the contemporary, and this often rather distorts his judgement on, for example, the cinema or, indeed, democracy.

Virginia Woolf wrote more than 400 essays, many of them literary critical, but rather than taking them towards a cool objectivity, she expanded the form towards the possibilities of fiction and her essayistic voice is very much one of a collaborative 'we' (Baldick 2004: 257). In one of her most famous literary critical works, 'Mr Bennett and Mrs Brown' (1924), where she sets out the distinctions she perceives between the Edwardians (Arnold Bennett, H. G. Wells and John Galsworthy) and the Georgians (here represented by T. S. Eliot and James Joyce), the 'Mrs Brown' section is a fictional encounter which demonstrates Woolf's argument about the creation of character in the novel (see Readers, obscenity and censorship, p. 16). For Woolf, essayistic rhetoric can neither reveal nor convince as powerfully as the poetic, ambiguous and inconclusive worlds of her fiction.

The techniques of the novel are used in many of her essays, not just her literary critical ones. In 'On Being Ill' (1926/30) Woolf playfully explores both the absence of illness as a subject from literature and asserts its freeing possibilities, 'with responsibility shelved and reason in abeyance' (Woolf 1993: 50). In particular, suggests Woolf, illness offers possibilities for being a certain kind of *reader* – one more dreamy, more directly receptive, less intellectual – and the essay ends with a slightly hallucinatory enactment of the way illness can expand our readerly pleasures.

The blurring of the boundaries between fact and fiction we can see in Woolf's essays can also be seen in the work of her friend and fellow Bloomsburyite, the biographer Lytton Strachey (1880–1932) (see The Bloomsbury Group, p. 96). His work of 1918, *Eminent Victorians*, eschews the careful, respectful tone and factual basis of nineteenth-century biography and uses wit, polemic and imaginative fabrication to produce deprecating portraits of four Victorian 'greats' – Cardinal Manning, Florence Nightingale, Dr Thomas Arnold and

General Gordon. The work, in particular with its creation of the interior monologue of his subjects and its
belief in the complexity of human character, moves very
near to the voice and techniques of the modernist novel.
*Eminent Victorians,* and Strachey's later *Queen Victoria*
(1921) and *Elizabeth and Essex* (1928), were hugely
influential on all types of non-fiction in the first half of
the twentieth century. After him, the personal, subjective voice was allowed in to pronounce on the most
serious and significant of topics.

The essays of D. H. Lawrence combine the personal,
subjective voice of Woolf's with the stringent aesthetic
judgements of Eliot's. However, with neither Eliot's
restraint nor Woolf's inclusiveness, Lawrence's essays are
bold and sermon-like, idiosyncratic and touched with
flashes of insight. During the 1920s, they dealt on the
whole with literary criticism, either on the novel and its
future, or on individual writers such as Edgar Allan Poe,
Nathaniel Hawthorne and Herman Melville (1819–91)
in *Studies in Classic American Literature* (1924). Unlike
Eliot, still less like the developing literary criticism
associated with I. A. Richards (1893–1979) and the
Cambridge School (see Modernism and contemporary
criticism (1818–39, p. 126), however, Lawrence's criticism utterly rejects a systematic or objective approach.

> Literary criticism can be no more than a reasoned account
> of the feeling produced upon the critic by the book he is
> criticizing. Criticism can never be a science: it is, in the first
> place, much too personal, and in the second, it is concerned
> with values that science ignores. (Lawrence 1998d: 210)

What most distinguishes Lawrence's essays from his
Victorian and Edwardian predecessors is the manner of
their address. While they do contain elements of the
sermon, as do, say, the essays of Carlyle and Ruskin,
unlike both these and the belle-lettrist essays of sophisticated charm, Lawrence veers between making no

attempt to connect with or seduce his reader and an almost child-like accessibility. Lawrence's expressed disregard for his audience – 'Saying my say and seeing other people sup it up doesn't amount to a hill o' beans, as far as I go' (Lawrence 1962: 876) – while perhaps hyperbolic, can be seen in his essays. His intensely personal style, rejecting the formal and the intellectual, privileges the spontaneous, the flash of insight rather than the careful argument.

## MOVEMENTS AND LITERARY GROUPS

### The Bloomsbury Group

The Bloomsbury Group was a loose association of men and women brought together through a belief in the importance of the individual, of personal relationships, and of questioning the morals and conventions of their parents' generation in order, as they believed, for the individual to live as honestly as possible and for the advancement of 'civilization'. Through a network of friendships and family relations, the group came to comprise a large number of the most significant artists and intellectuals in Britain in the first few decades of the twentieth century. It included the artist and critic Roger Fry (1866–1934), artists Vanessa Bell (1879–1961) and Duncan Grant (1885–1978), the art critic Clive Bell (1881–1964), the literary critic and biographer Lytton Strachey, the economist John Maynard Keynes (1883–1946), the philosopher Bertrand Russell, and the novelists Virginia Woolf and E. M. Forster (1879–1970). Indeed, as this list suggests, the groups' practices and beliefs included a commitment to the interrelation of the arts – writing, the visual arts and design – and as such were influential throughout a significant section of British society in the first half of the twentieth century.

The history of the Bloomsbury Group has its origins in

the history of one family – the Stephens – Vanessa Bell, her sister Virginia Woolf, and their brothers Thoby and Adrian. Their father, Sir Leslie Stephen (1832–1904), was an eminent figure in the world of Victorian letters. When he died in 1904 (their mother, Julia, had died in 1895), the four seized the opportunity to change their way of life. They moved to a house at 46 Gordon Square, Bloomsbury, an area of central London then associated by their own class with boarding houses and middle-class vulgarity. There they lived unchaperoned, much to the consternation of their remaining elder family members.

The Stephens began to meet regularly with Thoby Stephens' friends from his student days at Cambridge, including Lytton Strachey, Maynard Keynes, Clive Bell and Virginia Woolf's future husband, Leonard Woolf (1880–1969). At their regular 'Thursday evenings' at Gordon Square, the group would discuss the latest ideas in philosophy. Thoby Stephen and most of his friends had been members of the Apostles – a Cambridge secret society – and were influenced by the ideas of Cambridge philosopher G. E. Moore (1873–1958).

Moore's philosophy, based on the premise that the universe was godless and without meaning, attempted to propose a way of living in response to this that was humane and ethical. His *Principia Ethica* (1903) became a bible for the group. Moore emphasized the intellect and reason as a riposte to the demands of tradition and convention; reality must be faced honestly and truthfully. Of particular significance, Moore rejected nineteenth-century Utilitarian beliefs, and insisted that 'intrinsic good' could be found in the enjoyment of human relations and of beautiful things.

When Thoby Stephen died in 1906, the remaining Stephens continued to meet with his friends. In 1907 Vanessa married Clive Bell; the couple remained in Gordon Square, while Virginia and Adrian Stephen moved to a house in nearby Fitzroy Square and continued the 'Thursday evenings'. Increasingly, talk was dominated by questions of aesthetics. But perhaps more important was the *way* the group talked; the polite reticence of their parents' generation was abandoned for a commitment to the truth. This eventually included the freedom to discuss sexual matters, in particular homosexuality and extra-marital relations, subjects barely mentioned in respectable society. As Virginia Woolf later wrote in her memoir of the early Bloomsbury years, 'Old Bloomsbury' (1921/22), 'there was now nothing that one could not say, nothing that one could not do' (Woolf 1976a: 201).

Aside from personal relations, what most united the group was a shared understanding of aesthetics. The artists of the Bloomsbury Group were influenced very early (in terms of Britain) by European modernist painters, in particular Paul Cézanne, Henri Matisse (1869–1954) and Pablo Picasso. Indeed Roger Fry's writings on aesthetics, and his organization of the two Post-Impressionist exhibitions for the Grafton Galleries in London in 1910 and 1912, were some of the most important factors in the dissemination of modern art in Britain. Fry championed the work of modernist painters as more faithfully representing the life of the imagination, and as such as free from the morality of actual life: 'We must therefore give up the attempt to judge the work of art by its reaction on life, and consider it as an expression of emotions regarded as ends in themselves' (Fry 1925: 29).

However, for Fry and for Bloomsbury more generally, this didn't mean that the arts were amoral. Rather, all aesthetic experience worked to improve an individual through emotion rather than morality or reason. For Bloomsbury, aesthetics were of primary importance, and changing aesthetic experience was the most powerful way of changing the social and the political, indeed of bringing about 'civilization'.

Members of the group put this belief into practice in numerous ways, including the founding of the Omega

Workshop. This design centre was opened at 33 Fitzroy Square in July 1913, and run by Fry, Duncan Grant and Vanessa Bell. It was committed to the idea of showing the public that artists were capable of applying their skills to the decoration of everyday objects. It was also set up as a way of providing income for artists, and organized exhibitions to display their work. A number of artists were associated with Omega, including, for a while, Percy Wyndham Lewis, who left after disagreement with Fry, and set up Vorticist Rebel Art Centre (see Vorticism, p. 107).

While some Bloomsburyites were active in organized politics – Leonard Woolf was a committed socialist, was involved with the League of Nations after the First World War, and stood as a prospective Labour MP in 1922 – the group itself eschewed political slogans and what it saw as the vulgarity of political dogma. During the First World War, a number of the group were conscientious objectors, but their opposition to the war was a combination of what Hermione Lee has called 'snobbish detachment and courageous resistance' (Lee 1996: 344). At bottom, the war offended their sense of civilization – it was brutal, violent, and provoked the 'baser' passions of the mass of people.

The Bloomsbury Group, for all its interest in new ideas and new practices in the arts, remained in its dynamics and exclusion of outsiders a kind of family. This can be seen, for example, in the Hogarth Press, founded by Leonard and Virginia Woolf in 1917. They ran the press from their home in Richmond, Hogarth House, and while eventually the press's publications came to include the most innovative, provocative and up-to-date writing of the time – literary, political, economic, psychoanalytic – the people who worked at the press and who were published by it were dominated by friends and relations. Many of the press's titles, including all of Virginia Woolf's own works, had cover designs and illustrations by her sister, Vanessa Bell. These often sold in very small numbers, and to an audience made in their own image, but their publishing choices did affect more mass market publishers. As with the little magazines, the new and innovative was disseminated through a complex relation with consumer capitalism (see The 'little magazines', p. 118) (see Rainey 1998).

While most critics have not considered Bloomsbury as significant as the European avant-gardes (see p. 112) or even Vorticism (see p. 107) in terms of intellectual and aesthetic innovation, arguably the legacy of Bloomsbury has been more far reaching in the British context. The challenge to Victorian style and taste begun most obviously in Roger Fry's Omega Workshop produced a fundamental change in attitudes to interior décor in Britain's middle classes. In more abstract ways, too, the attitudes and lifestyles of Bloomsbury have affected middle-class lifestyles since. In their championing of personal freedom, in particular in sexual relationships, the Bloomsburyites challenged the Victorian patriarchal family and made personal relationships more flexible, more about individual happiness and less about hierarchy and tradition.

However, in this legacy we can see the origins of much criticism of Bloomsbury and its influence. The core of Bloomsbury was upper middle class, well connected and often with independent incomes. While the members of the group challenged the beliefs and lifestyles of their parents, they remained within their class, accepting its privileges and often reproducing its prejudices. In particular, Bloomsbury cultivated the exclusive atmosphere of a clique, but a clique which, for them, was *the* defender of civilization against the forces of barbarism. E. M. Forster called Bloomsbury the 'only genuine *movement* in English civilisation', while acknowledging that the outsider 'remains in a background of screaming farce' (Forster 1995: 79; emphasis in original).

A number of their modernist contemporaries – including D. H. Lawrence and Wyndham Lewis –

criticized the group for its privileged complacency. More recently, John Carey has argued that the artistic innovations associated with the group – as well as the other 'canonical' modernists, Pound, Eliot and Lewis – were the result of social snobbery and elitism; that the Bloomsbury aesthetic had its origin in a fear of mass culture (Carey 1992). Carey's argument is not just an aesthetic one, though, it is political too. Bloomsbury, from this point of view, did nothing to challenge the link between taste, a certain aesthetic and class position. Some critics have made claims for Bloomsbury as a modernist avant-garde (Froula 2005). However, their championing of individual freedom, even if it did involve sexual relations that were seen at the time as scandalous, can be seen in part as a continuation of nineteenth-century liberalism, with its fear of the collective, its denial of the importance of political inequality, and its ultimate reproduction of entrenched class privilege.

## Imagism

Imagism (or *Imagisme* as it was originally known) is a school of poetry developed, and most influential, in London between 1912 and 1917. Its poetics not only shaped what modernist poetry was to become (Eliot 1965: 58) (see Poetry, p. 69), but it was the first organized modernist English-language literary group, with a set of rules, and, in Ezra Pound, a champion and leader. The central Imagist poets were Pound himself, his fellow expatriate American H. D. (1886–1961), poet and later novelist Richard Aldington (1892–1962), and poet and translator F. S. Flint (1885–1960). Together, under Pound's sometimes challenged but always exuberant lead, they set out to create a new poetry that tore away established poetic niceties and conventions in order to restore a vigorous emotional power.

The origins of Imagism are complex. Indeed, another

of the reasons that Imagism is important is because it was one of the most salient meeting places for many ideas and debates about art going on in London in the five years before First World War. While Pound created Imagism as a group in 1912, this crucial moment for modern poetry had been prepared through the friendship between Flint and critic and poet T. E. Hulme (1883–1917) in 1909. The two men shared a passionate belief in the need to renew English poetry. Far from bringing language to life, as poetry should, they believed Edwardian poetry clung to clichés, to dead language. Hulme and Flint began meeting with others to talk about how to change poetry. Their group saw the Symbolists' renewal of French poetry some decades before as a model, and discussed how current English poetry might be replaced by '*vers libre*, by the Japanese tanka and haikai' (Flint 1915: 71).

Hulme's contributions to the discussions were influenced by his studies of the contemporary French philosopher, Henri Bergson (1859–1941) (see Henri Bergson and the rescue of humanity, p. 33). At the centre of Bergson's challenge to mainstream empirical thought was his concept of intuition, defined by him as a radical sympathy of subject for the object of perception. This relation was not intellectual, as intellectual knowledge demands distance from the object. Rather, the barriers between the subject and the object of perception needed to be broken down; for Hulme this meant that the poet needed to lose themselves and *become* the object. These ideas resonate with those of earlier poets, in particular the Romantic poet John Keats's (1795–1821) notion of 'negative capability'. It was exactly this strong sense of poetic practice, however, that Hulme and Flint believed had been lost in contemporary poetry. Hulme took from Bergson, too, the relation the image may have in the development of intuition. In his *An Introduction to Metaphysics*, Bergson argued that: 'Many diverse images, borrowed from very different orders of things, may, by the convergence of their action, direct consciousness to the precise point where there is a certain intuition to be seized' (Bergson 1913b: 14). The strong image could effect intuition through collapsing the distance between subject and object.

Following his arrival in London the previous year, Pound was introduced to Hulme and Flint's group in April 1909. Pound was already thinking along the same lines as them, and was developing a desire for poetry that used the direct language of speech rather than the rhetoric of mainstream poetry. Hulme's theories provided Pound with a solid foundation from which to launch his own assault on 'dead' poetry. While Hulme had used Symbolism as a model, however, Pound rejected its desire for poetry to aspire to the condition of music, and instead championed a poetry 'where painting or sculpture seems as if it were "just coming over into speech"' (Pound 1916: 95).

In the spring of 1912, after reading through new poems by H. D., Pound wrote at the bottom of her manuscript 'H. D. *Imagiste*'. Pound had recently been appointed 'foreign representative' of the small journal *Poetry*, based in Chicago and founded (in 1912) and edited by Harriet Monroe. Using this position to promote both his friends and his new 'movement', Pound sent poems by H. D. and Aldington to Monroe for publication. In his letter to her accompanying them in October 1912, he described them as: 'Objective – no slither; direct – no excessive use of adjectives, no metaphors that won't permit examination. It's straight talk, straight as the Greek!' (Pound 1971: 11). In the same month, Pound's volume of poems *Riposte* was published, and in an appendix the word *Imagiste* was used in print for first time.

For the next two years or so, Pound concentrated his efforts on the promotion of Imagism. The group's credo, 'Imagisme' (actually by Pound, although published under Flint's name), and 'A Few Don'ts by an

Imagiste' by Pound first appeared in *Poetry* in March
1913. 'Imagisme' begins by distinguishing the Imagists
from 'the Post Impressionists and the Futurists' (see The
European avant-gardes, p. 112) with whom they have
'nothing in common':

> They had not published a manifesto. They were not a revo-
> lutionary school; their only endeavour was to write in
> accordance with the best tradition, as they found it in the
> best writers of all time ... (Flint 1913: 199)

While the Imagists had nothing as vulgar as a manifesto,
they did have, the article goes on, a 'few rules':

1.  Direct treatment of the 'thing,' whether subjective or
    objective.
2.  To use absolutely no word that did not contribute to the
    presentation.
3.  As regarding rhythm: to compose in sequence of the
    musical phrase, not in sequence of the metronome.
    (Ibid.)

These three rules describe the eschewal of poetic conventions that is at the core of Imagism. Strict metre and
rhyme schemes, apostrophes, inversions, familiar figures
and metaphors had deadened the effect of poetry.
Imagism wanted to return to poetry a purity of language
which would provoke real emotion rather than clichéd
sentiment.

H. D.'s 'Oread' first appeared in the second anthology
of Imagist poetry, *Some Imagist Poets* (1915) and is referred to in Pound's essay 'Vorticism' (see Vorticism,
p. 107) as the ultimate Imagist poem:

> Whirl up, sea –
> Whirl your pointed pines,
> Splash your great pines
> On our rocks,

Hurl your green over us,
Cover us with your pools of fir. (H. D. 1915: 28)

The poem displays the restraint, precision and simplicity of diction crucial to Imagist poetics. It completely eschews the conventional tools of the poet – there are no similes, no symbols, no reflection, no expressed emotion, no fixed metre or rhyme, no abstractions and no narrative. The object of the poem, the sea/pines, overwhelms the subject – the poetic voice. The pronouns which refer to the voice of the poem are objects rather than subjects – 'us' rather than 'we'. They are the passive receiver of sea/pines' action.

In the rejection of simile in particular 'Oread' is evidence of the power of Imagist practice. The waves are not *like* pines, they *are* pines. This fusion of the object and an abstract idea of it create the image. The whole poem becomes the unit of meaning, rather than one simile or rhyme. The effect of this stripping away of poetic conventions, though, is evocative, resonant and haunting rather than flattening.

In 1914, under Pound's editorship, the first collection of Imagist poetry was published, *Des Imagistes: An Anthology*. The collection was not a success in terms of sales, and critically the reception was mixed. It lacked a preface or introduction which could explain the principles behind Imagism and the selection of poems, so left readers outside of the small groups who read the little magazines rather bemused. Dominating the anthology were poems by H. D. and Aldington, in free verse, spare and with classical subjects, but it is difficult to see how a number of the other poems included really qualify as Imagist at all. Overall, the poetry seems to paradoxically retain a strain of romantic yearning, if not in form and diction, then in the sense of the poetic voice as isolated and special. Indeed, neither of the two poems seen as most successfully Imagist, 'Oread' and Pound's 'In a Station of the Metro' (1913), appear in the collection.

Certainly, however, 1914 can be seen as the year that Imagism caught the literary imagination. In 1915, an issue of the *Egoist* was devoted to it, including Flint's 'History of Imagism'. This attention in some ways sealed Imagism as a movement, but also led to its eventual collapse. Pound's interests had already moved on, and he and Flint fell out over the 'History' article. From 1915, the American poet Amy Lowell (1874–1925) took on the role of champion and disseminator of Imagism. According to Pound, with his dismissive renaming of the movement as 'Amy-gism', this shift in personnel meant a loss of Imagism's precise definition and practice. However, the Imagist anthology, *Some Imagist Poets* (1915), put together by Lowell, is on the whole much better than Pound's from the previous year. Two more volumes followed, in 1916 and 1917, but by then Imagism was really over as a movement.

In many ways, the creation of Imagism was strategic. Pound's aims were not so much to create a school of poetry as to create an interest in new young poets and to aggressively challenge conventional expectations about poetry. Once this was done, Pound moved on and so, eventually, did the other original Imagists. That Imagism was short-lived is perhaps a sign of its success rather than its failure, however. While the principles of Imagism at their purest reduced the poem to the smallest unit possible, and really forbad the poet from commenting on the world, let alone seeing poetry as any kind of intervention in it, the influence of Imagism can be seen in the powerful modernist poetry of Eliot's *The Waste Land* (1922), Pound's *Cantos* (1917–69) and William Carlos Williams's *Paterson* (1946–58), and Imagist ideas have been assimilated into central assumptions about what poetry is during the twentieth century (see Poetry, p. 69).

## Vorticism

Vorticism is considered the most, and by some the only, important artistic movement based in Britain in the early twentieth century. It was the first British avant-garde movement (see Glossary: avant-garde), and was significant for its championing of abstraction in the visual arts, and its critique of both conventional British visual culture and current European avant-gardes (see p. 112). At its heart were the work and ideas of artist, writer and critic Percy Wyndham Lewis (1882–1957), and these were disseminated through Lewis's Rebel Art Centre and the short-lived journal *Blast*.

Lewis had worked as an artist and designer for Roger Fry's recently established Omega Workshop (see The Bloomsbury Group, p. 96), but he and a number of other artists left in October 1913 after a quarrel. Together they founded the rival Rebel Art Centre in March 1914 as a place for the exhibition, debate and discussion of the new and radical ideas and practices coming from Futurism, Expressionism and Cubism, rather than the Post-Impressionists championed by Fry (see The European avant-gardes, p. 112). While Lewis in particular had been developing this new kind of painting for a couple of years, the name Vorticism was given to the art being championed by Lewis by Ezra Pound in 1913. Pound developed the idea of the 'vortex' to convey his idea that artistic form – whether in the visual arts, writing or music – properly used expresses something universal, permanent and true. As in Pound's championing of the image during his involvement with Imagism, what is important for him is that any form be stripped of unnecessary ornament, sentiment and deadening convention; that any form is most powerful when it is most pure. Vorticism uses the 'primary pigment' (Pound 1916: 102). For each emotion or thought, there is only one form that can properly express it in art. What Vorticism is against is the use of 'secondary forms':

'Vorticism is art before it has spread itself into flaccidity, into elaboration and secondary applications' (ibid.).

While this formal purity suggests rigour and stasis, actually it is because of it that the Vortex is able to be 'a radiant node or cluster ... from which, and through which, and into which, ideas are constantly rushing' (ibid.: 106). For example, sculpture is Vorticist when its form is inseparable from the property of its basic medium – matter – rather than pretending to be something else. It is for this that Pound so praised the Vorticist sculptor Henri Gaudier-Brzeska (1891–1915). His *Red Stone Dancer* (c. 1913) represents a figure, but a figure pared down to its essential mass and lines, and a figure which recognizes the qualities of the material used. Painting, too, must concern itself with the underlying structures of the form, rather than just reproducing the surface of the world, as Lewis argues in a review of Vorticist art from 1914:

> All revolutionary painting to-day has in common the rigid reflections of steel and stone in the spirit of the artist; that desire for stability as though a machine were being built to fly or kill with; an alienation from the traditional photographer's trade and realization of the value of colour and form as such independently of what recognizable form it covers or encloses. (Lewis 1914: 9)

While the Vorticist artist concentrates on form rather than representation, for Lewis this is aligned not with an intellectualism, but with the supposed instinct of the 'primitive': 'The artist of the modern movement is a savage ...' (Lewis 2003: 202). The new, machine-dominated world which had begun in Britain was more akin to the jungle than a Futurist utopia, and the dynamism and violence of this world were most appropriately responded to by the vortex. Lewis's *Workshop* (1914), for example, was on the cusp between abstraction and representation of urban, technological modernity.

These ideas of Lewis and Pound were developed in response to wider aesthetic debates at the time, and Vorticism cannot be fully understood except in the context of these. In the five years or so before the First World War, the ideas and practice of a number of avant-garde European movements in the arts began to be known and talked about in London. Beginning with Roger Fry's Post-Impressionist Exhibition at the end of 1910, British artists and the British public could see for the first time the experiments in painting which had been going on in France for several decades. Along with a number of subsequent exhibitions of the Post-Impressionists, the ideas and paintings of the Italian Futurists were disseminated through a number of visits to London by Futurist founder and champion Filippo Marinetti (1876–1944) between December 1910 and 1914 and exhibitions of Futurist art in 1912 and 1913 (see The European avant-gardes, p. 112).

Lewis and the other soon-to-be Vorticists were already at the heart of a London art world that soaked up these new ideas and influences. The most important precursors to Vorticism in terms of the visual arts are indeed Futurism and Cubism, but Vorticism also constructed itself via its critique of these contemporary movements. From Cubism Vorticism took the fragmentation of the object into geometric planes, but criticized it for its conventional subjects and the way it ignored the realities of modernity, in particular the dominance of the machine. Vorticism seems to have more in common with Futurism in its embrace of dynamism, speed and the machine, but it tried to capture all this in one static image, rather than repeating Futurism's obsession with movement. As Lewis declaims in the first issue of *Blast*, 'Vorticist is at his maximum point of energy when stillest' (Lewis 2003: 163).

Linked to the Vorticist rejection of the Futurist

attitudes to speed and movement is their differing relation to the past. Futurism famously rejects the past completely. For Futurists, it is the future which is alive and which should be the focus for artists. Vorticism, in comparison, is not obsessed with either the past or the future, but with the energy of the present: 'The new vortex plunges to the heart of the Present. With our Vortex the Present is the only active thing. Life is the Past and the Future. The Present is Art' (Lewis 2003: 162)

While the Vorticists were quite clear about what Vorticism wasn't, there was less agreement about what it then was, and indeed over who had the authority to decide. For Pound Vorticism was a successor to Imagism. Imagism had gone flaccid, but Vorticism presented another opportunity to promote his theory of the image, and its importance in the recreation of poetry. The image was Vorticist because it was the 'primary pigment' of poetry. For Lewis, though, Vorticism was significant primarily for the visual arts. Although Lewis did write some Vorticist works – his play *Enemy of the Stars* (1914) and his novel *Tarr* (1918) – his focus was on revolutionizing the language of visual arts and, indeed, in claiming Vorticism as his own. Lewis was certainly its major theorist, publicist and champion. His publication of the two issues of *Blast* established the movement, with a manifesto and a declaration by those artists who signed up to it, but at the same time the journals provide evidence for the conflicts and contradictions at the heart of it.

The first issue of *Blast* appeared on 2 July 1914, just a month before the beginning of the First World War, and the second appeared a year later. They were edited and largely written by Lewis. In design and typography, as much as in content, the magazine shouted its departure from conventional aesthetics. The cover was bright pink, and the lines of text were chopped and irregular, using capitalization and line spaces for emphasis:

We will convert the King if possible.
A VORTICIST KING! WHY NOT?
DO YOU THINK LLOYD GEORGE HAS THE VORTEX IN
HIM? (Lewis 1998: 292)

The opening 20 pages of the 1914 issue consisted of the
Vorticist manifesto, signed by, among others, Lewis,
Pound, Richard Aldington, the sculptor Henri Gaudier-
Brzeska and artist Edward Wadsworth (1889–1949). The
artist David Bomberg (1890–1957) and sculptor Jacob
Epstein (1880–1959) did not sign, but their work featured in the journal alongside articles by Pound, a story
by Rebecca West, an extract from Ford Madox Ford's
*The Saddest Story* (published in 1915 as *The Good Soldier*), a
review of the artist Wassily Kandinsky's (1866–1944) *The
Art of Spiritual Harmony*, and many illustrations by Lewis
and others. The second issue of *Blast* included a short
play by Pound, Eliot's 'Preludes' and Gaudier-Brzeska's
'Vortex Gaudier-Brzeska', written from the trenches a
few weeks before he was killed in action.

A Vorticist exhibition was held in London in 1915,
and featured work by Lewis, Frederick Etchells (1886–
1973), Gaudier-Brzeska, Wadsworth, Jessica Dismorr
(1885–1939) and Helen Saunders (1885–1963), and
another took place in New York in 1917. However,
Vorticism was really over by then, killed by the First
World War and internal disputes. A number of the
Vorticists, including Lewis, joined up, and impetus was
lost. Not only that, but the war cast a new and horrific
light over the uses of machinery and its relation to the
human body, making Vorticist representations of technology look naive if not dangerous. Vorticist techniques
did inform some of the major paintings of the war, such
as those by war artist Paul Nash (1889–1946), but their
fragmentation evokes loss rather than exuberance. Following the war, Jacob Epstein remodelled his work *Rock
Drill* (1913–14) so that the robotic form, menacing and
masterful, became instead impotent and vulnerable.

## The European avant-gardes: Futurism, Dada and Surrealism

While the experimentalism of the Anglo-American modernists saw itself as new and challenging, it only sometimes echoed the movement-forming radicalness of the European avant-gardes. Certainly, internationalism was a defining characteristic of the broad group of people and practices which made up modernism, and Anglo-American modernists were aware of, and influenced by, the ideas of European experimental writers and artists. However, Anglo-American modernism never really produced a movement as influential as the most significant of the European avant-gardes. Futurism, Dada and Surrealism all produced manifestos and artworks which have shaped the arts, and in particular the visual arts, to this day.

Futurism's beginning was announced by its founder and principle champion, the Italian poet and editor F. T. Marinetti (1876–1944), in the French newspaper *Le Figaro* on 20 February 1909. This was followed in 1910 by the 'Futurist Painting: Technical Manifesto', shifting Marinetti's concentration from poetry to the visual arts, and by later manifestos on numerous other areas. The manifestos called for a new art, cut off from conventional understandings of the 'beautiful' and committed to re-seeing the world without the patina of nostalgia and sentiment. As Peter Nicholls suggests, 'The manifestos of Futurism would constitute a guide to almost every aspect of avant-garde activity to come' (Nicholls 1995: 84).

In strident language, Marinetti's 'Founding Manifesto' declared a new poetry which rejected the melancholy and introverted obsession with death which it saw in the poetry of the Symbolists and the Decadents, and instead sang of a love of the present, of speed and of the machine. It spoke of a violent rejection of the traces of the past in the present: 'Why should we look back ... .

Time and space died yesterday. We already live in the absolute, because we have created eternal, omnipresent speed ... We will destroy the museums, libraries, academies of every kind' (Marinetti 2003: 148).

For Marinetti, this celebration of the present meant that poetry could no longer be preoccupied with the self. Futurist poetry rejected the voice of conventional lyric poetry, and concentrated instead on the external world of activity and production. The removal of the unifying self of the poem is often coupled with a breakdown and fragmentation in the language, most clearly seen in Marinetti's own poetry. In *Zong Toomb Toomb* (1914), the insistent rhythms and sounds of the mechanical, not the emotions of the poet, dictate the form of the poem:

> my train train **tron**        **tron**        **tron**
> **tron** (iron bridge: **tatatlontlan) ssssssiii ssiissii**
> **ssissssssiii**        train        train        train
> fever of   my train   express-express-express-
> expresssssss....                (Marinetti 2002: 57)

The Futurist artists, centred in Milan and grouped around the painter and sculpture Umberto Boccioni (1882–1916), took Cubist techniques and remade them to fulfil their claim that '[t]he gesture which we would reproduce on canvas shall no longer be a fixed *moment* in universal dynamism. It shall simply be the *dynamic sensation* itself' (Boccioni et al. 2003: 150; emphasis in original). Boccioni soon moved from painting to sculpture, and in his *Unique Forms of Continuity in Space* (1913) can be seen Futurism's transformation of the human body into a hard, machine-like creature, no longer fleshly and vulnerable, but made for speed and action.

This celebration of technology and the present, however, led the Futurists into a problematic stance on gender. Marinetti's manifesto claimed 'scorn for woman' and that Futurists would fight feminism (2003:

148). He later explained this as scorn for that for which 'woman' conventionally stood – the domestic, the sentimental, the traditional – and not women as such, and the movement did include a number of women artists (Marinetti 2005: 9). However, despite Marinetti's partial recantation, the gender politics of Futurism's 'hard' aesthetics are indicative of the stance of all of the avant-gardes, for, as well as acting as a guide, as Nicholls suggests, the manifestos 'also encode some of [the avant-garde's] most problematic attitudes' (Nicholls 1995: 84).

Indeed, the link between aesthetics and a hierarchical politics more generally was integral to Marinetti's aims for Futurism through the promotion of new, specifically Italian art which would contribute to a new Italy. Futurism's links with fervent nationalism can be most clearly seen in Marinetti's association with Benito Mussolini and Italian fascism from 1919. Marinetti stood as a candidate for Mussolini's fascists in that year, and joined Mussolini in prison following their defeat. Futurism's most productive period was before Italy's entry into the war, when it was influential in Britain, Germany, the US, and especially in Russia.

The experience of the First World War was the most important factor in the creation of the next important European avant-garde, Dada, which used the previous examples of Futurism and Cubism, but recast their strategies and used them to proclaim a violent rejection of the European culture that had led to the horror of the war. Dada was not so much a redefinition of aesthetics, though, as these previous avant-gardes were, but an attempt to smash the aesthetic as such.

Dada was created in Zurich in around 1916. As a neutral country, Switzerland attracted many refugees and exiles during the war, including many intellectuals and artists. One of these was the German poet Hugo Ball (1886–1927), and the establishment of his Cabaret Voltaire really signalled the beginning of Dada as a movement. The Cabaret ran for just a few months in 1916, but the performances it staged proved enormously influential. As the artists involved travelled over Europe and beyond, especially after the war, Dada spread to Paris, New York, Berlin, and other German cities.

For Dada artists, reason, logic and meaning were responsible for the First World War, and their aim in their practice was to let irrationality loose, and destroy meaning. Hugo Ball's sound poetry, for example, which he performed live at the Cabaret Voltaire, radically challenged the coherence of the world that writing attempts to represent by making equal (non)sense in any language. One poem begins: 'gadji beri bimba glandridi laula lonni cadori/gadjama gramma berida bimbala glandri galassessa laulitalomini' (Ball 1977: n.p.).

Dada too had a manifesto, proclaimed by co-founder Tristan Tzara (1896–1963) in 1918, but rather than claiming or calling for certain things, as the Futurist Manifestos do, it is one long exercise in negation: 'I write a manifesto and I want nothing, yet I say certain things, and in principle I am against manifestos, as I am also against principles ...' (Tzara 2003: 253). For Tzara this negation was at the heart of Dada practice.

Dada practitioners did not attempt to create works which would be long-lasting, that would enter the tradition. The extremely influential experimental French artist Marcel Duchamp (1887–1968) was a central part of New York Dada after his move there in 1915. His most controversial work during this period negates the ideas of genius, inspiration and originality conventionally associated with the artist by placing everyday objects in the spaces of 'art' and by 'destroying' artworks seen as central to the European tradition. In 1917 Duchamp submitted a men's urinal, his work *Fountain* (1917), to a New York exhibition, and in 1920 he submitted to another in Paris a reproduction of Da Vinci's *Mona Lisa*, with beard and moustache added, his *L.H.O.O.Q.*

(1919). As is clear from these examples, laughter was an important element of Dada work. An explosion of laughter in response to a performance, poem or piece of visual art shattered the sacred reverence in which art was traditionally held.

Tzara moved to Paris in 1920, and continued to create and disseminate his own form of Dada. His ideas had already attracted many of the young, experimental writers working there at the time, including the future founders of Surrealism, André Breton (1896–1966), Philippe Soupault (1897–1990) and Louis Aragon (1897–1982). However, they were quickly frustrated by Tzara's Dada. While Dada saw itself as an attempt to expose the deathliness of European culture, for the soon-to-be Surrealists Dada had become part of that morbidity, a dead-end with no hope for the future. Breton, Surrealism's chief organizer and theorist, announced Dada dead in 1922 (Breton 2005a: 498–9).

Breton and the other Surrealists wanted to forge a theory and practice that broke through the deadened world identified by Dada, and find beyond it other possibilities. As the poet David Gascoyne claimed in his book introducing Surrealism to a British audience: 'Dada: negation. Surrealism: negation of negation; a new affirmation, that is' (Gascoyne 1970: 45).

Breton had worked as a stretcher-bearer during the war. Already interested in the ideas of Sigmund Freud (see Sigmund Freud and the unconscious, p. 29), he furthered his study of psychoanalysis by recording the dreams of shell-shocked men. Breton's eventual use of psychoanalysis in Surrealism was idiosyncratic, but for him Freud's theory of the unconscious allowed the possibility of another place, beyond the corrupt and absurd world of 'reality', from which the truth about human beings could be expressed, the place of 'surreality'. In ordinary life, this surreal is ignored and repressed, but it can be seen in areas generally deemed marginal or unimportant, in dreams and in children's imaginations. For the Surrealists, though, these are places of truth. In the first 'Manifesto of Surrealism' (1924), Breton states his belief in 'the future resolution of these two states, dream and reality, which are see-mingly so contradictory, into a kind of absolute reality, a *surreality*' (Breton 2005b: 723; emphasis in original). Surrealist practice was concerned with the opening up of the dream, the irrational and the child-like.

One way of doing this in literary works was through the practice of automatic writing, that is, writing in a trance-like state, where the writer is unaware of what his or her hand is writing until full consciousness returns. In 1920 Breton and Soupault had collaborated on *The Magnetic Fields*, the first work of automatic writing for literary purposes and generally seen as the first Surre-alist work. In the Manifesto, Breton recounts his 'dis-covery' of automatic writing through phrases which came to him on the point of sleep and an attempt to recreate Freud's method of 'free association'. He was trying to attain 'a monologue spoken as rapidly as possible without any intervention on the part of the critical faculties' (Breton 2005b: 727). It is this discovery which, Breton writes, led to the founding of his movement.

In the visual arts, the representation of this surreality extends from the amoeba-like forms of Joan Miró (1893–1983), to the hallucinatory images of the early works of Giorgio de Chirico (1888–1978), and those of René Magritte (1898–1967) and Salvador Dali (1904–89). In Magritte's work, for example, ordinary objects – a soberly dressed man, an apple – are made extraordinary through the use of incongruity, negation and dream-like distortions, juxtapositions and repetitions, as in *The Menaced Assassin* (1927).

Unlike Dada, Surrealism's search for truth and for 'absolute reality' led to its involvement with politics. Breton and Aragon joined the Communist Party in 1926 and the years between this and Breton's break with the party in 1935 were ones of schism and faction, as they attempted to work out the relationship between Surrealism and a communism increasingly committed to socialist realism, and suspicious of the experimental in the arts.

## The 'little magazines'

To a significant extent, Anglo-American modernism before the Second World War was the result of editorial and publishing decisions made by the owners and editors of numerous 'little magazines', some of the most significant of which were *The Dial, The Little Review, The Egoist, Blast* and *Poetry.* Although not constituting a movement or school as such, these magazines, in the US and the UK, often sold only by subscription and more often financially insecure, with small readerships and a high turnover of sometimes badly paid staff and unpaid contributors, shaped the idea of the experimental during the period, and braved censure and legal attack to publish the most challenging of contemporary work. Indeed, as Lawrence Rainey has suggested: 'It was in the little reviews ... that the principal masterpieces of the Anglo-American avant-garde would first be published' (Rainey 1998: 39). These magazines were central to the construction of modernism, both intellectually and in terms of its material practices and networks of production – that is, how new works got from the typewriters of their creators to the hands of their readers.

Magazine publishing generally changed significantly in the late nineteenth century. An expanding readership, changes in technology and the increased use of advertising meant potential changes in content, profitability and appeal. During the 1890s in particular, large numbers of new magazines and periodicals were established, such as the *Strand* (1891) and *Pall Mall* (1893). In contrast with the earlier Victorian quarterlies, many of these aimed to reach as great a readership as possible, in some cases beginning the practice of lowering cover prices considerably and relying entirely on advertising revenue for profit. While this meant more and more readers could afford to buy the magazines, it also meant that publishers became increasingly committed to accommodating rather than stretching the taste of the majority. This in turn often had a constricting effect on the content.

The late nineteenth century did see some magazines which attempted to publish work that challenged rather than followed public taste, such as the *Yellow Book* (1894), but it was the influence of new aesthetic and intellectual ideas from Europe, and especially from France, on Anglo-American intellectuals in the early twentieth century that spawned the little magazines which so contributed to the construction of modernism.

*The Dial* (1880–1929), although in some ways less radical, and certainly more financially secure, than many of the other little magazines, played a significant role in the dissemination of modernist works and ideas, and became one of the most influential little magazines in the 1920s. It had been founded in Chicago in 1880, and was for nearly four decades a mainstream review of current literature. However, after moving to New York in 1918, it was bought the next year by Scofield Thayer and J. S. Watson, who changed the editorial policy and tone of the magazine.

Thayer and Watson were in tune with new, experimental ideas and practice. They focused the magazine more on art and literature, and less on social and political issues, stressing the aesthetic as a separate, autonomous world with its own values, rules and effects. This meant that the magazine, in its layout and editorial decisions, made strong links between the literary and visual arts. Indeed Thayer was a major collector of contemporary art, and had strong connections with the experimental art world of Paris. *The Dial,* along with other little magazines, reflected strong links between the arts, but also shaped and put in place these connections. During the 1920s, *The Dial* published photographs of work by Henri Matisse, Amedeo Modigliani (1884–1920) and Pablo Picasso, as well as other leading figures in the European avant-garde.

The new owners were keen also to make their magazine more international, as were the editors of the other significant little magazines of the period. In this the magazines were crucial in shaping the character of modernism itself. In the 1920s *The Dial* published new work by T. S. Eliot (*The Waste Land* was first published jointly by *The Dial* and Eliot's own magazine, *The Criterion*, in the autumn of 1922), Ezra Pound and William Carlos Williams. Pound and Eliot wrote the 'Paris Letter' and 'London letter' respectively for *The Dial* in the 1920s. In these, they gave an overview of writing in their locales, but always within the context of wider, supranational issues of aesthetics, representation and form, as in Pound's 'Paris Letter' articles of 1922, which defended Joyce's *Ulysses* by placing it in the central tradition of European art (Pound 1922: 623–9).

The history of *The Dial* has a close connection with another of the most significant little magazines, *The Little Review* (1914–29). Its founder and editor, Margaret Anderson, worked as a reviewer for *The Dial* while it was still in Chicago. She began *The Little Review* in 1914, again in Chicago, as a mixture of essays, manifestos, poetry, fiction, and music and literary reviews. Her intention was to produce a magazine that represented 'the best conversation the world has to offer' (McKible 2002: 81) – an indication of both its international ambitions and its sense of a select audience. Anderson's move to New York in 1916 was motivated by her desire to make the magazine more international, and its change of subtitle soon after – from 'Literature, Drama, Music, Art' to 'A Magazine of the Arts: Making No Compromise with the Public Taste' – nicely expresses its aims.

Pound became foreign editor of *The Little Review* in 1917, bringing with him much needed financial support from New York lawyer and patron of the arts John Quinn. Pound came to the magazine after a stint as foreign editor of another little magazine, Harriet Monroe's *Poetry*, also based in Chicago. Since its beginning in 1912, *Poetry* had published many of the major modernist poets, but increasingly Pound had become frustrated with what he saw as its provincialism and lack of judgement. At *The Little Review*, though, Pound enjoyed the freedom to publish those who he saw as the most significant modern writers – principally James Joyce, T. S. Eliot and Wyndham Lewis – and indeed the years between 1917 and 1923 have been seen by critics as the magazine's greatest (McKible 2002: 79).

The histories of both *The Little Review* and *The Egoist* – the most significant British little magazine – reveal the importance of women in the construction and dissemination of modernism. Margaret Anderson and Jane Heap at the *Little Review*, Dora Marsden and Harriet Shaw Weaver at the *Egoist* – along with Harriet Monroe at *Poetry* – were just some of the women whose enthusiasm, brave publishing decisions and often financial support gave modernist writers an income and provided places for their work to be published (see Hanscombe and Smyers 1987; Marek 1995). *The Egoist* had been established by Dora Marsden in 1911 as *The Freewoman*, changing its name to *The New Freewoman* in 1913 and *The Egoist* in 1914 (see Mass democracy and the modernist response, p. 42). Again, Pound was influential in shaping the magazine as a forum for debate about experimental aesthetics, and as a place for the publication of new work by modernist writers; *The Egoist* published Joyce's *Portrait of the Artist as a Young Man* in serial form in 1914, and sections of *Ulysses* in 1918–19. However, the commitment and financial support of Harriet Shaw Weaver in particular was crucial in the creation of Anglo-American modernism, although her role, along with that of the other women, has too often been either invisible or seen as secondary.

Financial and censorship struggles dogged many of the little magazines during this period. Even at its height, *The Egoist*'s circulation was rarely more than 200 copies per issue. This, its commitment to publishing challenging material and its unwillingness to court advertising, meant serious financial difficulties. *The Egoist* ceased publication at the end of 1919 in order to concentrate on publishing books through its small publishing house, The Egoist Press. The main work of the press over the next two years was in the fraught attempts to publish *Ulysses* in book form. Although it was eventually published in Paris under the Egoist imprint towards the end of 1922, Weaver's struggles with printers reluctant to risk charges of obscenity further weakened the press financially.

Such financial difficulties shaped the histories of all the little magazines, and often brought together strange bedfellows. T. S. Eliot's own little magazine, *Criterion* (1922–39), was kept going by financial support from the wealthy Lady Rothermere, wife of the *Daily Mail*'s owner, the latter publication embodying everything that the little magazines loathed. By the end of the 1920s, *The Dial*, *The Little Review* and *The Egoist* had all ceased publication.

The most significant little magazine in the 1930s was *transition* (1927–39), founded and edited in Paris by Eugene Jolas. Committed to internationalism and experimentalism, to the 'Revolution of the Word', as it called it in a special issue of 1929, against the increasing pressure in the 1930s for the left to champion socialist realist work, *transition* published work by Franz Kafka, Samuel Beckett, Ernest Hemingway, William Carlos Williams, Rainer Maria Rilke, H. D., Djuna Barnes and Gertrude Stein, as well as experimental artists and architects. Of particular importance in *transition*'s 'revolution' was the work of James Joyce. From its first issue, *transition* published section by section Joyce's 'Work in Progress', published in 1939 as *Finnegans Wake.*

# 3

# Critical Approaches

---

Historical overview
Current issues and debates

---

## HISTORICAL OVERVIEW

As Marianne Thormählen suggests regarding the term 'modernism': 'No classifying concept has played a greater part in academic research on English poetry and fiction in the twentieth century' (Thormählen 2003: 1). For such an important term, however, its status, definition and credibility has since the beginning of its use been a matter of controversy and debate. 'Modernism' dominates Anglo-American criticism's idea of the writing of the first half of the twentieth century, as it still dominates the catalogues of academic publishers, the research of academics and university curriculum choices, but the dominance of the term has been seen by a number of critics as a great problem. Indeed, John Harwood has argued that the term has no existence outside the critical vocabulary of academics, that it has been constructed solely for purposes of academia (Harwood 1995).

For most writers and critics through the twentieth century, though, what has been most at issue is not so much whether the term should exist at all, but rather its definition, what it actually describes. At the heart of this, since the critical works of Anglo-American modernist writers themselves, has been a debate over the relation between modernist works and the world from and through which they are produced, and to which they are a response. While regular challenges to the existence of modernism are a necessary check, despite the debates and disagreements, it is possible to discern a certain coherence in writing which presents quite fundamental challenges to literary form and to the world it inhabits. However, what these challenges are, and how they are judged, has changed throughout the critical consideration of the work over the last 100 years.

While the term 'modernism' wasn't widely used in the way it is now until the 1960s, critics and writers themselves in the first decades of the twentieth century were certainly aware of the coherence of the ideas and the kinds of writing it has come to describe. One of the things which distinguishes what we now call modernism from many previous kinds of writing was the extent to which the literary and the critical were intertwined. Modernist writers were highly conscious of critical questions surrounding their writing, questions of how they wrote and what writing was for, and the links between themselves and other innovative writers. Indeed, one of the first uses of the term which corresponds to later critical uses is in the anthology of poetry put together by the poets Laura Riding and Robert Graves and entitled *A Survey of Modernist Poetry* (1927). In this, Riding and Graves see modernism as a 'movement', with its own techniques and concerns, even if their selection included poets who would not now be considered modernist (Riding and Graves 1927: 258).

In the 1930s Ezra Pound used a number of essays to give a retrospective form and shape to the 'movement' of experimental writing, a movement, of course, which he had helped create. For him, not only is it a 'movement to which no name has ever been given' (Pound 1932: 590), but its beginning is located in a different moment in different essays (Smith 1994: 2). Despite this slipperiness of origin and definition during the period usually associated with modernism, however, more recent critics such as Stan Smith, against Harwood's claims mentioned earlier, still see in the critical and literary work of the modernists a recognition of a theory and practice which distinguishes them from others. As Smith argues: '"Modernist" may be an epithet applied in hindsight to a disparate collection of writers, but it is also a real element in their discourse of themselves' (ibid.: 11). And for Smith, and many other critics who assert the existence of modernism or at least *modernisms*, that element is the coexistence of two moments 'of revolt and restoration', a 'dynamic instability in the fabric of modernism' (ibid.) explicitly acknowledged in the work of the modernists themselves.

## Modernism and contemporary criticism 1918–39

If for recent critics the *challenge* that is modernism has come to dominate its existence as a category, its definition and its significance (see below), modernism's enmeshment with criticism and the academy from the beginning had a very different tone. It is during what is usually seen as the modernist period in Anglo-American writing – from the end of the nineteenth century to the Second World War – that English literature as an academic subject began to establish itself in universities in Britain. Central to this process was what has come to be called 'Cambridge English' – English literature as an academic discipline as established at Cambridge University immediately following the First World War. Modernist writing played a large part in the shaping of Cambridge English, and Cambridge English played a large part in shaping subsequent understandings of modernist writing.

The work of one critic in particular dominated the construction of Cambridge English. I. A. Richards (1893–

1979) began lecturing on the theory of criticism in 1919, and taught at Cambridge until moving to Harvard University in 1944. His development through the 1920s of a theory and methodology for reading and assessing poetry both depended on and ended up championing modernist poetry, in particular that of T. S. Eliot.

Following the traumatic dislocations of the First World War, the study of English literature was seen by many as a potential way of uniting the nation and combating class divisions through a sharing of 'English' values and beliefs. Among the most influential propagators of this belief were the findings of a Royal Commission on the subject published in 1921, usually known as the Newbolt Report (see Baldick 1983). While ostensibly concerned with the nation as a whole, the Report focused in particular on the working class, implying that working-class life was unruly and lacked restraint. It argued that, if working-class people could read and appreciate literary works, works which were ordered according to certain values and principles, then their fundamental understanding of the world would be in harmony with other classes, rather than in conflict.

Richards shared this sense that the 'proper' appreciation of poetry demanded a regulation of the emotions, and could impose on the mind of the reader an orderliness and discrimination that would preclude misreading, disagreement and conflict. In *Practical Criticism* (1929), he set out his method for achieving this 'proper' reading. Its approach is described by him in the preface to his earlier *Principles of Literary Criticism* (1924):

> Extremely good and extremely bad poems were put *unsigned* before a large and able audience. The comments they wrote at leisure give, as it were, a stereoscopic view of the poem and of possible opinion on it. This material when systematically analysed, provides, not only an interesting commentary upon the state of contemporary culture, but a new and powerful educational instrument. (Richards 2001: x)

Richards' description makes clear a number of important assumptions about the reading of poetry and his own method. His intention in *Practical Criticism* was to use a systematic, indeed scientized, method to order and elucidate the emotional effects of poetry. The poetry itself was to be scrutinized outside of its historical or cultural context – it was not necessary to know when it was written or by whom in order to read it correctly. And to read correctly, readers needed to respond to the sense of the poem, its feeling, its tone and an implied authorial intention. The sense of a poem's value came from its ability to unite these harmoniously, to establish its own orderly world. While the poem's engagement with the actual world was immaterial to Richards' method (hence the rejection of historical and cultural context), this search for order meant that, in fact, a poem was judged valuable to the extent to which it reproduced the status quo, or could be read in that way. While Richards' 'interesting commentary', then, included a judgement that bad reading was an effect of contemporary cultural decline, paradoxically his method, by focusing on formal harmony, would not allow 'good' poetry to challenge that culture through a disruption of poetic effect.

It may seem strange, given this, that Richards' method became so linked, by him and others, with modernist poetry. His reading of modernist poetry, in particular his championing of Eliot, was based on his sense of the poetry as, though complex and ambiguous, finally static and orderly, as finally achieving in its language a harmony and hope that was not always present in the world. Indeed, Eliot's poetry is explicitly read by Richards as finally orderly and coherent. In *Principles of Literary Criticism*, he acknowledges that some have found Eliot's poetry nostalgic or pessimistic, but he claims that this is a misreading:

Both the bitterness and desolation are superficial aspects of [Eliot's] poetry ... some readers find in his poetry not only a clearer, fuller realization of their plight, the plight of a whole generation, than they find elsewhere, but also through the very energies set free in that realization a return of the saving passion. (Richards 2001: 278)

This reading of modernist poetry as ultimately attempting a kind of stasis, resisting the change and tumult of contemporary society, can, of course, be found in Eliot's own criticism. That subsequent critics have so taken Eliot at his word, and have read not only his work but all Anglo-American poetry in this way, is due to a significant degree to the influence of Richards' critical methods.

Among those whose anonymous responses to poetry were scrutinized by Richards in *Practical Criticism* was the literary critic, F. R. Leavis (1895–1978). Leavis and his wife Q. D. Leavis (1906–81) both taught at Cambridge, and through their criticism and through *Scrutiny*, the journal they set up in 1932, their ideas came to dominate English studies as it spread through other universities and, in particular, through schools.

Terry Eagleton has argued that the Leavises did such a good job in establishing literature as an object of academic knowledge that whereas in the 1920s 'it was desperately unclear why English was worth studying at all; by the early 1930s it was a question of why it was worth wasting your time on anything else' (Eagleton 1983: 31). Central to this sense of the importance of literature was Leavis's championing of modernist writing (although neither he nor Richards used the term), for example in his *New Bearings in English Poetry* (1932). For Leavis, for a literary work to be truly valuable, it must show a seriousness and sensitivity toward 'life' (a term never really defined by Leavis), and the way such 'life' is revealed in a 'living' language. In this demand, Leavis's sense of what is valuable in a literary work – a harmony and an organicism – has much in common with Richards', despite other differences in their approaches.

Much of Leavis's later criticism focuses on the novel, and in this he attempts to claim for that form the seriousness and importance of poetry. In this, he is at one with the claims of innovative novelists in English from Henry James onwards. In *The Great Tradition* (1948), Leavis proposes James and Joseph Conrad as the most significant recent contributors to the main tradition of the English novel, and later it is D. H. Lawrence's work that exemplifies the potential of the novel for seriousness, and for life-affirming comment on the contemporary world (Leavis 1955).

However, this demand for the novel to create a harmonious and 'whole' view of life through an organic language led to Leavis's rejection of other modernist writers. For him, neither Woolf, nor the wider Bloomsbury ethos, were sufficiently serious. Joyce's language games, especially in *Finnegans Wake* (1939), erred not only by treating language as a thing in itself rather than as a kind of glue which would cohere a fragmented society, but by actually fragmenting that language. As with Richards, Leavis's valuation of innovative writing demanded that its formal response to the perceived crisis in contemporary culture be a reassertion of harmony and wholeness. Again, writing that in its form disrupted and overturned conventional order – as in their different ways both Woolf and Joyce did – did not for Leavis offer possible ways of challenging that order, but was rather symptomatic of its decline.

In the United States, the most significant critical movement before and after the Second World War was New Criticism, and this too was both influenced by modernist poetry (as well as by the critical work of I. A. Richards and T. S. Eliot), and was in its turn influential in defining what 'modernism' was. The leading critics of New Criticism, in particular John Crowe Ransom (1888–1974), used the word 'modernism' to describe the poetry they admired throughout the 1930s, and it has been suggested that it is probably via this use that the term later entered American, and then British academic discourse (Smith 2003: 184). In their critical practices, New Critics rejected biography, social or historical context or literary history as frameworks through which to read a poem, and concentrated instead on considering the work itself as just 'the words on the page', as an autonomous, independent object. In this concentration on the purely verbal existence of a literary work – its figures, images and symbols – the focus was on the ambiguities and conflicts in the language of the poem, and in particular on the way such conflicts are resolved. This intensely formal reading of literature – the consideration of character, ideas and plot plays little part – is coupled with a belief that the value of a literary work is its final equilibrium, its reconciliation of paradox and opposition. This leads New Critics, along with Richards and Leavis, to ultimately conservative readings. Again such modernist poetry is read as finally orderly, balanced and static.

At the root of this conservatism was a failure to take on fully the question of a literary work's relation with the world, and to develop a thorough conceptual framework for understanding and critiquing that world. For Leavis, in particular, this was a paradoxical failure. Throughout the 1930s and 1940s his cultural criticism saw contemporary culture as destructive and in decline (Leavis 2000). He saw literature as an antidote to this, but his failure to try to work out what its relation to the world was, beyond his vague terminology of 'life', 'morality' and 'the organic', led him to a conservative and nostalgic reading of the literary that could not radically challenge contemporary society because it remained finally wedded to the status quo. What Leavis lacked was a *politics* that could both rigorously critique the world and explicate literature in relation to it, and this lack generally in Anglo-American criticism until the late 1960s meant that the disruptive challenge of modernist writing was denied.

## The 1960s and the creation of 'modernism'

The work of Richards, Leavis and the New Critics remained influential well into the 1960s. What did change, however, were the institutional needs of the academy. As the university sector expanded in both Britain and the US, the role of the academic changed to become more accountable and more 'professional'. While earlier critics such as Leavis had seemed to provide the academic with a moral and ethical basis on which to ground their activities, the changing cultural climate through the 1960s, with the rise in popular media such as television, and the increasing dominance of popular culture generally, began to challenge this basis. 'Modernism' as a fixed category for the purposes of teaching and research became entrenched through the 1960s in response to these changes. As Peter Faulkner notes in his own early work on the topic, the term 'was not used in 1961 in the volume of *The Pelican Guide to English Literature* discussing the twentieth century; but in *The Sphere History* in 1971 it is freely used' (Faulkner 1977: ix). Works such as Hugh Kenner's *Gnomon* (1958) and Graham Hough's *Image and Experience* (1960) recognized the coherence of the work of innovative writers from earlier in the century (although neither used the term modernist), and the poet Stephen Spender's *The Struggle of the Modern* (1963) began to set out a definition of modernism by opposing the idea of the 'modern' to the merely 'contemporary'. As with Richards and Leavis, though, this entrenchment in response to a surrounding world that was perceived as hostile led to a construction of a conservative modernism.

The American literary critics Lionel Trilling (1905–75) and Harry Levin (1912–94) were among the first to try to cohere a disparate set of innovative writers into a usable critical category, but for both, in opposing ways, their definitions merely reconfirmed the status quo – bourgeois, liberal and humanist. In his essay 'On the Modern Element in Modern Literature' (1961), Trilling defines the modern (or modernist) as a celebration of the irrational and the primal, as a disenchantment with culture itself, which he sees as synonymous with liberal humanism. He admits how wary he was of offering a course in modernist literature to his students, as the works seemed to represent unreason and irrationality in a way that he saw as threatening to social order (Trilling 1962). Trilling's reading of modernism here acknowledges its potentially disruptive effect, but works to diffuse or deflect it. For Trilling, the purpose of the literary critic is to uphold and reaffirm the central cultural beliefs of their society, and to read literary works in a way that does not threaten order and harmony.

Harry Levin, in the preface to his influential essay, 'What Was Modernism?' (first given as a lecture in 1960 and published in 1966), disagrees with Trilling's reading of modernist works, but not with his values. For him, modernist works are the progeny of the Enlightenment and its fundamental values of reason, rationality and progress; it is the contemporary, the 'postmodern', which is guilty of celebrating ignorance and irrationality. Modernism is rather a bulwark against such forces, an intelligent, high art compared to which recent writing is a falling away: 'Beckett, after Joyce, seems thin and strident and monotonous; [Henry] Miller looks like an amusing but crude burlesque of Lawrence ... It is difficult not to conclude, if we retain any perspective, that we have fallen among epigones' (Levin 1966: 273). In particular, modernism achieved these superior standards and values by 'working experimental transformations into traditional continuities' (ibid.: 287). Again, modernism must in the end be a confirmation of the status quo, and its formal innovation is subordinated to its supposed complicity with the orthodoxies of Western thinking.

Implicit in this drive to suggest a modernism which was a riposte to current decline, and a bulwark for the value of academic work, was its construction as *historical.* As Lawrence Rainey has pointed out, Ellmann and Feidelson, in their *The Modern Tradition: Backgrounds of Modern Literature* (1965), argue that modernism has 'passed into history' (Ellmann and Feidelson 1965: vi), and for Rainey this a 'key moment in modernism's passage to academic respectability' (Rainey 1998: 77). Modernism as a *current* disruptor of conventions and orthodoxies has to be over for it to be seen as itself orderly.

If the 'conservative' modernism of Anglo-American literary criticism until the 1960s was the result of a lack of a rigorous critique of contemporary culture, it was exactly such a critique that had been produced in Europe from the interwar years on by Marxist critics such as Walter Benjamin (1892–1940) and Theodor Adorno (1903–69). While neither Benjamin nor Adorno uses the term 'modernism', and their work primarily deals with European experimental writers and artists, for both such work was at the heart of their critiques. 'Modernist' works were significant in so far as they represented a radical challenge to the status quo. Crucially, what constituted this challenge for both Benjamin and Adorno was not *what* modernist works said, but *how* they said it (or indeed how they refused to say it).

Far from subordinating formal experimentation, as the Anglo-American critics did, for Benjamin and Adorno it was in the disruption of formal expectations that the possibility for subversion and revolutionary change lay. According to Benjamin, modernity is experienced by the individual as a series of 'shocks'; formal disruption can produce these shocks, for example in the editing techniques of cinema, or the collage effect of non-representational art, with revolutionary implications. Forms associated with modernity, especially film, produce 'a tremendous shattering of tradition', and emancipate art from its ritualized past into the political (Benjamin 1992: 215, 218). For Adorno, the 'autonomy' of experimental art did not mean a turning away from the world toward the purely aesthetic; it was rather an implicit critique of capitalist society: 'The emphasis on the autonomous work … is itself socio-political in nature … This is not the time for political works of art; rather, politics has migrated into the autonomous work of art' (Adorno 1992: 93–4).

## KEY ISSUES AND DEBATES

### The poststructuralist turn

The formation of modernism as an academic critical category in the 1960s in Anglo-American literary studies can be seen then in part as a defence against the increasingly 'postmodern' tenor of contemporary culture – with its emphasis on surface over depth, the present over the past, and its extreme scepticism towards the bourgeois liberal values of progress and civilization – and consequent anxiety about falling standards and cultural relativism. However, from the 1970s modernism's pre-eminence in the academy was fuelled by a quite contrary movement, poststructuralism, developed in the French academy through the 1960s, and this continues to have enormous influence on modernist studies right up to the present. It is via the work of poststructuralists that Anglo-American critics have come to reject the conservative modernism of their earlier compatriots, and begun to appreciate and use the work of Benjamin and Adorno, among others, to rediscover a modernism of subversion.

Poststructuralist theory has been most often associated with postmodernist work. Both challenge the central tenets of humanism and see meaning in language as fundamentally unstable, and constantly deferred. For poststructuralists and postmodernists, language is the primary determining factor of human subjectivity and human culture, and, as a consequence, both see the human subject as itself unstable, a fantasy constructed over lack, split and dissolution. Often influenced by Marxist thought, poststructuralist theorists suggest that this construction is ideologically driven. The human subject is made according to the requirements of bourgeois capitalism, and its need to fix and control the 'other' in terms of gender, class, sexuality and ethnicity.

Despite this overlap in the theoretical grounds of poststructuralism and postmodernism, in fact, the central poststructuralist theories of literature most often concentrate on modernist rather than postmodernist texts. (The term 'modernism' as understood in the Anglo-American academy is not used among European academics, but certainly French poststructuralists concentrate on writers, such as Proust and Kafka, who would be considered modernist by their English-speaking colleagues.) One reason for this is that, if language structures the human subject according to the demands of the dominant ideology, works which *undo* the commonsensical view that language is a transparent medium of communication, which play with language, break it down, make visible its own materiality, can be seen as in themselves radical and subversive. In his early work, *Writing Degree Zero* (1953), the French critic Roland Barthes (1915–80) assumes, unlike most Anglo-American critics of the time, that experimental writing occupies a privileged position. He is arguing against Marxist dogma of the time which condemns modernist writers as representing the pathology of bourgeois culture (for example in Sartre's *What is Literature* (1947) and Georg Lukács's *The Meaning of Contemporary Realism* (1957)). In 'The Reality Effect' (1968), Barthes argues that realism is as constructed, as determined by rules and conventions, as more 'visible' uses of language (Barthes 1982). Crucially, these rules and conventions demand the reproduction of the status quo, making realism an impossible vehicle for revolution.

Barthes' ideas inform (despite differences) a good deal of later, very influential, poststructuralist work on literature. In *Revolution in Poetic Language* (1974), and in the English translation of much of her work from the 1970s, *Desire in Language* (1980), Julia Kristeva uses Barthes and Lacanian psychoanalysis to suggest that writers such as the Symbolist poet Stéphane Mallarmé (1842–98) and James Joyce explore and break up language so that that which language is trying to repress is able to burst through; their aim is to 'wipe out sense through nonsense and laughter' (Kristeva 1981: 142).

In the work of Jacques Derrida (1930–2004), while it largely ignores the themes and questions which constitute the 'modernism' of Anglo-American critics, Joyce, Kafka and Mallarmé are also of importance. They are read as undoing the assumptions of Western philosophy and literary criticism, and Derrida's writing on them re-enacts their own disruption. In 'Ulysses Gramophone', he interrogates 'the *yeses* of *Ulysses* as well as the institution of Joycean experts' (Derrida 1992: 266), suggesting that the 'yeses' in Joyce's novel undo the conventional categorizations of linguistics, and make both possible and impossible a 'competent' scholarly 'reading' of the novel (ibid.: 254–5).

So, then, poststructuralist critics agree with Lionel Trilling – the formal and linguistic disruptions of modernist works *are* a threat to social order and dominant ideologies. For them, though, this is something to be welcomed and celebrated. Poststructuralist work recognizes and privileges modernism as disruptive and shocking. Indeed, a number of critics have seen poststructuralism as theory 'catching up' with modernist literary practice (Eysteinsson 1990: 47).

The Marxist literary critic Raymond Williams (1921–88) was one of the earliest British critics to be influenced

by French poststructuralist thought, and from this he was
led back to Marxist uses of modernism from the 1930s
onward, especially the work of Walter Benjamin and
Theodor Adorno (see previous section). Even though it
was not until his posthumously published work that he
looked at modernism as a specific critical category
(Williams 1989), throughout his work from the 1960s on
he sees Anglo-American criticism of experimental works
as having a conforming effect, making the works more
conservative than they are. It is Williams's assimilation of
French theory that allows this insight, and fuels his
challenge to the main strain of post-war Anglo-American
criticism. In his lecture from 1987, 'When Was Modernism?', the title a direct and ironic allusion to Levin's
lecture from nearly 30 years before (see above), Williams
argues that modernism has atrophied into a servant of
the capitalist market, and has lost its potentially subversive relation to the contemporary cultural moment:

> After Modernism is canonized ... by the post-war settlement
> and its accompanying, complicit academic endorsements,
> here is then the presumption that since Modernism is *here* in
> this specific phase or period, there is nothing beyond it. The
> marginal or rejected artists become classics of organized
> teaching and of travelling exhibitions in the great galleries
> of the metropolitan cities. 'Modernism' is confined to this
> highly selective field and denied to everything else in an act
> of pure ideology, whose first, unconscious irony is that,
> absurdly, it stops history. (Williams 1989: 34)

## Identity politics and the historical reclamation of 'modernisms'

Williams's sense of the importance of the historical
relation is significant in terms of the specifically British
assimilation of French theory. Poststructuralist theory,
while often influenced by Marx, tends to focus not so
much on historical context and dynamic, but on the

formal and linguistic aspects of a work. While the shift towards poststructuralist understandings of literary works in critical approaches to modernism began in the 1970s, a number of influential survey works were published in that decade that remained firmly within a historicist, rather than a theoretical, approach. Both Bradbury and MacFarlane's *Modernism 1890–1930* (1976) and Peter Faulkner's *Modernism* (1977) welcome the existence of modernism as a critical category within a particular historical period and attempt to define and characterize it using the methods of literary history. Although there are areas of contradiction between these two critical approaches, the historicist approach remains strong in British critical work on modernism up to the present (a more purely poststructuralist reading of modernism tends to be a characteristic of American criticism, although these distinctions are always blurred in the international field of academia). Much work combines a sense of the determinants of historical period, and the need to map and explicate complex networks of relation across the historical field, with the theoretical rigour and approaches to language learned from poststructuralism.

Indeed, throughout the 1980s, this combined approach was important in a modernist studies transformed through the influence of identity politics. This brought together poststructuralism's insistence on the radical potentialities of the language of 'othered' identities to disrupt the linguistic hegemony of bourgeois capitalism with a more materialist consideration of the historical determinants of class, gender, sexuality and ethnicity. In particular, the burgeoning of feminist literary studies during the decade produced a rethinking of the place of modernist women writers. Elaine Showalter's historicist (and biographical) approach to Woolf's work in *A Literature of Their Own* (1977) leads to a reading of Woolf's narrative strategies as 'ultimately unsuccessful' (Showalter 1978: 264) in terms of their vision of femininity and engagement with the world. Showalter argues that in the end they advocate 'a strategic retreat, not a victory; a denial of feeling, and not a mastery of it', and indeed a deathliness (ibid.: 285, 297). In contrast, those feminist writers who, by the 1980s, had assimilated poststructuralist understandings of language, in particular those linked to Lacanian psychoanalysis, are able to claim Woolf's complex aesthetic experimentation (and that of other marginalized modernists) as inherently disruptive of the oppressions of patriarchy, as political (Moi 1985; Minow-Pinkney 1987; Bowlby 1988; DeKoven 1991).

Much feminist work during the 1980s and 1990s also challenged the gender politics of those writers thought to be at the centre of Anglo-American literary modernism, Wyndham Lewis's 'men of 1914' – Eliot, Pound, Joyce and Lewis himself – whose centrality had been institutionalized by critics from the beginning: by Richards, Leavis, Richard Ellmann and Hugh Kenner, for example. The title of Bonnie Kime Scott's *Refiguring Modernism: The Women of 1928* (1995) alludes to the 'men of 1914', and her study attempts to undermine their hegemony in modernist studies. She argues that: 'Well into the 1980s, the modernist era was managed for the academy by men who paid little critical regard to gender and had little interest in giving space in the canon to women, among other outsider groups' (Scott 1995: 80). In challenging the defining power of the 'men of 1914' and their critical successors, such work often goes on to assert the claims of 'marginalized' women writers to a place in the central 'canon' of modernism.

However, as part of the opening up of the category of modernism, a number of critics have come to question this tactic. As argued by Thormählen, it merely reinforces the valorization of modernism which she sees as the central problem with the term: 'Being designated as "modernist" has undoubtedly raised the prestige of a literary text or writers, a practice which has had two unfortunate consequences: works on which the label has not seemed to fit have been unfairly neglected, and the area of applicability has been stretched to (and sometimes beyond) the limit of meaningfulness' (Thormählen 2003: 6). Baldick, in his revisionary account of the period 1910–40, which eschews modernism as the central, privileged mode, sees this tactic – 'if you can't beat them, join them' – as defeatist and attributes the extreme privileging of modernism to the influence of poststructuralism and its assertion of experimental writing as politically subversive. For him, the valorization of modernism is due to the political dogma of much of the academy over the last 30 years, 'where admiration for the realist tradition may still be regarded as political backsliding' (Baldick 2004: 399, 400). Criticism that does not acknowledge this, then, but is complicit in seeing this privileging as somehow objective or natural, is severely flawed. For others, the privileging ignores the extent to which an 'outsider's' experience of modernity is unrepresented in mainstream modernism, and the extent to which modernity itself is problematically linked to certain ideas of gender, class and ethnicity by many modernist writers (Felski 1995).

While in the previous section the approaches of Leavis and the New Critics are seen in opposition to those of Adorno, what they do have in common is effecting a sharp division between an elite culture and mass culture. From the 1990s until now, work on modernism has seen strong challenges to this division, and a consequent challenge to the category of modernism itself. Much important work has stressed the divisions and tensions within modernism, indeed has insisted that we think of *modernisms* (Nicholls 1995). Marshall Berman's *All That Is Solid Melts Into Air* (1983) is an early antecedent of this type of work. In it, he broadens the definition of modernism to include 'any attempt by modern men and women to become subjects as well as objects of modernization, to get a grip on the modern world and make

themselves at home in it' (Berman 1983: 5), hence
allowing nineteenth-century figures such as Dickens,
Marx, Dostoevsky and Baudelaire to be unquestioningly
'modernist'. While Berman's argument has been criticized for its downplaying of the significance of the specifically formal innovations of modernists in the early
twentieth century (Anderson 1984), this questioning of
the boundaries of the category of modernism has been
central in recent critical work.

Over the last 20 years or so, modernism's 'others' have
returned and forced a rethinking of the aesthetic, political and ethical underpinnings of canonical modernism. Much of this work has found that mainstream
modernism is more implicated in and enmeshed with
these 'others' than previously admitted. An important
forerunner to this, and a study with which much of it has
been in dialogue, is Andreas Huyssens' *After the Great
Divide: Modernism, Mass Culture, Postmodernism* (1986).
Huyssens argues that modernism's relation with mass
culture, far from being straightforwardly oppositional,
has always included 'a plethora of strategic moves
tending to destabilize the high/low opposition from
within', even though such strategies in the end only have
temporary effects (Huyssens 1986: vi). This argument,
and the work that has responded to it, have both re-
explored modernism's claim to an aesthetic which is
autonomous from the market (Dettmar and Watt 1996:
Rainey 1998), and brought to attention those areas of
culture – such as popular fiction, the middlebrow and
the effects of professionalization on English culture –
that have been ignored as a consequence of the dominance of a certain view of modernism in the academy
(Ardis 1990; Strychacz 1993; DiBattista and McDiarmid
1996; Trotter 2001). As Ardis herself argues in *Modernism
and Cultural Conflict,* her work is an attempt to recover 'a
turn-of-the-century cultural landscape in which modernism did not (yet) throw gigantic shadows' (Ardis
2002: 4). As with Ardis, much of this work, whatever its

focus, is influenced by and indebted to feminist questionings of modernism from the 1980s on.

Other work in this mould has focused on areas that, while not specifically eclipsed by modernism as conventionally read, have been suppressed for the way they open up modernism to scrutiny and critique, or suggest a more subversive modernism. Work on suppressed sexualities has both reread mainstream modernists, such as Woolf, and looked at previously somewhat ignored writers such as Djuna Barnes and H. D. (Collecott 1999; Galvin 1999; Hackett 2004). A related focus on modernism and the body – in relation, for example, to technology, to 'race' and to sex – has suggested a corporeality at the heart of modernist experimentation which challenges both the revolt at the flesh of many of the mainstream modernists, and the focus on the text of the New Critics and later formalist critics (Doyle 1994; Froula 1996; Armstrong 1998; Daly 2004).

While many earlier studies of modernism stress the international characteristics of the movement, and the role of exile in many modernist writers' lives and work, recent studies have begun to question modernism's relationship to place, nation and nationalism, and as a consequence to rethink its politics (Peppis 2000; Garrity 2003). Linked to this, very recent work has begun to use postcolonial approaches and theories to consider modernism. Booth and Rigby, in the introduction to their collection, suggest that it is 'the first book-length study that seeks to explore the pervasive but complex interrelations between British colonialism and the modern movement' (2000: 1). While they cite precursors in Chinua Achebe (1930–), Edward Said (1935–2003) and Fredric Jameson (1934–), they suggest that critics are really only just beginning to fully consider and challenge, for example, the place of the 'primitive' in certain kinds of modernism, to call attention to the central place of 'other identities' in the constructions of both modernity and modernism, and to reformulate modernism's relation to colonial politics. Over the last few years, a number of critics have responded to this challenge (Adams 2003; Hackett 2004; Marx 2005).

Much work on modernism continues to consider themes that have been central in critical work from the beginning – the influence of French writing or the impact of the First World War, for example – although with new perspectives and awareness. The often repeated criticism is still, however, that modernist criticism continues to 'read modernism from within its own politics and prejudices' (Jacobs 1994: 277), but work such as that of Rado (1997), Armstrong (1998) and Ardis (2002) has begun to create a reading of modernism that goes far beyond that stipulated by either the modernists' own prescriptions or previous literary critical conventions.

Much of the recent rethinking of modernism can be seen in relation to the wane in the critical fortunes of 'postmodernism'. One of the emerging issues in modernist studies over the last decade or so has been the sense that modernism has been read via postmodernism, for example as still championing the 'grand narratives', and therefore misread (Ellman 1995: vii–viii; Nicholls 1995: vii). While indebted to poststructuralist work for the impulse to read modernism politically, much of the work surveyed above can be seen as an attempt to read modernism beyond the textual focus of postmodernist critics, and to reground modernism in its history.

# 4

## Resources for Independent Study

Chronology of key historical and cultural events
Glossary of key terms and concepts
Further reading and resources

## CHRONOLOGY OF KEY HISTORICAL AND CULTURAL EVENTS

| Date | Literary Events | Other Significant Events |
|---|---|---|
| 1900 | Joseph Conrad, *Lord Jim* <br> W. B. Yeats, *Shadowy Waters* | Independent Labour Party founded in Britain <br> Sigmund Freud, *The Interpretation of Dreams* (published end of 1899, dated 1900) <br> Friedrich Nietzsche, *Ecce Homo* <br> Max Planck's Quantum theory <br> *Daily Express* founded |
| 1901 | W. B. Yeats, *Poems* | Queen Victoria dies, Edward VII succeeds <br> First wireless communication between Europe and US <br> Max Planck's law of radiation |
| 1902 | Joseph Conrad, *Heart of Darkness* <br> Henry James, *The Wings of the Dove* <br> W. B. Yeats, *Cathleen Ní Houlihan* | Boer War ends <br> William James, *Varieties of Religious Experience* <br> *Times Literary Supplement* founded |

| 1903 | Henry James, *The Ambassadors* | G.E. Moore, *Principia Ethica* Daily Mirror launched Wright brothers' first flight Women's Social and Political Union founded by the Pankhursts |
|---|---|---|
| 1904 | Joseph Conrad, *Nostromo* Henry James, *The Golden Bowl* | Abbey Theatre founded in Dublin |
| 1905 | E. M. Forster, *Where Angels Fear to Tread* | Liberal government formed in Britain Sinn Fein founded in Dublin Albert Einstein's Special Theory of Relativity |
| 1906 | | Women's suffrage movement becomes activist Labour Party founded in Britain |
| 1907 | Joseph Conrad, *The Secret Agent* James Joyce, *Chamber Music* | Henri Bergson, *Creative Evolution* First Cubist exhibition, Paris Pablo Picasso, *Desmoiselles d'Avignon* |
| 1908 | E. M. Forster, *A Room with a View* Ezra Pound, *A Lume Spento* Getrude Stein, *Three Lives* W. B. Yeats, *Collected Works I and II* | H. H. Asquith becomes Prime Minister in Britain Old age pensions in Britain for first time Ford Madox Hueffer (later Ford) founds *English Review* |
| 1909 | F. T. Marinetti's first Futurist Manifesto Ezra Pound, *Personae and Exultations* | Henri Bergson, *Matter and Memory* Sigmund Freud lectures on psychoanalysis in the US Henri Matisse, *The Dance* |
| 1910 | E. M. Forster, *Howard's End* | Edward VII dies, George V succeeds Roger Fry's first Post-Impressionist exhibition in London |

**1911** Joseph Conrad, *Under Western Eyes*
T. E. Hulme, 'Romanticism and Classicism'
D. H. Lawrence, *The White Peacock*
Katherine Mansfield, *In a German Pension*

Political unrest in Britain: strikes, suffragette action and campaign for Home Rule in Ireland
Ernest Rutherford's nuclear theory of the atom
Frederick Taylor, *The Principles of Scientific Management*

**1912** D. H. Lawrence, *The Trespasser*
Ezra Pound, *Ripostes*
Beginning of Imagism
Poetry magazine founded in Chicago

Second Post-Impressionist exhibition in London
First Futurist exhibition in London
Sinking of *Titanic*
Death of Scott of the Antarctic
Marcel Duchamp, *Nude Descending a Staircase*

**1913** D. H. Lawrence, *Sons and Lovers*
Marcel Proust, *À la récherche du temps perdu* (–1927)
Gertrude Stein, *Portrait of Mabel Dodge at Villa Caronio*
William Carlos Williams, *The Tempers*

Omega Workshop opened in London
Umberto Boccioni, *Unique Forms of Continuity in Space*
Igor Stravinsky, *The Rite of Spring*; Diaghilev's production with the Ballets Russes provokes riots when it opens in Paris
The Armory Show, New York
Sigmund Freud, *Totem and Taboo*
First time signal transmitted around the world from the top of the Eiffel Tower

**1914** Joseph Conrad, *Chance*
James Joyce, *Dubliners*
D. H. Lawrence, *The Prussian Officer*
Percy Wyndham Lewis, *Enemy of the Stars*

Beginning of the First World War

Ezra Pound (ed.), *Des Imagistes*
Gertrude Stein, *Tender Buttons*
W. B. Yeats, *Responsibilities*
First issue of *Blast*
*The Egoist* begins publication
*The Little Review* begins publication

| 1915 | Joseph Conrad, *Victory* | D. W. Griffith, *Birth of a Nation* |
| | Ford Madox Ford, *The Good Soldier* | |
| | D. H. Lawrence, *The Rainbow* | |
| | Amy Lowell (ed.), *Some Imagist Poets* | |
| | Ezra Pound, *Cathay* | |
| | Dorothy Richardson, *Pilgrimage* (first volume) | |
| | Virginia Woolf, *The Voyage Out* | |
| 1916 | H. D., *Sea Garden* | Dada begins in Zurich |
| | James Joyce, *Portrait of the Artist as a Young Man* | The Battle of the Somme |
| | Ezra Pound, *Lustra* | Easter Rising in Dublin |
| | W. B. Yeats, *Reveries over Childhood and Youth* | Albert Einstein's General Theory of Relativity |
| 1917 | T. S. Eliot, *Prufrock and Other Observations* | USA enters the war |
| | D. H. Lawrence, *Look! We Have Come Through* | Bolshevik Revolution in Russia |
| | Ezra Pound, *Cantos* (–1969) | |
| | W. B. Yeats, *At the Hawk's Well*, *The Wild Swans at Coole* | |
| 1918 | James Joyce, *Exiles* | First World War ends |
| | D. H. Lawrence, *New Poems* | Ernest Rutherford splits the atom |
| | Percy Wyndham Lewis, *Tarr* | Women over 30 given the vote |

Katherine Mansfield,
*Prelude*
Gertrude Stein, *Mary, He
Giggled*
Lytton Strachey, *Eminent
Victorians*
Tristan Tzara, Dada
Manifesto
Rebecca West, *Return of
the Soldier*
W. B. Yeats, *Per Amica
silentia Lunae*

**1919** T. S. Eliot, *Poems,*
'Tradition and the
Individual Talent'
May Sinclair, *Mary
Olivier: A Life*
Virginia Woolf, *Night and
Day*, 'Modern Novels'
W. B. Yeats, *Two Plays for
Dancers*

John Maynard Keynes, *The
Economic Consequences of the Peace*
Relativity scientifically proved
Nancy Astor is first woman MP to
take her seat in British
Parliament

**1920** Joseph Conrad, *The
Rescue*
T. S. Eliot, *The Sacred
Wood*
D. H. Lawrence, *The Lost
Girl*
Katherine Mansfield,
*Bliss and Other Stories*
Ezra Pound, *Hugh Selwyn
Mauberley*
W. B. Yeats, *Michael
Robartes and the Dancer*
William Carlos Williams,
*Kora in Hell*

Roger Fry, *Vision and Design*
Sigmund Freud, *Beyond the
Pleasure Principle*
League of Nations founded

**1921** T. S. Eliot, 'The
Metaphysical Poets'
D. H. Lawrence, *Women
in Love*
Lytton Stratchey, *Queen
Victoria*

Irish Free State established

W. B. Yeats, *Four Plays for Dancers*

| | | |
|---|---|---|
| **1922** | T. S. Eliot, *The Waste Land*<br>James Joyce, *Ulysses*<br>Katherine Mansfield, *The Garden Party*<br>May Sinclair, *Life and Death of Harriett Frean*<br>Virginia Woolf, *Jacob's Room*<br>W. B. Yeats, *Later Poems*<br>*Criterion* begins publication | BBC founded<br>Friedrich Murnau, *Nosferatu*<br>Benito Mussolini comes to power in Italy |
| **1923** | D. H. Lawrence, *Studies in Classic American Literature, Kangaroo*<br>Wallace Stevens, *Harmonium*<br>William Carlos Williams, *Spring and All* | USSR established<br>Stanley Baldwin becomes Prime Minster of Britain<br>BBC radio begins transmission |
| **1924** | Ford Madox Ford, *Parade's End*<br>E. M. Forster, *A Passage to India*<br>D. H. Lawrence, *England, My England*<br>I. A. Richards, *Principles of Literary Criticism*<br>Virginia Woolf, 'Mr Bennett and Mrs Brown'<br>André Breton, first Surrealist Manifesto | First Labour government under Ramsay MacDonald in Britain<br>Italian fascist state established |
| **1925** | T. S. Eliot, *Poems, 1905–25*<br>F. Scott Fitzgerald, *The Great Gatsby*<br>Gertrude Stein, *The Making of Americans*<br>Virginia Woolf, *The Common Reader, Mrs Dalloway*<br>W. B. Yeats, *A Vision* | Adolf Hitler, *Mein Kampf*<br>Josef Stalin's rise to power begins<br>Sergei Eisenstein, *Battleship Potemkin*<br>Charlie Chaplin, *The Gold Rush* |

| | | |
|---|---|---|
| **1926** | H. D., *Palimpsest* | General strike in Britain |
| | T. S. Eliot, *Sweeney Agonistes* (/1927) | Fritz Lang, *Metropolis* |
| | Ernest Hemingway, *The Sun Also Rises* | |
| | D. H. Lawrence, *The Plumed Serpent* | |
| | Ezra Pound, *Personae* | |
| **1927** | Robert Graves and Laura Riding (eds), *A Survey of Modernist Poetry* | First solo flight across Atlantic First 'talkies' |
| | James Joyce, *Pomes Penyeach* | |
| | D. H. Lawrence, *Mornings in Mexico* | |
| | Percy Wyndham Lewis, *Time and Western Man, The Wild Body transition* begins publication | |
| | Virginia Woolf, *To the Lighthouse* | |
| | W. B. Yeats, *October Blast* | |
| **1928** | James Joyce, *Ann Livia Plurabelle* | Women enfranchised in Britain on equal terms with men |
| | D. H. Lawrence, *Lady Chatterley's Lover* | Sergei Eisenstein, *October* |
| | Percy Wyndham Lewis, *The Childermass* | |
| | Lytton Strachey, *Elizabeth and Essex* | |
| | Virginia Woolf, *Orlando* | |
| | W. B. Yeats, *The Tower* | |
| | Djuna Barnes, *Ladies Almanack* | |
| **1929** | Richard Aldington, *Death of a Hero* | Wall Street Crash Beginning of Stalin's dictatorship |
| | William Faulkner, *The Sound and the Fury* | |
| | Ernest Hemingway, *A Farewell to Arms* | |

I. A. Richards, *Practical Criticism*
Virginia Woolf, *A Room of One's Own*
W. B. Yeats, *The Winding Stair*
Second Surrealist Manifesto

| | | |
|---|---|---|
| **1930** | W. H. Auden, *Poems*<br>John Dos Passos, *U.S.A.*<br>T. S. Eliot, *Ash Wednesday*<br>William Faulkner, *As I Lay Dying*<br>D. H. Lawrence, *The Virgin and the Gipsy*<br>F. R. Leavis, *Mass Civilization and Minority Culture*<br>Percy Wyndham Lewis, *The Apes of God* | Sigmund Freud, *Civilisation and its Discontents*<br>Television begins in the US |
| **1931** | Virginia Woolf, *The Waves, The Second Common Reader* | Formation of National Government in Britain<br>Abandoning of Gold Standard in Britain<br>Fritz Lang, *M*<br>Charlie Chaplin, *City Lights* |
| **1932** | T. S. Eliot, *Sweeney Agonistes Scrutiny* founded | |
| **1933** | T. S. Eliot, *The Use of Poetry and the Use of Criticism*<br>Gertrude Stein, *The Autobiography of Alice B. Toklas*<br>W. B. Yeats, *The Winding Stair* | Adolf Hitler becomes Chancellor of Germany |
| **1934** | Samuel Beckett, *More Pricks Than Kicks*<br>T. S. Eliot, *After Strange Gods* | |

|        |                                                                                                            |                                                                                                                    |
| ------ | ---------------------------------------------------------------------------------------------------------- | ------------------------------------------------------------------------------------------------------------------ |
|        | Percy Wyndham Lewis, *Men Without Art* Ezra Pound, *The ABC of Reading*                                     |                                                                                                                    |
| 1935   | T. S. Eliot, *Murder in the Cathedral, Four Quartets* (1942) Wallace Stevens, *Ideas of Order*             | Italy invades Abyssinia British government begins policy of Appeasement                                             |
| 1936   | Walter Benjamin, *The Work of Art in the Age of Mechanical Reproduction* W. B. Yeats (ed.), *The Oxford Book of Modern Verse, 1892–1935* | BBC Television founded Abdication crisis in Britain Spanish Civil War begins Beginning of Stalin's 'Great Purge' Charlie Chaplin, *Modern Times* |
| 1937   | Djuna Barnes, *Nightwood* Percy Wyndham Lewis, *Blasting and Bombardiering* Wallace Stevens, *The Man with the Blue Guitar* Virginia Woolf, *The Years* | Pablo Picasso, *Guernica* Policy of Appeasement continued by Neville Chamberlain in Britain                         |
| 1938   | Samuel Beckett, *Murphy* Virginia Woolf, *Three Guineas*                                                    | Organized pogroms against Jews in Germany                                                                           |
| 1939   | T. S. Eliot, *The Family Reunion* James Joyce, *Finnegans Wake*                                             | Second World War begins                                                                                             |

# Glossary of Key Terms and Concepts

Words in **bold** direct the reader to other entries within the glossary.

## Allusion

An allusion is a reference to something external to a work – a person, historical event, or another literary work – without any explicit identification. It can take the form of an indirect reference, the use of a few lines from another source, such as the lines used from Wagner's opera *Tristan und Isolde* in Book 1 of *The Waste Land* (1922), or a large formal borrowing, such as James Joyce's use of Homer's *Odyssey* in his *Ulysses* (1922).

In modernist poetry direct or indirect allusion to other literary works is much used, and is often seen as contributing to a poem's obscurity or difficulty, as, unlike the use of allusion in poetry of previous ages, the general reader is unlikely to share the wide knowledge evidenced by copious allusion. T. S. Eliot, in his essay 'The Metaphysical Poets' (1921), argues that the poetry of the contemporary age is bound to be difficult. The age is one of 'great variety and complexity' and in response the poet 'must become more and more comprehensive, more allusive, more indirect, in order to force, to dislocate if necessary, language into his meaning' (Eliot 1975c: 65).

The allusive techniques of both Eliot and Ezra Pound

have often been seen as a comment on the relation between the present age and the cultural past of Europe. The implied comparisons between Shakespeare's Cleopatra and Lil in Book 2 of *The Waste Land* are strongly ironic, and leave the present seeming poor, facile and vulgar. At the same time, the invocation of classical antiquity or the Elizabethans can be seen as an attempt to remake the supposed unity and vibrancy of poetic tradition through a living relationship to it, and as an attempt to use past forms to provide a stability absent in the contemporary world, as suggested by Eliot in his essay '*Ulysses*, Order and Myth' (1923) (see **myth**).

## Avant-garde

This phrase was originally the French military term for 'advance-garde'. In the nineteenth century it came to be applied to art which championed new ideas, and in the early twentieth century to writers and artists whose work was self-consciously experimental, and whose experimentation was in direct opposition to the conventional techniques and institutions of the arts. During this period, avant-garde work, in its attempt to set itself against these conventions, was often associated with the use of primitivism, profanity, 'nonsense' and verbal or physical violence, and worked towards shocking its audience. Marcel Duchamp's *Fountain* (1917), for example, brings mass production, the everyday and the 'lower' functions of the body into the rarefied space of the art gallery.

Over the last 30 years or so, there has been a lively critical debate over the definition of the term. In particular, the question of the relation between the idea of an avant-garde and modernism has been much debated: is the avant-garde a synonym for modernism, is it a subset of it, or is it in opposition to it? Linked to these questions is that of *when* the avant-garde was. Is it a historical phenomenon, as modernism is usually understood to be, and like modernism located only in the early twentieth century, or is it ahistorical? In Peter Bürger's influential work (1974), the avant-garde is sharply in opposition to modernism; whereas modernism attacks conventional *techniques*, the avant-garde attacks the very institutions through which all art is made (1984: vx). It is more radical in its attempt, not to separate art from life, but to insert art into life and transform both, with the use, for example, of the manifesto borrowed from the political sphere, or the technique of collage. Other critics, such as Rainey (1998), dispute this characterization of modernism, arguing that modernism's relation to the world is more complex than this suggests.

## Classicism

A number of Anglo-American modernist poets, most notably T. S. Eliot, saw themselves as classicist in as much as they rejected what they saw as the previous tradition of English poetry from the Romantics through the Victorians. At its worst, they characterized this as sentimental, as giving too great a place to the individual voice of the poet, and as undisciplined in poetical form. 'Classicism' denotes a desire to return to more austere practices in terms of voice and form. Its most influential articulation comes in T. E. Hulme's essay 'Romanticism and Classicism' (1911/12). The age of Romanticism is nearing its end, argues Hulme with much satisfaction, not least because its assumptions about the nature of human beings has led to a misuse of language (Hulme 1994: 61). For classicists, the individual was rather a limited thing who only achieved their best when made aware of their constraints, and when disciplined by rules and order.

These beliefs had very particular consequences for poetry. In Romanticism, language is a tool for the destruction of boundaries and barriers. For the classicist, on the other hand, the poet must struggle with language, not because what he or she has to say belongs to the realm of the infinite beyond the remit of language, but because language, as earth bound as ourselves, resists the precision and freshness crucial to the best poetry. The relation between writer and language is not one of easy, natural symbiosis, but of conflict and struggle. The poets who were influenced by Hulme in the years before the First World War, and saw themselves as classicist, such as Pound and the Imagists, rejected the elaborate diction of nineteenth-century poetry, and replaced it with the use of quotidian language.

## Dissociation of sensibility

The term comes from T. S. Eliot's essay 'The Metaphysical Poets' (1921), where Eliot cites the English Civil War as the moment where sensibility became split between the intellectual and the emotional, the rational and the experiential. For him, the Metaphysical poets were the last to exemplify a unity of sensibility – 'a thought to Donne was an experience; it modified his sensibility' (Eliot 1975c: 64) – and subsequent poetry expressed either thought or feeling, but not both as a unity. It was Eliot's aim to achieve a reunification in his own poetry.

The New Critics took up Eliot's idea, and in particular attributed the dissociation to the spread of scientific views of the world from the seventeenth century on. The idea was also taken up and expanded by the literary critic F. R. Leavis. For him, the shared and stable values of an 'organic community' had been lost through industrialization, secularization and mass democracy. Leavis believed that contemporary literature could provide a place of shared values, thus restoring social cohesion and harmony (Leavis 2000).

## Epiphany

Originally referring to the moment in the Nativity story when Christ and the meaning of his birth is revealed to the wise men, and meaning more generally the revelation of a spiritual reality beyond the material or everyday, the term has come to be associated with moments in modernist prose where a character's consciousness goes beyond the boundaries of quotidian reality to grasp an important and sometimes shattering truth. In modernist works, indeed, such moments of revelation can be destructive to the extent that they lay bare the relative, unstable and tenuous foundations of such a reality, but at the same time such a realization can be also a moment of liberation and joy as they affirm, not an external spiritual reality, but an internal psychological force.

The most influential origin of the term as related to modernist writing is in the early work of James Joyce, where he defines the term as 'a sudden spiritual manifestation' occurring through a particular kind of experience of the vulgar or ordinary which 'the man of letters' should 'record with extreme care, seeing that they themselves are the most delicate and evanescent moments' (Joyce 1969: 216). Here, the revelation occurs through the observation of a 'symptom' of some truth about contemporary life. Crucially, Joyce's epiphanies were the result of random urban encounters, rather than the contemplation of nature, as may be found in Romantic writings, and in later uses of the revelatory moment by Joyce, Virginia Woolf and Katherine Mansfield, for example, the emphasis shifts to what is revealed about the observer. Modernist epiphanies do not so much serve to reveal either the divinity or degradation of the observed object, but rather the ambiguities, multiplicities and blind spots of the observing self. In Joyce's 'The Dead', set around the Christian feast of Epiphany, Gabriel is forced to confront his own limitations through an epiphanic encounter with the reality of the lives of the dead (Joyce 1975: 220).

## Free indirect style

This is a narrative technique where the voice of the narrative, although in the third person, uses the language and point of view of a character. This has the effect of merging the identities of both character and narrator, evincing a sympathy for the former, but at the same time paradoxically creating an ironic distance. The character's view of the world is ventriloquized by the narrator in order to imply its limitations and shortcomings through the reader's sense that there is an (unspoken) alternative view. So, for example, a direct representation of a character's thought – 'She thought, "I do not love him. I will leave him"' – would be rendered indirectly as: 'She did not love him, and would soon leave him.'

While this is not an exclusively modernist technique, it became a central technique of much modernist prose fiction, and is used by modernist writers – in Virginia Woolf, and in the short stories of James Joyce and Katherine Mansfield – to great effect to root their narratives in the individual psychological reality of their characters while at the same time allowing a critical stance.

## Free verse

This describes poetry which rejects the regular metre and rhyme of conventional verse. The French Symbolists championed free verse (*vers libre*) as part of their attempt to move poetry away from the verbal and rational and towards the musical and sensual. These predecessors were taken up by Anglo-American modernist poets in their attempts to free poetry from what they saw as the dead weight of much Victorian poetry. However, for

most modernist poets, free verse comprises only one
element of their poetic techniques, and most continued
to make some use of conventional metre and rhyme.

Indeed, the relation to ideas of free verse among the
modernists is varied. Pound's rejection of conventional
metre and rhyme was not a licence to write expressive,
formless poetry, for which he had contempt, but to
explore alternative forms, such as those borrowed from
Chinese and Japanese writing. T. S. Eliot explicitly
rejected the term 'free verse' (Eliot 1975a). Although
some of his own early poetry is often characterized as
free verse, his poetry generally uses regular rhyme and
metre, although irregular line lengths.

In contrast, in the poetry of D. H. Lawrence from his
collection *Look! We Have Come Through* (1917) on, free
verse is taken up exuberantly to allow for his championing of the unfettered individual expressing himself
amid the flux and change of nature. In his essay 'Poetry
of the Present' (1919) he characterizes free verse as
spontaneous creation of the body (Lawrence 1998a: 78–
9).

## Interior monologue: see stream of consciousness

## Irony

Irony could be said to be the dominant mode of the
Anglo-American modernists. Irony works to reveal a split
– between what is thought and what is said, between
surface meaning and what is really the case, between a
particular view of reality and reality itself – and is indeed
itself evidence of that rupture. Central to the view of
many modernist writers was the perception that split and
rupture – between the past and the present, between the
individual and society, between convention and reality –
characterized **modernity** and as such their works are
often founded on a profoundly ironic worldview.

Irony in a literary work can be created in a number of ways, from the specific narrative detail of the **free indirect style** or the use of ironic **allusion**, to large structural ironies of plot or character. All these are certainly present in literary works other than the modernist, but the centrality of the sense of rupture and fragment (whether welcome or profoundly mourned) brings irony to the heart of modernist experimentation.

Contrary to this reading of irony in modernism, though, literary critic I. A. Richards defined irony in poetry as the balancing of opposites, and as a characteristic of poetry of 'the highest order' (Richards 2001: 234). The New Critics took up this usage from Richards, and for them irony within a poem is evidence of a superior position, one that is aware of opposite attitudes, but manages nevertheless to create a whole that stabilizes such an opposition.

## Mock heroic

The mock heroic is constructed when writers take up traditional, heroic forms of writing, which deal with momentous events and the actions of the gods, and apply them to everyday occurrences in order to prick pretension and self-illusion. However, while previous writers may have wished to belittle the pretensions of some, modernist writers used the technique more loosely to undercut human illusions in a more radical way by questioning the position of the human being per se in contemporary culture.

In T. S. Eliot's poem 'The Love Song of J. Alfred Prufrock' (1917), the speaker of the poem, despite his self-aggrandizing initial 'J' and his rather precious attitude to both his self-grooming and his questioning of life's big questions, finally admits 'No! I am not Prince Hamlet, nor was meant to be' (l. 114). The façade attempted by the speaker crumbles, and he is unmasked as inadequate. The tone of the poem up to that point has been mock heroic. Even before the speaker's admission of failure, his self-aggrandizement is undercut – the 'J' might attempt authority but 'Prufrock' suggests a narrow priggishness. The mock heroic undermines pretension and claims to grandeur; it unmasks the individual as small, weak and fallible.

Unlike poetry, the novel can be seen as an inherently mock-heroic genre. From Cervantes's *Don Quixote* (1605), the novel has defined itself against the earlier forms of epic and romance and located its interest in the everyday. In the modernist novel, however, the everyday is transformed through new understandings of psychology, history, the complexities of human relation, and the operations of language. James Joyce's *Ulysses* (1922) has often been described as mock heroic, but whereas in Eliot's poetry it is clear that it is the present day that comes off badly in the comparison with the 'heroic', *Ulysses* is more ambiguous. The link made between Leopold Bloom, Joyce's protagonist, and Odysseus does not diminish Bloom's value, but rather infuses him with significance. Joyce's handling of Bloom is one of pathos rather than bathos.

## Modernity

As a name describing a period of time, there is some variety in the use of 'modernity'. For some, the term is used to name the period from the seventeenth century through to the twentieth century. For others, its use is more specific, referring either to the late nineteenth and early twentieth centuries, or to the twentieth century until around the 1960s. What is implied by the term, however, is more cohesive, whatever period of time is chosen. Modernity distinguishes a world that is modern in that its principle authority is science, its principle economic mode is capitalist, and its principle means of production industrial, with radical consequences for the experiences of work, of time, of relations to the past, of relations between different groups of people, and of the self. 'Modernity' describes those parts of the world where religion, feudalism and agriculture are seen on the whole as playing a minor role, if not actually as reactionary and retrogressive. The city, progress, the dominance of reason and the rise of the importance of the individual are some of the central locations and modes of modernity.

Such changes had consequences that were material, political and epistemological. Some critics have argued that modernity has been constructed as an opposition to other modes of thought and existence, and has defined itself by setting itself against, for example, the 'primitive', the traditional, the superstitious, the 'barbaric'. While the privileged narrative of modernity is one of enlightenment and liberalism, this oppositional definition has paradoxically been seen to place oppression at the heart of modernity, for example in the slave trade, in imperialism and in the Holocaust (Adorno and Horkheimer 1997). Others have rather stressed the positive side of the Enlightenment project (Habermas 1987).

The relationship between modernism and modernity is one that has been much discussed and debated. Is modernist writing complicit in the privileging of rationality and evidence that is seen as central to modernity, or is it against modernity in its focus on fragmentation, the unconscious and nonsense? In attempting to answer such questions, any idea of modernism as a single and coherent entity becomes impossible, but it can be said that modernism is marked by an acute and anxious awareness of the complex and contradictory conditions of modernity.

As suggested above, many critics see the period of modernity as coming to end in the second half of the twentieth century, giving way to a postmodernity in which the supposedly stable assumptions of modernity – the belief in progress, in the authority of science, in the benevolent effect of liberal humanism – have obviously crumbled away (Lyotard 1984; Jameson 1991).

## Myth

A myth is a story that explains the world to its hearers, such as the story of God's creation of the world and the Fall of humanity at the beginning of Genesis. Within **modernity**, such a story is generally seen as containing a poetic rather than empirical truth, and as in some sense in opposition to both scientific and historical accounts of the world. While, because of this, modernity is often seen as disparaging the value of the mythical, the relationship between them as revealed in literary modernism (and elsewhere) is far more complex.

Modernist uses of myth are various, but all display an ambiguous relationship to modernity's belief in progress, science and rationality. In his essay '*Ulysses*, Order and Myth', T. S. Eliot reads James Joyce's novel as an attempt to use a 'mythical method' to achieve an artistic order within the 'futility and anarchy which is contemporary society' (Eliot 2005b: 167). Far from the past lacking in comparison to the present (as is implied in the idea of progress), the use of myths from the past provides a balance and coherence missing from the present. In Eliot's *The Waste Land* (1922), he uses a number of myths, such as that of the Fisher King, to provide a structure and imagery.

A very different use of myth can be seen in the work of D. H. Lawrence. For him, industrialization, secularization and democracy have killed something essential and living in human beings. In order to revitalize that thing, art needs to come close to the beliefs, rituals and practices of those people who, it is believed, have not lost the connection with essential things. In *The Plumed Serpent* (1926), for example, Lawrence uses the beliefs and myths of Mexico to indicate the dark and disturbing truths which have been lost by desiccated, over-intellectual Western 'man', by industrialization and democracy.

However, Lawrence's use of myth, and similar uses by other modernists, have been seen as problematic by more recent critics. Their primitivism, their celebration of the 'otherness' of non-Western people, has been seen as actually one of the gestures by which the West denigrates and makes secondary those from other cultures. In asserting the 'closeness to nature' of other peoples, primitivism in fact places them on the side of animals, in opposition to the human and to culture. In an extreme version, such privileging of the non-rational, the supposedly essential, 'natural' and hierarchical attracted a number of modernist writers to fascism in the years between the two world wars.

## Primitivism: see **myth**

## Stream of consciousness/Interior monologue

The term comes from the philosopher and psychologist William James, and was used in his influential work *Principles of Psychology* (1890) to describe the continuous flow of memories, thoughts, feelings and perceptions through the waking mind. It is thought to have been first applied to the narrative methods of prose fiction by May Sinclair, in her review, first published in *The Egoist* in 1918, of the first three volumes of Dorothy Richardson's *Pilgrimage* (1915–38). Sinclair describes the novel as being entirely made up of the protagonist's, Miriam Henderson's, 'stream of consciousness going on and on' (Sinclair 1990: 444); the narrative contains nothing but her thoughts, perceptions, memories and feelings. Although Richardson does include descriptive third-person narrative in her novel, the narrative voice never speaks 'over the head' of Miriam to the reader, and the description contains nothing that would not be in Miriam's consciousness.

Although there had been novels written before the early twentieth century which included passages of introspection, where all that is recorded is that which passes through one character's consciousness, the use of this technique by a number of modernist writers is an indication of the extent to which the interior life of the subject was a central concern for them. The view of the world given is not the God-like, panoramic vision of the omniscient narrator, but the limited, partial and fallible one of the individual. More than this, not only in the consciousness of the individual, but in everything flux and change are fundamental to certain modernist views of the world.

Indeed, modernist uses of the method often have the effect of suggesting how fragile any ordered meaning is. In *Ulysses*, James Joyce too mixes sections of stream of consciousness with direct third-person narrative, but at the same time, his method makes clearer than Richardson's the extent to which the stream of consciousness is a choppy, fragmented narrative, where relations between thoughts and ideas are not those of conventional cause and effect and grammatical order, but looser, more indirect, more associative, as in the passages where we are immersed in Leopold Bloom's thoughts, such as in Book 8, 'Lestrygonians' (Joyce 1986: 124)

Often in these passages, the flow of Bloom's thoughts leads to memories, emotions and ideas which are difficult or painful for him, and the flow veers off again toward safer waters. In this, as in the origin of the term itself, literary uses of the idea of a 'stream of consciousness' link modernist writing closely with contemporary work in psychology. Freud's method of 'free association' encouraged his patients to talk in just such a loose, indirect and seemingly random way, based on the belief that an evasion of the conventional ordering techniques of both thought and language would eventually allow repressed memories and thoughts to emerge.

Some critics are keen to make strong distinctions between stream of consciousness narrative and interior monologue, insisting that a piece of prose fiction is only properly the latter if fragmented and unpunctuated, eschewing nearly all of the rules of the ordering of written language. For such critics, the examples quoted above would not be interior monologue. On this definition, true interior monologue can be seen in very few works of prose, but most famously in the last book of *Ulysses*, Molly Bloom's soliloquy (Joyce 1986: 609).

# Further Reading and Resources

## FURTHER READING

Below are some suggested critical sources that will help your further research into various aspects of modernism. With the exception of the section 'Introductions to modernism', works present in Works Cited are not reproduced below.

## Introductions to modernism

There are a number of introductions to modernism which are excellent next steps from this guide.

Armstrong, Tim (2005) *Modernism: A Cultural History*, Cambridge: Polity.
   A detailed yet comprehensive analysis of modernism as related to its intellectual and material history, including sections on the First World War, eugenics, science and technology, cinema, and gender.
Ayers, David (2004) *Modernism: A Short Introduction*, Oxford: Blackwell.
   Approaches the subject through specific and detailed close readings of a number of texts, both mainstream and less well known. A useful chapter on Walter Benjamin and Theodor Adorno.
Baldick, Chris (2004) *The Modern Movement*, The Oxford English Literary History, vol. 10, 1910–1940, Oxford: Oxford University Press.

This surveys the whole of British culture during the period, and explicitly contests the privileging of modernism in literary history. A useful challenge to modernism's seemingly unquestioned centrality in literary studies.

Bradshaw, David (ed.) (2003) *A Concise Companion to Modernism*, Oxford: Blackwell.

Each chapter is a comprehensive essay on subjects significant to modernism's intellectual history, such as physics, eugenics, technology and psychoanalysis.

Bradshaw, David and Kevin Dettmar (eds) (2006) *A Companion to Modernist Literature and Culture*, Oxford: Blackwell.

A comprehensive introduction, divided into four parts, with essays on intellectual origins, movements, readings of specific texts, and 'other modernisms'.

Childs, Peter (2000) *Modernism*, London: Routledge.

The various sections give an introduction to important figures in the construction of modernity (such as Marx, Darwin and Freud), on the different genres of writing, the visual arts, and film, and then a more detailed look at important themes (such as gender and epistemology) via a number of modernist works.

Goldman, Jane (2004) *Modernism, 1910–1940: Image to Apocalypse*, Basingstoke: Palgrave.

A particularly good demonstration of the role of the 'little' magazines, and useful on the relations between modernism and the avant-garde.

Trotter, David (1993) *The English Novel in History, 1895–1920*, London: Routledge.

A useful survey of the period in which the early modernist novel flourished, setting it alongside a detailed look at the non-modernist novel.

## Modernism and culture

The following works all investigate the complex relation between literary modernism and the developing culture of consumption and the market.

Cooper, John Xiros (2004) *Modernism and the Culture of Market Society,* Cambridge: Cambridge University Press.

Demoor, Marysa (ed.) (2004) *Marketing the Author: Authorial Selves, Narrative Selves and Self-fashioning, 1880–1930,* Basingstoke: Palgrave.

Turner, Catherine (2003) *Marketing Modernism Between the Two World Wars,* Amherst: University of Massachusetts Press.

For a very good analysis of the relationship between modernism and difficulty, locating its analysis in some useful historical examples, such as the Armory Show in New York in 1913:

Diepeveen: Leonard (2002) *The Difficulties of Modernism,* London; Routledge.

## Modernism and philosophy

Banfield, Ann (2000) *The Phantom Table: Woolf, Fry, Russell and the Epistemology of Modernism,* Cambridge: Cambridge University Press.

Gillies, Mary Ann (1996) *Henri Bergson and British Modernism,* Montreal, Kingston, London and Buffalo: McGill-Queen's University Press.

Thatcher, David S. (1970) *Nietzsche in England, 1890–1914,* Toronto: University of Toronto Press.

The following books look at the relation between modernism and the less 'respectable' philosophies of the period, such as spiritualism and the occult.

Materer, Timothy (1995) *Modernist Alchemy: Poetry and the Occult,* Ithaca: Cornell University Press.

Sword, Helen (2002) *Ghostwriting Modernism,* Ithaca: Cornell University Press.

Surette, Leon (1993) *The Birth of Modernism: Ezra Pound, T. S. Eliot, W. B. Yeats and the Occult,* Montreal and Kingston: McGill-Queen's University Press.

## Modernism and politics

Most of the work on modernism and politics focuses on the difficult questions surrounding modernism's links to right-wing politics generally, and to fascism in particular.

Ferrall, Charles (2000) *Modernist Writing and Reactionary Politics*, Cambridge: Cambridge University Press.

Hewitt, Andrew (1993) *Fascist Modernism: Aesthetics, Politics and the Avant-Garde*, Stanford: Stanford University Press.

Morrison, Paul A. (1996) *The Poetics of Fascism: Ezra Pound, T. S. Eliot, Paul de Man*, Oxford: Oxford University Press.

Tratner, Michael (1995) *Modernism and Mass Politics: Joyce, Woolf, Eliot, Yeats*, Stanford: Stanford University Press.

## Modernism and the First World War

Booth, Allyson (1996) *Postcards from the Trenches: Negotiating the Space Between Modernism and the First World War*, Oxford: Oxford University Press.

Fussell, Paul (1975) *The Great War and Modern Memory*, New York and London: Oxford University Press.

Sherry, Vincent B. (2003) *The Great War and the Language of Modernism*, Oxford: Oxford University Press.

Tate, Trudi (1998) *Modernism, History and the First World War*, Manchester: Manchester University Press.

## Modernism and science

The following trace the influence of scientific ideas on modernist writing.

Schleifer, Roland (2000) *Modernism and Time: The Logic of Abundance in Literature, Science and Culture*, Cambridge: Cambridge University Press.

Vargish, Thomas and Delo E. Mook (1999) *Inside Modernism: Relativity Theory, Cubism and Narrative*, Yale: Yale University Press.

Whitworth, Michael H. (2002) *Einstein's Wake: Relativity, Metaphor, and Modernist Literature,* Oxford: Oxford University Press.

## Modernist writing

Flora, Joseph M. (ed.) (1985) *The English Short Story, 1880–1945,* Boston: Twayne.

Levenson, Michael (1984) *A Genealogy of Modernism: A Study of English Literary Doctrine,* Cambridge: Cambridge University Press.

—— (ed.) (1999) *The Cambridge Companion to Modernism,* Cambridge: Cambridge University Press.

Marker, F. J. and C. Innes (eds) (1998) *Modernism in European Drama: Ibsen, Strindberg, Pirandello, Beckett,* Toronto: University of Toronto Press.

Matz, Jesse (2004) *The Modern Novel: A Short Introduction,* Oxford: Blackwell.

May, Charles E. (2002) *The Short Story: The Reality of Artifice,* London: Routledge.

Nicholls, Peter (1995) *Modernisms: A Literary Guide,* London: Macmillan.

Stevenson, Randall (1998) *Modernist Fiction,* 2nd edn, London: Prentice Hall.

## Modernist groups and movements

Black, J. et al. (2004) *Blasting the Future!: Vorticism in Britain, 1910–1920,* London: Philip Wilson.

Edwards, Paul (ed.) (2000) *Blast: Vorticism, 1914–1918,* Aldershot: Ashgate.

Perloff, Marjorie (1986) *The Futurist Moment: Avant-Garde, Avant Guerre, and the Language of Rupture,* Chicago: University of Chicago Press.

Rosenbaum, S. P. (1998) *Aspects of Bloomsbury: Studies in Modern English Literary and Intellectual History,* London: Macmillan.

—— (2003) *Georgian Bloomsbury: The Early Literary History of the Bloomsbury Group, 1910–1914*, Basingstoke: Palgrave.

Scheunemann, Dietrich (ed.) (2000) *European Avant-Garde: New Perspectives*, Amsterdam: Rodopi.

## Modernism and the visual arts

Butler, Christopher (1994) *Early Modernism: Literature, Music and Painting in Europe, 1900–1916*, Oxford: Oxford University Press.

Harrison, Charles (1997) *Modernism*, London: Tate Publishing.

## The critical reception of modernism

Brooker, Peter (1992) *Modernism/Postmodernism*, London: Longman.

Litz, A. Walton, Louis Menand and Lawrence Rainey (eds) (2000) *The Cambridge History of Literary Criticism: Modernism and the New Criticism*, Cambridge: Cambridge University Press.

# WEBSITES

All URLs were correct at time of going to press.

Thousands of websites contain comment and information on modernist writers and their work. However, not all of them are of good quality. The website of the Literary Dictionary and Encyclopedia, while it is necessary to subscribe, contains many articles on modernist writers and specific modernist works that are all of a high critical standard. This can be found at www.litencyc.com.

Websites are a particularly useful way of seeing reproductions of artworks. www.artchive.com contains many good quality reproductions (or links to sites that contain them), plus biographies of artists, critical writing on them, and suggestions for further reading.

It is also always a good idea to look at the websites of the large art galleries, such as the National Gallery, the Tate, the Guggenheim, the Museum of Modern Art in New York, and so on. Particularly good is the Tate website, which contains reproductions of 65,000 works, plus information about artists and individual works. This can be found at www.tate.org.uk.

The following websites contain reproductions of the work of specific artists and individual artworks mentioned in the book:

### Chapter 1, Historical, Cultural and Intellectual Context
For examples of the work of Édouard Manet see
   www.artchive.com/artchive/M/manet.html

For examples of the work of Paul Cézanne see
   www.artchive.com/artchive/C/cezanne.html

For examples of the work of Vincent Van Gogh see
   www.artchive.com/artchive/V/vangogh.html

For examples of the work of Paul Gauguin see
   www.artchive.com/artchive/G/gauguin.html

For Paul Nash's paintings of the First World War, see
   www.art-ww1.com/gb/peintre.html#N

Robert Delaunay, *Eiffel Tower* (1911), www.guggenheim
   collection.org/site/movement_work_md_ Orphism_39_3.html
   *The City of Paris* (1912), http://artyzm.com/e_obraz. php?
   id=312
   *Sun, Tower, Airplane* (1913), http://www.albrightknox.
   org/ArtStart/Delaunay.html

### Chapter 2, Modernist Literature
For examples of Cubist work by Pablo Picasso and Georges Braques, see www.tate.org.uk/collections/glossary

Henri Gaudier-Brzeska, *Red Stone Dancer* (c. 1913), www.tate.
   org.uk/servlet/ViewWork?workid=4984&tabview=image
Percy Wyndham Lewis, *Workshop* (1914), www.tate.org.uk/

servlet/ArtistWorks?cgroupid=999999961&artistid=1502&
    page=1
Jacob Epstein, *Rock Drill* (1913–14), www.tate.org.uk/servlet/
    ViewWork?cgroupid=999999961&workid=4122
Umberto Boccioni, *Unique Forms of Continuity in Space* (1913),
    www.tate.org/servlet/ViewWork?workid=1208
Marcel Duchamp, *Fountain* (1917),
    www.tate.org.uk/servlet/ViewWork?workid=26850
Marcel Duchamp, *L.H.O.O.Q.* (1919), www.studiolo.org/
    Mona/MONA11.htm
Joan Miró, for examples of his work see
    www.artcyclopedia.com/artists/miro_joan.html
Giorgio de Chirico, for examples of his work see
    www.artcyclopedia.com/artists/de_chirico_giorgio.html
Salvador Dali, for examples of his work see
    www.dali-gallery.com
René Magritte, *The Menaced Assassin* (1927), see
    www.moma.org

# Works Cited

Adams, David (2003) *Colonial Odyssey: Empire and Epic in the Modernist Novel,* Ithaca: Cornell University Press.

Adorno, Theodor (1992) *Notes to Literature,* vol. 2, Shierry Weber Nicolsen (trans.), New York: University of Columbia.

—— and Max Horkheimer (1997) *Dialectic of Enlightenment* (1944), John Cumming (trans.), London: Verso.

Anderson, Perry (1984) 'Modernity and Revolution', *New Left Review,* March–April, 144.

Ardis, Ann L. (1990) *New Women, New Novels: Feminism and Early Modernism,* New Brunswick: Rutgers University Press.

—— (2002) *Modernism and Cultural Conflict, 1880-1922,* Cambridge: Cambridge University Press.

Armstrong, Tim (1998) *Modernism, Technology and the Body,* Cambridge: Cambridge University Press.

—— (2005) *Modernism: A Cultural History,* Cambridge: Polity.

Arnold, Matthew (1982) 'Culture and Anarchy' (1869), *Selected Prose,* P. J. Keating (ed. and intro.), London: Penguin.

Baldick, Chris (1983) *The Social Mission of English Criticism, 1848–1932,* Oxford: Clarendon.

—— (2004) *The Modern Movement: 1910–1940,* vol. 10, The Oxford English Literary History, Oxford: Oxford University Press.

Ball, Hugo (1977) *Seven Sound Poems,* London and Stockholm: Writers Forum.

Barthes, Roland (1982) 'The Reality Effect' (1968), in Tzvetan Todorov (ed.), *French Literary Theory Today,* Cambridge: Cambridge University Press.

—— (1997) *Writing Degree Zero* (1953), Annette Lavers and Colin Smith (trans.), Preface by Susan Sontag, New York: Hill and Wang.

Bell, Clive (1914) *Art*, London: Chatto & Windus.

Benjamin, Walter (1992) 'The Work of Art in the Age of Mechanical Reproduction' (1936), *Illuminations*, Hannah Arendt (ed.), London: Fontana.

Bergson, Henri (1911a) *Creative Evolution*, Arthur Mitchell (trans.), London: Macmillan.

—— (1911b) *Matter and Memory*, Nancy Margaret Paul and W. Scott Palmer (trans.), London: Swann Sonnenschein.

—— (1913a) *Time and Free Will*, F. L. Pogson (trans.), New York: Harper and Row.

—— (1913b) *An Introduction to Metaphysics*, T. E. Hulme (trans.), London: Macmillan.

Berman, Marshall (1983) *All That Is Solid Melts Into Air: The Experience of Modernity*, London: Verso.

Boccioni, Umberto et al. (2003) 'Futurist Painting: Technical Manifesto' (1910), in Charles Harrison and Paul Wood (eds), *Art in Theory: 1900–2000: An Anthology of Changing Ideas*, Oxford: Blackwell.

Booth, Howard J. and Nigel Rigby (eds) (2000) *Modernism and Empire*, Manchester: Manchester University Press.

Bowen, Elizabeth (1937) *The Faber Book of Modern Stories*, London: Faber.

Bowlby, Rachel (1988) *Virginia Woolf: Feminist Destinations*, Oxford: Blackwell.

Bradshaw, David (2003) 'Eugenics: "They should certainly be killed"', in David Bradshaw (ed.), *A Concise Companion to Modernism*, Oxford: Blackwell.

Breton, André (2005a) 'After Dada' (1922), in Lawrence Rainey (ed.), *Modernism: An Anthology*, Oxford: Blackwell.

—— (2005b) 'Manifesto of Surrealism' (1924), in Lawrence Rainey (ed.), *Modernism: An Anthology*, Oxford: Blackwell.

Bürger, Peter (1984) *Theory of the Avant-garde* (1974), Michael Shaw (trans.), Minneapolis: University of Minnesota Press.

Carey, John (1992) *The Intellectuals and the Masses: Pride and*

*Prejudice Among the Literary Intelligentsia, 1880–1939*, London: Faber

Chekhov, Anton (1977) 'Gooseberries' (1898), *The Portable Chekhov*, Avrahm Yarmolinsky (ed.), London: Penguin.

Childs, Donald (2001) *Modernism and Eugenics: Woolf, Eliot, Yeats and the Culture of Degeneration*, Cambridge: Cambridge University Press.

Clarke, Bruce (1996) *Dora Marsden and Early Modernism: Gender, Individualism, Science*, Ann Arbor: University of Michigan Press.

Collecott, Diana (1999) *HD and Sapphic Modernism, 1910-1950*, Cambridge: Cambridge University Press.

Conrad, Joseph (1998) *Heart of Darkness and Other Tales*, Cedric Watts (ed.), Oxford: Oxford World's Classics.

—— (1985), *Tribute to Freud*, Manchester: Carcanet.

Daly, Nicholas (1999) *Modernism, Romance and the Fin de Siècle: Popular Fiction and British Culture, 1880–1914*, Cambridge: Cambridge University Press.

—— (2004) *Literature, Technology and Modernity, 1860–2000*, Cambridge: Cambridge University Press.

DeGroot, Gerard J. (1996) *Blighty: British Society in the Era of the Great War*, London: Longman.

DeKoven, Marianne (1991) *Rich and Strange: Gender, History, Modernism*, Princeton, New Jersey: Princeton University Press.

Derrida, Jacques (1992) *Acts of Literature*, Derek Attridge (ed.), New York and London: Routledge.

Dettmar, Kevin J. H. and S. Watt (eds) (1996) *Marketing Modernisms: Self-promotion, Canonization and Rereading*, Ann Arbor: University of Michigan Press.

DiBattista, Maria and Lucy McDiarmid (1996) *High and Low Moderns: Literature and Culture, 1889–1939*, Oxford: Oxford University Press.

Doyle, Laura (1994) *Bordering on the Body: The Racial Mix of Modern Fiction and Culture*, Oxford: Oxford University Press.

Eagleton, Terry (1983) *Literary Theory*, Oxford: Blackwell.

Edel, Leon and Gordon N. Ray (1958) *Henry James and H. G. Wells: A Record of their Friendship, their Debate on the Art of Fiction, and their Quarrel*, London: Rupert Hart-Davis.

Eliot, T. S. (1965) *To Criticize the Critic and Other Writings*, New York: Farrar, Straus & Giroux.

—— (1975a) 'Reflections on Vers Libre' (1917), in Frank Kermode (ed.), *Selected Prose of T. S. Eliot*, London: Faber.

—— (1975b) 'Tradition and the Individual Talent' (1919), in Frank Kermode (ed.), *Selected Prose of T. S. Eliot*, London: Faber.

—— (1975c) 'The Metaphysical Poets' (1921), in Frank Kermode (ed.), *Selected Prose of T. S. Eliot*, London: Faber.

—— (1985) *The Collected Poems of T. S. Eliot 1909–1962*, London: Faber and Faber.

—— (2005a) 'London Letter: November 1922 (Marie Lloyd)' (1922), in Lawrence Rainey (ed.), *Modernism: An Anthology*, Oxford: Blackwell.

—— (2005b) '*Ulysses*, Order and Myth' (1923), in Lawrence Rainey (ed.), *Modernism: An Anthology*, Oxford: Blackwell.

Ellman, Maud (1995) 'Preface' to Rainer Emig, *Modernism in Poetry: Motivations, Structures and Limits*, Harlow: Longman.

Ellmann, Richard and Charles Feidelson Jnr (eds) (1965) *The Modern Tradition: Backgrounds of Modern Literature*, New York: Oxford University Press.

Eysteinsson, Astradur (1990) *The Concept of Modernism*, Ithaca: Cornell University Press.

Faulkner, Peter (1977) *Modernism*, London: Methuen.

Felski, Rita (1995) *The Gender of Modernity*, Cambridge, MA: Harvard University Press.

Flint, F. S. (1913) 'Imagisme', *Poetry*, vol. 1, no. 6, March, 198–200.

—— (1915) 'The History of Imagism', *The Egoist*, 1 May, 70–1.

Ford Madox Ford, (1933) *It Was the Nightingale*, London: Heinemann.

—— (1996) *The Good Soldier* (1915), Manchester: Carcanet.

Forster, E. M. (1995) 'Bloomsbury, An Early Note' (1929), in S. P. Rosenbaum (ed.), *The Bloomsbury Group: A Collection of Memoirs and Commentary*, revised edn, Toronto: University of Toronto Press.

Freud, Sigmund (1953) *The Interpretation of Dreams* (1900), *Standard Edition,* vols IV and V, London: Hogarth Press.

—— (1957) 'On the universal tendency to debasement in the sphere of love' (1912), *Standard Edition,* vol. II, London: Hogarth Press.

—— (1961) *The Ego and the Id* (1923), *Standard Edition,* vol. XIX, London: Hogarth Press.

—— (1963) 'Fixation to traumas: the unconscious' (1917), *Standard Edition,* vol. XVI, London: Hogarth Press.

—— (1964) *The Future of an Illusion* (1927), *Standard Edition,* vol. XXI, London: Hogarth Press.

Froula, Christine (1996) *Modernism's Body: Sex, Culture and Joyce,* New York: Columbia University Press.

—— (2005) *Virginia Woolf and the Bloomsbury Avant-Garde: War, Civilization, Modernity,* New York: Columbia University Press.

Fry, Roger (1925) *Vision and Design,* 2nd edn, London: Chatto & Windus.

Galvin, Mary (1999) *Queer Poetics: Five Modernist Women Writers,* Westport, CT: Praeger.

Garrity, Jane (2003) *Step-Daughters of England: British Women Modernists and the National Imaginary,* Manchester: Manchester University Press.

Gascoyne, David (1970) *A Short Survey of Surrealism* (1935), London: Frank Cass.

Gaudier-Brzeska, Henri (2003) 'Vortex Gaudier-Brzeska (Written From the Trenches)' (1915), in Charles Harrison and Paul Wood (eds), *Art in Theory, 1900–2000: An Anthology of Changing Ideas,* Oxford: Blackwell.

Gilbert, Geoffrey (2004) 'The origins of modernism in the haunted properties of literature', in Nicola Bown, Carolyn Burdett and Pamela Thurschwell (eds), *The Victorian Supernatural,* Cambridge: Cambridge University Press.

Gilbert, Sandra and Susan Gubar (1988) *No Man's Land: The Place of the Woman Writer in the Twentieth Century,* vol. 2, Yale: Yale University Press.

Gilbert, Stuart (1952) *James Joyce's Ulysses* (1930), New York: Vintage.

Gillies, Mary Ann (2003) 'Bergsonism: "Time out of mind"', in David Bradshaw (ed.), *A Concise Companion to Modernism*, Oxford: Blackwell.

Goldman, Jane (2004) *Modernism, 1910–1945: Image to Apocalypse*, Basingstoke: Palgrave.

Green, Christopher (1995) *The European Avant-Gardes: Art in France and Western Europe 1904–c1945*, London: Zwemmer.

Habermas, Jürgen (1987) *Philosophical Discourse of Modernity: Twelve Lectures* (1985), Frederick Lawrence (trans.), Cambridge: Polity in association with Blackwell.

Hackett, Robin (2004) *Sapphic Primitivism: Productions of Race, Class and Sexuality in the Key Works of Modern Fiction*, Piscataway, NJ: Rutgers University Press.

Hanscombe, Gillian and Virginia L. Smyers (1987) *Writing for Their Lives: The Modernist Women, 1910–1940*, London: The Women's Press.

Harwood, John (1995) *Eliot to Derrida: The Poverty of Interpretation*, London: Macmillan.

H. D. (Hilda Doolittle) (1915) 'Oread', in Amy Lowell (ed.) *Some Imagist Poets: An Anthology*, London: Constable.

Head, Dominic (1992) *Modernist Short Story: Study in Theory and Practice*, Cambridge: Cambridge University Press.

Hobsbawm, Eric (1994) *Age of Extremes: The Short Twentieth Century, 1914–1991*, London: Michael Joseph.

Hulme, T. E. (1994) 'Romanticism and Classicism' (1911/12), *The Collected Writings of T. E. Hulme*, Karen Csengeri (ed.), Oxford: Clarendon Press.

Huyssens, Andreas (1986) *After the Great Divide: Modernism, Mass Culture, Postmodernism*, Bloomington, IN: Indiana University Press.

Hynes, Samuel (1979) *The Auden Generation: Literature and Politics in England in the 1930s* (1976), London: Faber and Faber.

Innes, Christopher (2003) 'Shifting the Frame – Modernism in the Theatre', in Marianne Thormählen (ed.), *Rethinking Modernism*, Basingstoke: Palgrave.

Jacobs, Deborah (1994) 'Feminist Criticism/Cultural Studies/Modernist Texts: A Manifesto for the '90s', in Lisa

Rado (ed.) *Rereading Modernism: New Directions in Feminist Criticism*, New York: Garland.

James, Henry (1914) 'The Younger Generation', *Times Literary Supplement*, 19 March and 2 April.

Jameson, Fredric (1991) *Postmodernism*, London: Verso.

Joyce, James (1969) *Stephen Hero* (1944), London: Jonathan Cape.

—— (1975) *Dubliners* (1914), London: Penguin.

—— (1986) *Ulysses* (1922), London: Penguin.

Keating, Peter (1991) *The Haunted Study: A Social History of the English Novel 1875–1914*, London: Fontana Press.

Kern, Stephen (2003) *The Culture of Time and Space, 1880–1918*, 2nd edn, Cambridge, MA and London: Harvard University Press.

Kristeva, Julia (1981) *Desire in Language: A Semiotic Approach to Literature and Art* (1980), Leon S. Roudiez (ed.), Thomas Gora, Alice Jardine and Leon S. Roudiez (trans.), Oxford: Blackwell.

—— (1984) *Revolution in Poetic Language* (1974), Margaret Waller (trans.), New York: Columbia University Press.

Lawrence, D. H. (1960) *Psychoanalysis and the Unconscious and Fantasia of the Unconscious*, introduction by Philipi Rieff, New York: The Viking Press.

—— (1962) *The Collected Letters of D. H. Lawrence*, Harry T. Moore (ed. and intro.), vol. 2, London: Heinemann.

—— (1998a) 'Poetry of the Present' (1919), *Selected Critical Writings*, Michael Herbert (ed.), Oxford: Oxford World's Classics.

—— (1998b) 'Morality and the Novel' (1925), *Selected Critical Writings*, Michael Herbert (ed.), Oxford: Oxford World's Classics.

—— (1998c) 'Art and Morality' (1925), *Selected Critical Writings*, Michael Herbert (ed.), Oxford: Oxford World's Classics.

—— (1998d) 'John Galsworthy' (1927), *Selected Critical Writings*, Michael Herbert (ed.), Oxford: Oxford World's Classics.

Leavis, F. R. (1955) *D. H. Lawrence: Novelist*, London: Chatto & Windus.

—— (2000) 'Mass Civilization and Minority Culture' (1930), in Ian Hamilton (ed.), *The Penguin Book of Twentieth-Century Essays*, London: Penguin.

Lee, Hermione (1996) *Virginia Woolf*, London: Chatto & Windus.

Levin, Harry (1966) 'What Was Modernism?' (1960), *Refractions: Essays in Comparative Literature*, Oxford: Oxford University Press.

Lewis, Percy Wyndham (1914) 'The Cubist Room', *The Egoist*, vol. 1, no. 1, 1 January, 8–9.

—— (1998) 'Long Live the Vortex!' (1914), in Vassiliki Kolocotroni, Jane Goldman and Olga Taxidou (eds), *Modernism: An Anthology of Sources and Documents*, Edinburgh: Edinburgh University Press.

—— (2003) 'Our Vortex' (1914), in Charles Harrison and Paul Wood (eds), *Art in Theory, 1900–2000: An Anthology of Changing Ideas*, Oxford: Blackwell.

—— (2005) 'Manifesto' (1914), in Lawrence Rainey (ed.), *Modernism: An Anthology*, Oxford: Blackwell.

Lindberg, Kathryne V. (1987) *Reading Pound Reading Nietzsche: Modernism After Nietzsche*, Oxford: Oxford University Press.

Luckhurst, Roger (2002) *The Invention of Telepathy*, Oxford: Oxford University Press.

Lyotard, J. F. (1984) *The Postmodern Condition*, Geoff Bennington and Brian Massumi (trans.), Manchester: Manchester University Press.

McKible, Adam (2002) *The Space and Place of Modernism: The Russian Revolution, Little Magazines and New York*, New York and London: Routledge.

Mansfield, Katherine (1962) *Bliss and Other Stories*, London: Penguin.

Marek, Jayne E. (1995) *Women Editing Modernism: 'Little' Magazines and Literary History*, Lexington, KY: University Press of Kentucky.

Marinetti, F. T. (2002) 'Zong Toomb Toomb' (1914), *Selected Poems and Related Prose*, selected by Luce Marinetti, Elizabeth R. Napier and Barbara R. Studholme (trans.), New Haven and London: Yale University Press.

—— (2003) 'The Foundation and the Manifesto of Futurism' (1909), in Charles Harrison and Paul Wood (eds), *Art in Theory: 1900–2000: An Anthology of Changing Ideas*, Oxford: Blackwell.

—— (2005) 'Contempt for Women' (1911), in Lawrence Rainey (ed.), *Modernism: An Anthology*, Oxford: Blackwell.

Marwick, Arthur (1991) *The Deluge: British Society and the First World War*, 2nd edn, London: Macmillan.

Marx, John (2005) *The Modernist Novel and the Decline of Empire*, Cambridge: Cambridge University Press.

Miller, Jane Eldridge (1994) *Rebel Women: Feminism, Modernism and the Edwardian Novel*, London: Virago.

Minow-Pinkney, Makiko (1987) *Virginia Woolf and the Problem of the Subject*, Brighton: Harvester.

Moi, Toril (1985) *Sexual/Textual Politics: Feminist Literary Theory*, London: Methuen.

Nicholls, Peter (1995) *Modernisms: A Literary Guide*, London: Macmillan.

Nietzsche, Friedrich (1988) *Twilight of the Idols* (1889), R. J. Hollingdale (trans.), London: Penguin.

—— (1993) *The Birth of Tragedy* (1872), Michael Tanner (ed.) and Shaun Whiteside (trans.), London: Penguin.

—— (2001), *The Gay Science* (1882), Bernard Williams (ed.) and Josefine Nauckhoff (trans.), Cambridge: Cambridge University Press.

Oppenheim, Janet (1985) *The Other World: Spiritualism and Psychical Research 1850–1914*, Cambridge: Cambridge University Press.

Ouditt, Sharon (1994) *Fighting Forces, Writing Women: Identity and Ideology in the First World War*, London: Routledge.

Panek, Richard (2005) *The Invisible Century: Einstein, Freud and the Search for Hidden Universes*, London: Fourth Estate.

Peppis, Paul (2000) *Literature, Politics and the English Avant-garde: Nation and Empire, 1901–1918*, Cambridge: Cambridge University Press.

Poe, Edgar Allan (1994) 'Review of *Twice-Told Tales*' (1842), in Charles E. May (ed.), *The New Short Story Theories*, Athens: Ohio University Press.

Pound, Ezra (1913) 'A Few Don'ts by an Imagiste', *Poetry*, vol. 1, no. 6, March, 200–6.

—— (1916) 'Vorticism' (1914), *Gaudier-Brzeska: A Memoir*, London: John Lane.

—— (1922) 'Paris Letter', *The Dial*, June, 623–9.

—— (1932) 'Harold Munro', *Criterion*, July, 590.

—— (1971) *The Selected Letters of Ezra Pound, 1907–1941*, D. D. Paige (ed.), London: Faber and Faber.

—— (2005) 'Song of the Bowmen of Shu' (1915), in Lawrence Rainey (ed.), *Modernism: An Anthology*, Oxford: Blackwell.

Pugh, Martin (1999) *State and Society: A Social and Political History of Britain 1870–1997*, 2nd edn, London: Arnold.

—— (2002a) *The March of the Women: A Revisionist Analysis of the Campaign for Women's Suffrage, 1866–1914*, Oxford: Oxford University Press.

—— (2002b) *The Making of Modern British Politics, 1867–1945*, 3rd edn, Oxford: Blackwell.

Rado, Lisa (ed.) (1997) *Modernism, Gender and Culture: A Cultural Studies Approach*, New York: Garland.

Rainey, Lawrence S., (1998) *The Institutions of Modernism*, Yale: Yale University Press.

Richards, I. A. (1929) *Practical Criticism*, London: Kegan Paul, Trench, Trubner.

—— (2001) *Principles of Literary Criticism* (1924), London: Routledge.

Richardson, Dorothy (1979) *Pilgrimage: Vols 1–3, Pointed Roofs, Backwater, Honeycomb* (1915, 1916, 1917), London: Virago.

Riding, Laura and Robert Graves (1927) *A Survey of Modernist Poetry*, London: Heinemann.

Scott, Bonnie Kime (1995) *Refiguring Modernism: Vol. 1 The Women of 1928*, Bloomington, IN: Indiana University Press.

Showalter, Elaine (1978) *A Literature of Their Own: From Charlotte Brontë to Doris Lessing* (1977), London: Virago.

Sinclair, May (1990) 'The Novels of Dorothy Richardson' (1918), in Bonnie Kime Scott (ed.), *The Gender of Modernism: A Critical Anthology*, Bloomington, IN: Indiana University Press.

Smith, Andrew and Jeff Wallace (eds) (2001) *Gothic Modernisms*, Basingstoke: Palgrave.

Smith, Helen Zenna (1988) *Not So Quiet* ... (1930), London: Virago.

Smith, Stan (1994) *The Origins of Modernism: Eliot, Pound, Yeats and the Rhetorics of Renewal*, London: Harvester Wheatsheaf.

—— (2003) 'The Disconsolate Chimera: T. S. Eliot and the Fixation of Modernism', in Marianne Thormählen (ed.), *Rethinking Modernism*, Basingstoke: Palgrave.

Strychacz, Thomas (1993) *Modernism, Mass Culture, and Professionalism*, Cambridge: Cambridge University Press.

Taylor, Frederick (1911) *The Principles of Scientific Management*, New York and London: Harper and Bros.

Thormählen, Marianne (ed.) (2003) *Rethinking Modernism*, Basingstoke: Palgrave.

Thurschwell, Pamela (2001) *Literature, Technology and Magical Thinking, 1880-1920*, Cambridge: Cambridge University Press.

Trilling, Lionel (1955) *Freud and the Crisis of Our Culture*, Boston: Beacon.

—— (1962) 'On the Modern Element in Modern Literature' (1961), in Stanley Burnshaw (ed.), *Varieties of Literary Experience*, New York: New York University Press.

Trotter, David (2001) *Paranoid Modernism: Literary Experiment, Psychosis, and the Professionalisation of English Society*, Oxford: Oxford University Press.

Tzara, Tristan (1977) *Seven Dada Manifestos and Lampisteries*, Barbara Wright (trans.), London: John Calder.

—— (2003) 'Dada Manifesto 1918', in Charles Harrison and Paul Wood (eds), *Art in Theory: 1900–2000: An Anthology of Changing Ideas*, Oxford: Blackwell.

Underhill, Evelyn (1995) *Mysticism (1911)*, 14th edn, London: Bracken.

Valentine, Kylie (2003) *Psychoanalysis, Psychiatry and Modernist Literature*, Basingstoke: Palgrave.

West, Rebecca (2005) 'What Is Mr. T. S. Eliot's Authority as a Critic?' (1932), in Lawrence Rainey (ed.), *Modernism: An Anthology*, Oxford: Blackwell.

Williams, Louise Blakeney (2002) *Modernism and the Ideology of History: Literature, Politics and the Past*, Cambridge: Cambridge University Press.

Williams, Raymond (1989) *The Politics of Modernism: Against the New Conformists*, Tony Pinkney (ed. and intro.), London: Verso.

Winter, J. M. (1998) *Sites of Memory, Sites of Mourning: The Great War in European Cultural Memory*, 2nd edn, Cambridge: Cambridge University Press.

—— (2003) *The Great War and the British People*, 2nd edn, London: Palgrave.

Woolf, Virginia (1976a) 'Old Bloomsbury' (1921/22), *Moments of Being*, Jeanne Schulkind (ed.), London: Triad/Panther.

—— (1976b) *Mrs Dalloway* (1925), London: Granada.

—— (1982) 'Saturday 27 June 1925', *The Diary of Virginia Woolf, Vol. 3 1925–30*, Anne Oliver Bell (ed.), London: Penguin.

—— (1986) 'Mr Bennett and Mrs Brown' (1924), in Peter Faulkner (ed.), *A Modernist Reader: Modernism in England, 1910–1930*, London: Batsford.

—— (1992) *Between the Acts* (1941), London: Vintage.

—— (1993) 'On Being Ill' (1926/30), *The Crowded Dance of Modern Life: Selected Essays, Volume 2*, Rachel Bowlby (ed.), London: Penguin.

Yeats, W. B. (1990) *W. B. Yeats: Collected Poems*, London: Picador.

—— (2005a) '"Introduction" to *Certain Noble Plays of Japan*' (1916), in Lawrence Rainey (ed.), *Modernism: An Anthology*, Oxford: Blackwell.

—— (2005b) 'Rapallo' (1929), in Lawrence Rainey (ed.), *Modernism: An Anthology*, Oxford: Blackwell.

# Index

Words in **bold** refer to entries in the glossary

# Riding to Newport

# Riding to Newport

Donnie Lamon

Copyright © 2010 Donnie Lamon
All rights reserved

ISBN: 1-4196-1339-1

To order additional copies, please contact us.
rglamon@aol.com
Printed by Pulp
Bound by Kingsport Book, Inc.

# Riding to Newport

# Through The Years

### by Jane Nolan

Let's go in memory to our childhood
To the places where we used to go.
Let's live again those childhood memories
with the people that we both loved so.

Let's go in memory to the church house
to the chapel where we said, " I Do."
Let's live again each happy hour.
Each hour has been happy, dear, with you.

Let's stop and linger by the cradle
Where our children brought us so much joy.
Let's count them as our richest blessing;
three little girls and two little boys.

Now that we both are growing older.
As the golden hair turns to gray.
Every day Heaven seems a little closer
and our love grows stronger every day.

## In Loving Memory

## June Nolan

May 8, 1927 – October 28, 2002

## Jane Nolan

June 22, 1929 – May 10, 2006

Tonight, I heard the dark decree:
The crier, in sad soliquays,
Hearkened unto his sad duty to tell
And felled his words as foes to his heart.
Still, he cried on, as his new impart
Fell as shadows from mouth of friend.

Though none could escape, none wanted to hear
The weight of the words that fell on their ears,
And slipped hands to those organs to prove their denial.
Meanwhile, the crier, though beckoned to cease
Found in his bowels the urge to increase.
With lips of full trembling, he sounded again.

His voice, though tepid was not impaired,
And found its mark swiftly in everyone there.
Then slowly, so slowly in shadows they came;
All lame and impotent in their grief-stricken states,
Wide eyed and weeping, pondering their fates;
Hopeless and lost, they started to sing.

First one, then two, then three and then all,
They joined in their anthem, for Heaven to call.
For hours and hours they chanted their dirge;
Converged into one melody of remorse.
In sackcloth and ashes, they stayed to their course,
Weeping, lamenting the death of the king.

# Prologue

*Walking up the grassy incline, the wind cool and hard on my face, the* grass wet and soaking through my tennis shoes. The sun, like a vagrant wandering up from behind a curtain of trees, floating aimlessly into the white smeared, azure sky. A southern morning rising slowly, as if its life will last forever. My breath is heavy against the brooding onslaught of daylight. I lean heavily on the walking stick. All around me are the boundless shadows of the fallen. Marble slabs catch pieces of sunlight and sparkle like life. Names and dates etched into their faces. Dates separated by tiny dashes. Little lines carved into stone. The expanses of lives condensed into tiny dashes. All the joys and pains and the triumphs and tragedies, the mistakes and the beauty and the ugliness. Everything. This is our life. This dash. This is what we have. All of it. Silent and still. Etched in concrete. Commemorated in stone, carved there by some worker we don't even know. Living his own life. Etching his own mark for someone else to immortalize in stone. The measure of a man's life. A dash between two numbers.

And I walk on. Mesmerized by the sweet intoxicant. The silent sadness that is palpable in a graveyard. Passing the markers of friends and relatives. Ancestors and strangers. There are flowers all over the place. Draped over the headstones. Lining the graves. They are placed there to make the passer forget about death. To make him think of life. Of birth. Of new beginnings. There are little plastic angels everywhere. Baby cherubs playing flutes and dancing on grave grass. Little bright and shining faces to fend off the uneasiness. But the birds sing sadly in the trees. They know of death. And our pretty flowers and plastic angels will not silence their dirges. The fool-hearty clouds are

overhead. Watching. Passing slowly. Casting giant shadows over the green ground, as if force-feeding their sadness to the world.

When I come to my destination, I stop slowly. I look down slowly. A name. Two dates. A dash. I put the bag on the ground beside me. I put my hand into my pocket . . .

*For My Family*

# I

*Saturday morning. No duties. Monday morning and school are a* thousand years away as I lie in the calm warm womb of my bed. In my fetal position, I have pulled the covers about my head. Snuggled into nothingness. Thinking nothing. For there is nothing to think about on Saturday mornings. The house is cold. And this drives me deeper into my warm nothingness. My nonexistence. Birds chirp a gleeful cadence outside my window. They are already up and at work. They know nothing of Saturdays. And they try to goad me into joining them. But I will not hearken yet. There is still lots of nothing to do in my bed. And I will not rise until it is done. A sliver of sunlight pokes its fingers through my window and into my eyes. It moves across the covers and lumbers lethargically to the wall. It beckons me to get up. To frolic with it. But again I will not heed. Not yet. There is no need to greet the world now. School is a forgotten memory. The grass has been mowed. All homework is done. Every obligation is fulfilled.

I hear feet walking dutifully down the hall. Adults are waking and going to work. Not knowing what work to go to, but instinctually rushing toward it. They have lost the secret of Saturday mornings. And at sixteen, I know that I too will soon lose it. But for now it is mine. And I will keep it as long as I can.

A few more minutes of non-committal bliss and I hear the coffee pot purring in the kitchen. Gurgling and spitting forth its fuel in dark brown waves. It is a signature sound at my house. It usually begins before the sun comes up. But on Saturday mornings even its routine is made latent by lethargy. More feet are moving. And chairs scoot across the linoleum floor in the kitchen. The pungently welcoming aroma of coffee wafts its

swarthy trail down the hall and seeps under my door. Behind it is another smell. A smell much more likened to my taste. It arouses in me the desire to get up and eat, but nothing more. It is the smell of sausage gravy and butter melting over hot biscuits. Not the kind of biscuits from a can. The kind that are pressed out with the top of a glass. I fight for some time with my wont to remain anonymous in my bed and the growing urgings of my belly. Soon the decision will be made for me, for I hear the doorknob turn. The door opens slightly and morning floods into my room. I know what she is going to say even before she says it. "Wake up sleepy head. Breakfast is ready."

I roll about for moment, and moan slightly, as if I have just awakened. I cast my covers off my head and rub my eyes. Letting them see the morning only in bits and pieces. When she sees that I am getting up, my mother retreats to her duties but leaves the door open to stifle any temptations of further slumber. I throw the covers to the floor and lie unsheltered in my bed for a moment. Having thrown off my barriers, I am smitten into rising by the morning. I pull on a pair of jeans and push the first shirt my fingers find down over my head and down about my waist. I pass my bedroom mirror and glance at myself, letting my eyes absorb my disheveled image. My hair is askew and sticking out in every direction. I have never been blessed with good morning hair, but I pay this little heed on Saturday mornings.

Staggering down the hallway, half blind with sleep, I pass the myriad of pictures that line it like the hallowed halls of some sacred institution. Each photo holding some consecrated image from the past. Placed there to remind the passers that life was lived here. Birthday parties and pony rides. Ten-pound catfish and baseball teams. Weddings. Graduations. Baptisms. Basketball players. Cheerleaders. Vacations in Myrtle Beach. Little lives lived out behind little panes of glass. I scrub my bare feet along the shag carpet because I like the sound and the feel of it. This drives my mother crazy but it is too early on a Saturday morning for her to mind. As I near the kitchen I can hear forks grating against plates and the hushed banter of a reporter on the

television set. It is almost always turned on simultaneously with the coffee pot. It is always on the news. The only exception is Sunday mornings, when it is changed to *The Mull's Singing Convention*, a live program featuring Southern Gospel singing groups. On Saturdays though, it is the news. The local news, for nothing but local news matters on Saturday mornings. I pass the television set in the living room, my eyes still basking in the warm darkness of the house. My family believes in turning on lights one at a time. The only light on now is the kitchen light. I glance at the clock on the wall. It is 7:30 A.M.

The kitchen is a world of light and fragrances. It fights the night off me in bright iridescent waves. There is a table at the center of it. We do not have a *dining room* proper. We eat in the kitchen, where the food is cooked, as we feel that the two cannot, or should not be separated. My dad sits over his empty, greasy plate, studying yesterday's paper. When he hears my uncommitted footfalls he looks up and says what he says every Saturday morning: "Well, look who decided to get up."

I scratch my head and do not respond. I never respond to this, for I have yet to find a suitable response. The rudimentary truth of the statement leaves little room for debate or contemplation. I sit next to my sister, Tammy, who looks up from her plate and acknowledges my presence silently. We are both at the awkward ages where verbal acknowledgments to peers are lofty considerations not to be taken lightly. My momma gleefully brings my breakfast to me on the same plates I have eaten from every day of my life. We have changed very little in sixteen years. Momma gets her plate. Sits down with us. She eats last. She always has.

We finish our breakfast and momma clears the dishes away into the sink. She fills the left sink basin with hot soapy water and lets the dishes soak in it while she sips her coffee. Dad puts his paper down, fills another cup with coffee and walks into the living room, where he turns on the light and turns the news up a little. Tammy retreats to her room and to whatever secret things fourteen-year-old girls do in their rooms.

When momma finishes her coffee, she starts on the dishes.

I sit on the love seat in the living room, listening to the weather on the news. The weatherman says it's going to be cold. Talks about how cold it's going to be. Better bundle up. Better make sure you've got lots of firewood stacked. Check the antifreeze in your car. There's lots of work to being cold. I think of what Mark Twain said: "Everyone complains about the weather, but no one does anything about it." Dad is leafing through a TV Guide. He turns to me and says, "What are your plans for the day?"

I shrug my shoulders. I can see in his eyes that he is thinking of something for me to do. Having nothing to do in his house is a cardinal sin. I see an idea behind his eyes and I know that his mind is flirting with some fledgling idea to keep me occupied for the day. I know that I have to think of something quickly or my Saturday will be wasted on some form of manual labor. He is about to speak when the phone rings. I offer a quick, silent prayer of thanksgiving as my hand darts for the phone.

I know who it is even before I hear his voice. There is only one person in our family who will call at 8 o'clock on a Saturday morning. Papaw.

"What do ye know?" He asks, as if he has been awake for hours. Mornings are nothing to him, as days are nothing. His life transcends days and nights and months and years. He lives in his own time.

And I say, "Not much." As I always do.

"What've ye got planned fer today?" He asks.

I tell him I that I have no plans, and I can hear him smile across the phone line.

"Well, that's good." He says, laughing lightly. "I've always thought well of a man that ain't afraid to do nothing."

I laugh at this.

"Well, since you ain't doin nothing, how 'bout runnin me up to Newport?"

Now, Newport is a euphemism, really. While there is an actual town of Newport, just east of Gatlinburg, and we will eventually make it there, what he is really asking me is if I will take

him to town. Which is also a euphemism for *Lets go somewhere.*
You see, there are some people who believe that Saturdays are
set aside to finish the work that could not be completed
through the week. And there are some who believe that Saturdays are set aside to do household chores. And there are those
who believe that Saturdays are set aside to do nothing. But my
grandfather is of a different persuasion. He believes that Saturdays are set aside for adventures.

"Alright," I say. "But I don't have any money for gas."

"Ye've got enough to git here, don't ye?" He asks, and this
is a joke, for his house is just across the road.

I laugh again. "I guess I do."

"Well, just get on over here. I've got enough gas money to
make it to Newport."

"Let me ask my mom and dad." I say, out of habit, but I
know what their answer will be. I have only been driving for
about four months, and my parents are hesitant to let me venture too far from home, but they always let me drive my grandfather around on Saturdays. He is only in his sixties, but an
uninsured car accident a few years ago left him without a
driver's license and he has been traveling on the good will of
family members ever since. One would think that his inability
to drive would have been a fatal blow to his rambling nature,
but it seems to have only provoked it to a greater ferocity. He
has always loved to go, but now he has to go with someone else,
which is an even greater joy to him. There is too much to see
alone.

"Let me talk to yore momma." He says, as he cannot call
our house without talking to his daughter. She is standing beside me now, for she knows who is on the phone and that it will
soon be her turn to talk. I hand her the receiver and the two
chatter for a while. When they are finished she returns the
phone to me. We pick up our conversation as if there has been
no interruption.

"Come on over." He says. "I'll be waitin on ye." He says
this with an air of finality.

"It'll be a few minutes. I've got to get ready first."

"Well, don't take too long. We've got people to see and things to do."

We are finished speaking, but we never say *goodbye*. We always say, *See you*.

I get ready, which is to say that I put on my socks and shoes, pull a hat over my head, pushing my wild hair into conformity, and don my winter coat. There is little formality involved in these Saturday excursions. There is no one to impress. And we wouldn't have cared if there were. I wave goodbye to my mom and dad as I leave, and there are no admonishments or cautions thrown at me. They know that this day I will be in good hands.

I walk outside and let my lungs fill up with the invigorating life of the cold. I have always loved it. The cold. It seems more real. More honest. It makes you feel alive. It gets in you and pushes everything to the surface. I exhale and my breath, visible, like smoke, cuts through the cold air and hangs in it and rises like helium. I start my pickup truck, and automatically turn the volume all the way down on my stereo. Papaw does not care to listen to music while we are driving. It distracts, he says. It offers competition to his voice, and he loves to hear himself talk. Almost as much as I do. But there is another reason I turn off my stereo, even before I reach his house. My papaw is lost in his *time*. A perfect time that has not dissipated, but grown more solid over the years. He believes that I live in this time as well, that I *love* this time, as he loves it, and I would not want to transgress his dream by allowing him to know that I sometimes like things from my own time as well. I turn up the heat and let my truck idle for a while, so it will be nice and warm for him. My papaw is one of those men that for some unexplainable reason, you just like to please.

The descent down our long steep driveway, from my time to his, is an easy one. I slip into it like slipping into an oversized pair of old shoes. My truck is a five speed, and I let it ride first gear all the way down our mountain to the bottom, touching neither brake nor the accelerator. I learned to drive on mountain roads long before I learned to drive on flat ones. The engine

whines in the cold and my tires sing happily against the frost-covered concrete. Our driveway ends at Shield's View Road, which lies like a great gulf between me and my grandparents. It is a reminder of the Now, and the world where that time exists. I inch my truck toward it, and then in it, unsafe for a brief time as I cross it, adrift in the sea of the Now. But I am soon across and safe on the dusty, gravel-strewn driveway of my destination. I start up their mountain. It is as long and as steep and as narrow as my own, but my tires are singing a different tune now. Older and more melodic. The song of dirt and stones. Pebbles prick the underbelly of my man-made metal beast, playing rhapsodically, children of eons built. Trees line the driveway like sober sentinels. Trees of perpetual green. Losing no life to the mutable seasons. There are bare trees as well, their arms outstretched and frozen upwards, as if caught in the act of praying for one more chance at life. I like the green trees. Green has always been my favorite color. It is a deep hue, three dimensional and porous. The fingers want to touch it, the eyes, the mouth, the nose, and the ears. Green is the color of all five senses. Around a curve, through the perpetual green, and the road levels out to my grandparents' house, which sits like a castle atop this small mountain.

It is a castle to me, and has always seemed as such. It is filled with and surrounded by mythical effigies, which to a boy seem to be made of magical stuff. Cars are dreamily lazily here and there. Some that run. Some that do not. For now, that does not matter. They are filling their places. They are filling their times. You can only drive one car at a time, anyway. To my left is a rust colored 1972 Chevrolet Nova, the sun feasting hungrily on its paint-splotched roof. It sits with its silent story in contentment, and relents to the sun's teeth amidst some ambitious weeds, which have not yet met their Armageddon of weed-eater blades. There is a 1979 Buick next to it, up on blocks, its rims amputated and transplanted long ago. It waits, perched atop its pedestals, waiting for its chance to fly again. A red Datsun sits with its hood perpetually open, hungry for attention. There are a few more, scattered here and there like long dead and forgotten soldiers. Some belong to papaw. And some belong to my

uncle Kip. But they all belong here. Two vehicles hold special places of prominence in the yard, off by themselves. The weeds carefully trimmed around them. They sit in silent glory, known only to those who care to look and listen. One is not too much to look at. Just the shell of an old 1956 Ford truck. It rests on cinder blocks, like a monument, and that is what it is. My uncle Gerald placed it there, and it is his dream in emergence. Materializing in bits and pieces before our very eyes. It is just the shell and nothing more. No engine block. No wheels. No seats. The wooden floor of its bed has long ago been eaten away by rot. Ever so often though, one will see an addition to it. A mirror on the windshield that was not there yesterday. A gas cap. A hood ornament. A front bumper. My uncle is building his dream one piece at a time.

The other vehicle is a white 1969 Chevy truck. Contained in it is a piece of sacred history. A story talked about enough so that it has reached mythical proportions. There has even been a whisper of supernatural heroism attached to the truck. It was a couple of years ago, when Papaw, Kip and Gerald were clearing off a portion of lake property that papaw had recently purchased. They drove out early that morning in that old white truck. As the morning progressed, they cleared away many trees. Kip, the Keeper of the Chainsaw, felled the trees. Trimmed off the branches. Cut the trees up into little stove-wood sized pieces. Gerald carried them up out of the holler and cleared the brush away. There was a rudimentary road cut into the mountainside, leading down into the holler from the higher portion of the property, and Papaw stood there. High above. Supervising the labor. Some time during the day, Kip went to cut up a felled tree. Unbeknownst to him, on its way down the great tree had pushed over another tree. This smaller tree had not separated from its base. It lay waiting like a cocked rifle underneath the larger tree. When Kip made his first incision into the tree, the smaller one was unleashed and came catapulting upward, catching him on the underside of his nose. He went flying backwards onto a pile of brush and fell unconscious. Blood pouring from his mangled face. The chainsaw fell silent at his side. Gerald saw all of this,

and cried, "Daddy!" At which, Papaw came running. They carried Kip up out of the holler and placed him in the truck. Gerald, who had never learned to drive, hopped up into the bed and Papaw climbed behind the wheel. He threw the truck into reverse and slung mud and rocks out from the front of the vehicle as he floored the accelerator. He navigated the truck across the old road that led from the lake like an expert. Like a spider on a spider web. They pulled out onto the highway, Gerald being thrown back and forth in the back of the truck, holding on to his store-bought hair as waves of careless wind swept over the hood of the truck, across the cab and into the bed. Kip lay with his head on the window. Blood pouring down the front of his shirt in frightening torrents. Papaw never lifted his foot from the gas pedal, and the truck sped down the highway, weaving in and out of traffic as the engine roared from the fury of its conscription. We will never know the specifics of the conversation in the cab of that truck. The words of comfort offered to Kip. The prayers that wafted up through the roof, for papaw is reluctant to talk about it. He never likes to talk about things that scare him.

They were but a few miles from the hospital when the truck's big 8-cylinder engine could take no more. It began to heave and lurch beneath the hood, and a warring, discordant symphony of unseen metallic intestines began to break free and rattle. Not long after that, waves of black, acrid smoke billowed out from beneath the hood. But still, the truck sped on. It looked like a crazy white locomotive tearing down the highway. They pulled into the emergency room parking lot and the truck finally gave up its ghost. Papaw was able to coast the thing into a parking space, and then the truck would move no more of its own accord. We had to tow it back to the house, where it sits now. We are romantics. We believe that the old truck gave its life for Kip. We believe that it has earned its place, far removed from the others, a testament to the devotion of steel and glass and rubber.

There are other things as well. Half built lawnmowers. A one-handled wheelbarrow. An outboard motor. A broken tiller. A golf cart with three flat tires. Built and half-built bicycles here and there. A child of the Great Depression, my grandfather has

always put more faith in things than in money. I park my truck behind a gold colored Oldsmobile Cutlass.

The front door of the house opens before I can pull up my emergency brake, and behind the screen door is Gerald, smiling. He has an uncanny ability to hear a vehicle coming from a mile away, and when he does hear one coming, he always stands by the door until he can confirm that his intuition is correct. Then he will turn and announce to everyone who is coming. He is the herald of the family. As I approach the door, I can hear him inside the house. "It's Donnie, daddy."

He opens the door for me. It creaks loudly in the cold air, crawling against the silent damp. Its metallic refrain is soothing. I enter and it slams fitfully closed. There is no sound in the world like the sound of a screen door opening and closing.

"Hidey, Pal-Pal!" He exclaims. This is what he calls me, and always has. I suspect that he will still be calling me this when I am thirty years old. He has nicknames for all of his nieces and nephews. We don't mind. Gerald is different. He is more like the children than anyone else in the family. And that is why the children love him so much. He is content in his own time, with his own ways, just like his father. The children grow, mature, and change, just as the world does, but Gerald stays the same. He is one of the few constants in our universe. He is short and very thin, but his body is lined and sinewy with ropy muscles that covet a physical strength one would not suspect such a diminutive frame could possess. He wears his store-bought hair with more pride that if it were his own natural locks. The most prominent thing about Gerald is his beard. It hangs down from his face in a great, flowing wave of black and gray. With his beard and his thin, sharply enunciated features, he looks a lot like the pictures of mountain men you see. Or perhaps a nineteenth century romantic poet.

"Come on in the house!" He says, loudly. Everything he says is loud and excited. He smiles as if he has not seen me in twenty years. "Look who's come to see us, momma!"

Mamaw smiles from somewhere in the dark kitchen.

There is little light in the house. They like to conserve en-

ergy. (They *have* to conserve energy). and so lights and outlets
are used only when needed. My senses are flooded with familiar
sensations. The smell of wood burning in the stove. The sounds
of pine knots crackling in the fire. The gold warmth of fire-heat.
The sparse everyday artifacts of the lives there in their usual
places. But this being Saturday morning, there is another sound
which is not heard through the week. It is the sound of the local
radio program, *The Swap and Shop*. On the program, sellers call
in with whatever they have to sell, state a starting bid, and then
the moderator takes calls from bidders. Papaw loves this program, but he rarely calls in. We are all convinced that he is afraid
to hear his voice on the radio. But he loves to listen to the various prices that people are willing to pay for things. It gives him
ideas. He is a man of ideas. He has a new one every day. You can
see it in his eyes first thing in the morning. He wakes up every
morning to cigarettes, coffee and ideas.

The radio announcer says: "All right caller, what'cha got to
sell this morning?"

The next voice is slow. Unsure of itself: "Yeah, this here is
L. T. Maynard, and I got——" There is muffled giggling in the
background. "Lenora! Keen't you see if you keen't keep 'ese kids
quiet fer a minute? I'm 'a tryin to talk to this man on the radio."

"Go ahead caller." The announcer says, with a hint of perturbation and amusement in his voice.

"Well." The caller continues. "I got me this here tractor
here to sell. It's been a perty good 'un. I bought in new in '74
and I ain't really had no trouble with it, but to tell you the truth,
I need some money a sight bad. It's this old no account feller
my oldest daughter went and married. He hailed from Florida.
And I tole her not to trust him, not to never trust no boy from
Florida what has hair longer than hers and what never says please
or thank ye. But she just wouldn't listen. I tell ye what's the
truth, young 'uns nowadays don't keer a bit about what their
mommas and daddies tell 'em. Anyhow, this old boy wudn't no
account. I seen it right from the start. Sometimes daddies just
know, you know? He quit his job over at Cherokee Mill and run
off somers down around St. Louis, last I heard. Left my daughter

Pearline and her three young 'uns all alone. The bank repossessed their trailer and all four of 'em had to move in with me and Lenora. Now, Lenora ain't my wife. My wife been dead four years. Come down with a bad case of the gout and never got—"

"Why don't you tell the listeners about your tractor, Mr. Maynard?" The announcer asks. Curtly. Still with perturbation in his voice, but no amusement this time.

"Anyhow, like I was sayin, Lenora comes over and does my cookin and cleanin fer me. She don't spend the night, though. I jest wont to make sure everybody knows that. Anyhow, I've got to build on to my house to make room for Pearline and her kids, and I got to studying on the prices of lumber and other sech things and I figgered I'd better come up with some more money somehow. That's why I'm 'a sellin this here tractor."

"It'd probably sell a lot better if you told us about it." The announcer says, not even trying to hide the sarcasm in his voice.

"Well, it's a Massey Ferguson. A 165 diesel with a MF32 front-end loader attachment that works good. It's got spin out rims, four remotes. Let's see here . . . it's a three speed. Uh, three point rear weights and fenders."

"Anything else?"

"It's got power steering. That really comes in handy fer an old feller like me. I had a hard time steerin my other tractor. The one I had before I got this one. I got a touch of arthritis in my elbow, and I really had to wrastle that old tractor to git it to turn. It was a John Deere. I ain't never keered too much for them, but I got a pretty good deal on it. They's this old widder woman had it. Her husband had passed on from cancer. Had it a sight bad. He was all eat up with it from what I heerd."

"What's your starting bid?" The announcer asks.

"Well, I'z wontin to git at least nine hundred dollars fer it. I—"

"All right then, folks. You heard him—"

"I got a right good picture of it. If ye wont I can bring it down there to the radio station."

"Thank you caller." The announcer says, gleefully, finally silencing the caller. "Bring that picture on down and I'll show it

on the radio. This is auction number 63 folks. And it's for a Massey Ferguson farm tractor. The starting bid is nine hundred dollars. What do you say callers?"

Mamaw emerges from the kitchen, wiping her hands on a dishtowel. She is smiling, on the verge of laughter, as if she has just thought of a joke. This is how she always looks when you first see her. Mamaw was born in the mountains as papaw was. She is one of the most humble people I have ever known. She is the oldest daughter of Verless and Cora Morton.

The announcer says: "You're on Swap and Shop caller, go ahead."

"Yeah, I'd like to bid on that farm tractor. Auction 63, I think it is. Nine hundred dollars."

"Thank you, caller. You are now the high bidder."

"Well, there's Donnie!" Mamaw says, as if it is some big surprise. I am at their house almost every Saturday, and many days in between, but still it is like a big surprise to her. She always has a certain way of making you feel like you are the most important person in the world to her. I bask in her warm happiness for a moment. I am falling into their time already, and the outside world seems a million miles away.

Papaw comes out of his place in the living room: a great, brown second-hand recliner. Sitting as it has for the past four years, just next to the stove where it's warm. Most of the things in their house are second-hand. I can rarely remember them buying anything new. Papaw and mamaw likes to keep things that were in their family like the old trunk filled with things money can't buy that Papaw's Grandmother gave to him when he was young. He just can't see paying money for something new when there are plenty of used things just as good, and for less money. Papaw is not one to give up on things so easily. The old couch from somebody's yard sale. The old coffee table left over from somebody's move. The goliath television on a trade from somebody who needed something that wasn't a television set. It must have weighed two hundred pounds. Set in this big oak cabinet with doors that you could close when you weren't watching TV. The volume knob had long since fallen away. If you wanted to

adjust it, you have to get the little pliers from the top of the set and work it into the hole, grab the post and turn. No cable. There is a wire running from the back of the television set up the wall and through the roof to a tall, brass colored antennae that juts up from the corner of the house. In good weather they get three channels. In poor weather they get one or none. You have to turn the antennae to get better reception. We take turns. There would be a thunderstorm outside. Lighting and thunder and rain in sheets. We would all be inside trying to watch the race or something. And then the reception would go blurry. Someone would ask, "Whose turn is it to turn the antennae?" And nobody would answer. Everyone would say that they did it last time. Me being the youngest, I was usually volunteered to do it. I would go outside, wrap my hands around the cold antennae, look up at the top (it seemed to go up forever, into the clouds, even.) and start turning. Someone would yell from the inside, "Wait! Go back! Turn it the other way!" And I would reverse directions. Then they would yell, "Too far! Go back the other way!" And I would. This would go on for some time, until finally I would hear them yell, "Hold up! Slow down! A little more! A little more! Hold it right there!" And I would go back inside and get to watch about five minutes of the race, or whatever we were watching, and then the screen would go fuzzy again and I would have to do it all over again. I don't think I ever watched a complete television program in all the time I spent up there.

"You're on Swap and Shop. How 'bout it, caller?"

"Nine hundred and fifty dollars on that tractor."

Papaw hobbles over toward me, as if he is in pain. I am never really sure if he is really in pain, or just pretending. I know that he has arthritis, but the word is a vague notion to me, an abstraction of age that I cannot yet fully comprehend. Besides, he is always joking, anyway. He is a big man, six-foot three, with a stocky, but not fat frame. His broad shoulders stretch out larger than life, like he is, superimposed on the world. His face is thick, but the features are sharp. The dignified, prominent nose, a trait that has woven its way down through his long ancestry. The defined chin. The high cheekbones. He has the

shadow of a handsome man under his face. An eighteenth century Scottish nobleman, perhaps. A sparse crop of ivory hair crowns his head. As long as I can remember, he has always worn it the same way, slicked straight back with hair oil.

"Ten-twenty-five on the Massey Ferguson." A caller says.

Papaw says in his loud, always laughing voice, "Take yer coat off and stay a while."

I do, and place it on the cardboard box filled with firewood, beside the door. Mamaw asks me if I have eaten yet, just like she always does. It is a comforting feeling to know that there is always at least one place in the world where I will always be able to get something to eat. I thank her, but tell her I have already eaten. I look at papaw. He is standing now. Listening to the radio. Thinking.

"Fourteen hundred on the tractor." Another caller says.

Papaw stirs from his contemplation and says, "Come on over here and set a spell. I've got to call a man before we go."

I sit on the couch. An old, comfortable thing that swallows me up in its warmth. Papaw returns to his chair and pulls his billfold from his back pocket. He sifts through it and then his fingers settle on a little slip of paper, torn from an old *Reader's Digest* cover. He picks up the receiver of an old rotary-dial telephone.

"Jane." He says, struggling to read his own handwriting written there. "Come over here and dial this man's number for me."

My grandmother goes to him, dutifully. He hands the paper to me and says, "See if you keen't read this writin."

"Who wrote it?" I ask.

"I did, but I done forgot what I wrote. I keen't hardly read, no how." He can't see very well, or so he says. I never really know if it is true or one of his little jokes that he plays to amuse himself and me. I take the paper and study it. Mamaw is poised with her fingers over the phone, waiting for my instructions. I read the number aloud, and she dials it.

She and I sit on the couch while he conducts business. We talk of different things while his voice overshadows us. His

voice is always there in the house. It is the most prominent
thing there, and everything else must be carried out beneath it.
His only competition is Gerald, who speaks continually of
things others would probably find trivial, bits of useless knowledge to the outside world, but rare pearls of truth to him.

"This is June Nolan." Papaw says. Loudly. Into the phone.
This always tickles me. How he thinks the further away you are
from the person on the other line, the louder you have to talk.
"I'z over at Ralph Barnes' house the other day and he said you
had a tractor yore wontin to sell."

He is silent for a moment. I can hear a muffled voice
through the receiver, and then Papaw laughs.

"Well, that's good." He says. "A man's got to do what he
can to survive in this day and age. Life's getting awful hard on a
pore man. Ye know it? 'Specially with 'at Reagan runnin us all
into the pore house."

There is laughter and then more indiscernible words from
the phone. They carry on as if they have known each other their
whole lives.

"I might be." He says. "I'z sortie looking fer a good tractor
to have around the house."

There are more words from the receiver.

"Huh? Well, no. I ain't got me a big farm, but I thought I
might need to git me a tractor in case I ever do decide to get a
big one. Man would hate to have a big farm and no tractor."

Kip comes down the hall, scratching his head and yawn-
ing. He is tall, but thinner than his father. He is handsome, the
possessor of the looks that now shadow Papaw's face, but with
something else, the softness and genteel countenance of his
mother. He is thin but athletic and full of life. Like his father, he
loves to laugh and make people laugh. If Papaw is the voice of
the house, and Mamaw is the heart of the house, and Gerald the
memory of the house, then Kip is the life of the house.

"Well, if it ain't Donald Eugene Gibson." He says. This is
not my name. But for some reason, which I have never really
understood, he always calls me this. "What'che up to this morning?"

"About six-foot four." I say, and we both laugh. "I'm carryin Papaw up to Newport." I say this with pride. It is an important endeavor in our family.

"Well, don't lose him." He says, walking into the kitchen to eat breakfast.

I hear Papaw's voice behind me. "Maw, where's Gerald?"

"He's outside feedin the dogs."

"Tell him to siphon some gas out of that old Buick and pour it in Donnie's truck's tank."

She does, and Gerald obeys. A few minutes later, he comes back into the house and shakes the cold from him by rubbing his hands together and blowing warm air into them. "Hey Pal-Pal." He says to me. "Do you remember that old 1-ton truck that daddy traded Chin McCarter out of back when yore daddy worked at Tinker's Service Station?"

"Why Gerald!" Mamaw reprimands. "Donnie wudn't even born then."

"I don't know." I say to Gerald, because I know that he is going to tell me whether I remember it or nor. His memory is profound.

"You should have seen the steam roller that I built on the front of it. It was a sight!" For some reason, steamrollers on the front of trucks have always fascinated Gerald. His eccentric tastes have always been a bit on the odd side. There were steam rollers on the front of trucks, round houses, locomotive engines, dirt race tracks, hybrid farm tractors, and any car or truck over twenty years old (excluding Cadillacs and Lincolns.) "You remember that, don't chee, Kip?"

"Yep." Kippy says, from the kitchen.

Gerald walks over to the television set and retrieves a pouch of Bugler tobacco from the top and proceeds to roll himself a cigarette. "Momma," he says, "tell daddy to pick me up some ready rolls when he gits to town."

"You art not smoke." She chastises, like she always does, but to no avail. She is the only one in the house who does not smoke. She is trapped in a walled prison of fumes and vapors.

Gerald immediately changes the subject. "Tell me, Pal-Pal,

are you still excited about that trip that you and me and Kip and Paul made over to Chattanooga? Remember when we saw the Chattanooga Choo Choo and went down inside that big cave with the lake in the bottom of it?"

"I sure do." I say. This trip took place about four years ago, but to Gerald, it could have happened yesterday.

"Remember them big old fish that was swimmin in the lake?"

"Yup."

"They took us around in a glass bottomed boat. Didn't they, Kip?"

Kippy doesn't hear him.

"Well, where do ye live at?" Papaw asks, into the phone. "Are ye gonna be there fer awhile? Alright. We'll be there atter awhile. We'll see ye." He hangs up the phone and gets up slowly from his chair and does a little dance in which he kicks up one leg slightly into the air while bouncing on the other. Then he changes legs and repeats the process. "You ready to go, big boy?" He asks me.

"Is that what you call dancing?" I ask.

"That's called dancin a jig." He says, reaching for his coat draped over the couch.

"I low are ye likin yer Nissan truck, Donnie?" Gerald asks, as if he does not know that we are about to leave. "Ye know, they build 'em right here in Tennessee."

"Yeah, I know it." I say, starting for the door. "I like it pretty good, I guess."

My truck has a history, just like the other two. It is mine. My truck, because I am paying for it. Daddy bought it new. He traded a Subaru Brat for it, which we had more than outgrown. There were four of us, and only that little two-seater truck to carry us around. It had two little plastic seats in the back and if it was warm, my sister and I would ride back there, and mom and dad up front. If it was cold or raining, we all four crammed ourselves into the cab, me sitting in between the bucket seats on the emergency brake and my sister on my mother's lap. Seat belt laws were not strictly enforced back then. The new Nissan truck,

however, had a new addition to it called the *king cab*. Which was a little space behind the bucket seats, where two little foldout seats came out of the side for my sister and I to sit on. We were still crammed in there, but it seemed like we had more room. At least there were seatbelts for everyone. Daddy kept that truck and put three hundred thousand miles on it, and it never once went into a garage, other than for regular repairs: oil changes, brake jobs, tune-ups and such. When I turned sixteen, Daddy had paid the truck off, and I just figured, being the firstborn and all, that the truck was now mine. Daddy had other plans. He took me down to his bank one morning and co-signed on a loan for eighteen hundred dollars. The bank gave me the money and I gave it to Daddy and he gave me the keys to the truck. I worked summers and some weekends to pay off that loan, but when I did, the truck was mine. It was no one else's, and I cherished it like a firstborn child.

"Well, let's go." Papaw says, impatiently. "I've got people to see. They might be worried about me."

Mamaw takes hold of my arm lightly. "Donnie, won'tchee come in here and see if you can wear some of these old shirts that don't fit daddy or Kip no more?" She loves to do this, for I am the only grandchild that is about the same size as Papaw, and she loves to know that I can wear his clothes.

"I'll look when I get back." I say.

"Well, let's go." Papaw repeats.

Kippy comes in from the kitchen with a plate of eggs and bacon in his hand. "Hey Donnie," he says, "have you ever read *Robinson Caruso?*" He loves to read, and loves to talk about what he has read. Mamaw instilled a love for reading in him, for she was once a schoolteacher. She taught elementary classes at the old Glades School. It was a one-room schoolhouse. She took her first paycheck and paid to have electricity put into her mother and father's house. But that is a different story. She was made the teacher because she was the only one in the community who had finished high school. People used to come by and have her read letters, and write letters, and do their figuring for them. People say she could figure in her head faster than a

calculator. His name, Joseph Kipling Nolan, is an homage to one of Mamaw's favorite authors, Rudyard Kipling. He does not like the name Kip, and would much rather be called Joseph, but at sixteen, I think that Kip is the coolest name I have ever heard. He is sometimes very erudite in his reading. He is the only person I know that has read all 26 volumes of the Encyclopedia Britannica, as well as Webster's Dictionary, from cover to cover.

"I read that in the third grade." I say. "As a matter of fact, it was the first real book I ever read. (actually the bible was the first) I didn't read the kiddy version, either. It was unabridged and complete, with all the hard words and lengthy narratives included."

"That's good." He says. "That's one of them books that pulls you in and won't let you go."

"I'm reading *King Lear* now." I say.

"I don't bleeve I've ever read that one. What's it about?"

"It's Shakespeare's darkest work. He explores the gamut of human depravity. He—"

Let's go if we're goin!" Papaw says, again.

Gerald says to me: "Hey Donnie, how 'bout hookin up that contraption so I can watch *Thunder Road*? It will be the forty-ninth time I've seen it."

By *contraption*, he is referring to the Betamax, an ancient forerunner of the VCR. It is a huge, silver box sitting atop the television set. They had received it from someone last Christmas, and none of them knew how to work it. The movie he is referring to, *Thunder Road*, is an old black and white drama starring Robert Mitchum. It is the story of a mountain family of bootleggers who lived around this area. Gerald watches it religiously for its extensive back road car chase scenes.

I go to the Betamax, locate the tape, and set it up for him. "Just press this button when you want to watch it." I say. "And make sure the television is on channel three."

Papaw is pacing the floor, anxious to leave. Gerald walks over to him and whispers in his ear, "Daddy, pick me up some ready rolls when you git to town."

"Alright Gerald. Well, are we ready to go, or not?"

"I bleeve I'll fix me a cup of coffee." Gerald says. "How 'bout you, Donnie? You want a muck-in-the-cup?"

I shake my head.

"You want one, daddy?"

"I want to leave." Papaw says, "While there's still daylight."

"What kind of tractor you gonna git, daddy?"

"It's a Massey Ferguson, Gerald." He starts for the door again. "Come on, Donnie."

"Oh boy!" Gerald exclaims. "That's just what we need out at the farm. Hey Donnie, did I ever tell you about that tractor that Mouse Martin had? It was a Ford and a Massey Ferguson put together. We called it a Fassey Merguson."

"I'm pretty sure you've told me about it." I say.

Papaw grunts loudly, and says, "That feller ain't gonna wait on us all day."

Mamaw says to me, "Just come in here and look at these shirts right quick. It won't take but a minute, and I'd hate to just throw 'em away."

"My goodness!" Papaw sighs, "I'll be waitin out in the truck."

It is always hard to leave their house.

I open the door of my truck. He is seated in the passenger seat, smoking a cigarette with his walking stick leaning between his legs.

"Do you really need that stick?" I ask him. "You look to me like you can walk just fine."

"This stick ain't for walkin. I'm bringin it in case I have to knock some hard-headed man upside his noggin."

"What if he's got a bigger stick?" I ask, laughing.

"We'll run. Now, hop on up in here and let's go."

I start to get in behind the wheel, and then I stop. "How much gas did Gerald put in my truck?"

Papaw shrugs his shoulders. "About a gallon, I guess."

"Have you got some gas money?"

"I near 'bout forgot. They had me all tore up in there. Go over there in the carport and git two or three of 'em crates of dope bottles. 'At arta git us enough gas to git there and back."

In the dark carport, I navigate my way through a maze of misbegotten treasures. Items from everywhere, forgotten, neglected, but somehow all migrating their way home to a small carport in Gatlinburg, Tennessee. There are ancient looms here and there, with broken treadles and dangling harnesses. Looms have always been a staple there. Mamaw sitting behind one, weaving and singing. One loom is the loom my great-great grandmother wove on. There are fishing poles, bicycle tires, chainsaw parts, boxes of thread, remnants of a fifty-year-old Singer Sewing Machine, half-full metal boxes, a carburetor pulled from a 1958 Dodge, a hand plow nicknamed Bessie by Gerald, a wooden crate with an assortment of bolts and screws, a cardboard box of *American Legion* magazines, keeping their stories of war and heroes in silence. Great and myriad are the treasures laid out before my eyes. I feel as though I have stepped into Aladdin's fabled cave, and I would love to forage through it, but I cannot tarry. I go to the back of the carport, where there are stacks of wooden crates, each one filled with empty soda bottles. They bear the labels of Coca-Cola, Royal Crown, Mountain Dew, Mellow Yellow, Pepsi, A&W, and most of the other soda manufacturers. The most important marking on the bottles is a relief in the glass itself, just above the labels, where the words *.10 deposit* appear. I pick up two of the crates. A spider scurries out from under them, his home having been excavated, and he searches diligently for more cover. The boxes are heavy, and my back, though young and strong, cries out from its conscription. I navigate my way through the carport, careful not to disturb anything from its slumber, and then put the boxes gingerly in the bed of my truck. From his place, Papaw taps on the inside of my rear window. I walk around to his side. He asks me how many bottles I have. I judge that I have about 40 bottles, so another trip will be necessary. Maybe two more. I go back, until I have about a hundred bottles. I secure them in the bed. I get in and start the truck and Papaw and I set out with ten dollars worth of empty soda bottles for Newport.

# II

*Going down their driveway, the truck is warm and we have left every-*thing behind. People carry too much stuff with them, or so Papaw has always said. They are heavy laden, and walk slowly from the cumbersome weight. That is why they are missed so badly when they are gone. They leave nothing behind for others. They leave nothing to mark their existence. People walking around all day long, carrying everything they own: Troubles and laughs and memories and tears, having no place to set them down. He carries his walking stick, and I carry his bottles for him, and that is all that we need.

When we get to the bottom of the driveway we are faced with a decision, which is really no decision at all, but I always like to offer it to him anyway, even though I know what his answer will always be. A person can take comfort in a thing like that. "Which way do you want to go?" I ask. "Through town, or up the creek?"

"Up the creek." He answers. "I don't bleeve I kin handle goin through town this mornin. I ain't had my nerve pill yet."

When he says, *Up the Creek,* he is referring to an intricate system of back roads, which will eventually lead us to Byrd's Creek Road. Byrd's Creek Road is a ridge road, cut alongside a mountain. I have heard rumors that there is a creek beneath it, Byrd's Creek, but in sixteen years I have yet to see it. I turn left, and we start up Shield's View Road, climbing higher and higher into the canopy of green trees that line it. Where I am from, you are always either going up or down. This is probably a metaphor for life, but I am too young to recognize it.

The truck's engine is winding up in low gear, and we ride in silence for a while. The inside is very warm now, and Papaw

fumbles with the switches on the dashboard. "How do ye turn this thing down?" He asks, frustrated.

I turn the fan down. He lights a cigarette, and it hangs from his lips, dancing in quick little spasms as he talks. I watch the cigarette in innocence, not hearing its faint warning, its premonition of a death it would bring about from its child-like, treacherous little charade, a death that I would know for many years now. Even if I had heard it, I would not have listened. We are segregated from abstractions like death and birth and life. We are lost in the safety of his time, and the world goes on outside the metal shell of my truck. We pass it, oblivious to it. Somewhere in the world things are happening. Over in Germany, the Berlin Wall is falling. In China, a lone student is defying the tyranny of tanks and suited men in Tiananmen Square. An earthquake is rocking San Francisco, while Hurricane Hugo is pummeling the east coast. Somewhere in Panama, General Manuel Noriego is being led, handcuffed, out of his mansion by United States forces. Off the coast of Alaska, the *Valdez* is bleeding its black blood out upon the aboriginal shore. But in my truck, we are going to Newport, and for all we are concerned about, these things could be happening on another planet.

"Let me ast ye a question." Papaw says, startling me out of my lofty contemplations. "Would ye d'ruther be a coonrod, or a messer?"

He asks me this all the time, and while I am not sure what either of them is, I always manage to answer. Two years later, I will meet a young man in Fort Jackson, South Carolina, whose last name will actually be Coonrod. His name will be right there emblazoned on his uniform. I will wonder if this is what Papaw meant by the term, and if so, I will be thankful that I did not turn out to be one. For Coonrod will prove to be a very rude and singularly loathsome person. Still, I will not be able to help laughing at the thought of arranging a meeting between the two of them, just to see how Coonrod will respond.

"I bleeve I'd d'ruther be a messer." I say. I speak in his vernacular when I am with him. I have coached myself away from my natural dialect, and after much practice, have developed the

ability to let it shine through only when I want it to. When I started kindergarten, I was made fun of by my classmates, most of whom were not even from the area. I was made to feel foolish in my own world for being *from* my own world. I decided then and there that I would lose my Appalachian accent. Here in the truck though, in his time, in his *world*, the air is untainted by outsiders, and I feel the freedom to speak without thinking about it. It is a tremendous relief.

"Well, that's good." He laughs. The sound is heavier than the air in the truck, but it hangs there just the same. "I've never thought too much of coonrods, myself."

We top the hill, where Shield's View Road merges with Ownby Circle, and then start down a very sharp curve. He tosses his cigarette through his partially lowered window, and pushes his fingers into his shirt pocket. He always dresses the same way: A simple, button up dress shirt and dark polyester slacks and a green Co-Op hat. He retrieves a package of Rolaids, flips one out with his thumb, and pops it into his mouth. He eats Rolaids like candy. He is afflicted with chronic stomach problems, and has suffered under their relentless torture most of his life. The stories always came to me in vague, whispered innuendoes, and I never really grasped the seriousness of the affliction until one day I saw the evidence for myself. I came over to his house one morning, very early, and I accidentally caught a glimpse of him climbing out of bed without his shirt on. A series of deep, ugly, red scars ran the length of his stomach. It was very hard to look at, so I looked away.

He offers a Rolaids to me. I decline, never having cared for their chalky taste. He returns the package to his pocket and then slaps both hands against his knees. "Well," he says, "what d'ye think about Reagan runnin us all into the pore house?"

Papaw is a die hard, sanctified, baptized and confirmed Southern Democrat, and will not be dissuaded from his persuasion regardless of the amounts of logic or facts that you throw in his face.

"I don't know." I answer. "There are a lot of people who think he is one of the best presidents of this century."

"What about Franklin Roosevelt? He was the best president we've ever had. He brought this country out of the Great Depression. He carried us through the biggest war this country's ever seen. He wudn't like Reagan. He know'd how to work fer a livin. He know'd what it was like to be pore. That's why he's always lookin out fer the pore man."

I start to tell him that Franklin Roosevelt came from a very wealthy family, but I decide not to. Once he has made up his mind on a matter, he will not budge.

"Roosevelt couldn't even walk." He continues. "He had a hard life. He wudn't no Hollywood movie star, havin everthing give to him on a silver platter."

"Well," I say, "don't blame me. I didn't vote for Reagan or Roosevelt."

Softly, almost to himself, he says, "I don't know what this country was thinkin, puttin a man like Reagan in the White House."

Softly, almost to myself, I say, "They put him there twice."

"I didn't vote for him either time." Papaw says.

"See," I say, "you didn't vote, so you can't complain about who gets elected."

He looks sternly at me. "Now, you know as well as I do that the Clique won't let me vote."

Now, the *Clique* is an interesting entity. While imaginary, it is as real in Papaw's mind as anything else. I say it is imaginary, but in truth I have never been able to either confirm or discount its existence. In simple terms, the Clique is an intricate system of people and factions seeking to bring Papaw's life to ruin. No one knows exactly how it started, for he is very vague with details. The only certain thing about it is that every idea in his mind that has failed was thwarted by this entity. I abide his idea of the Clique, because like many of his others, I know that there is no harm in letting him believe it. Also, I am never really sure whether he is doing it for his amusement or for mine.

"What about Jimmy Carter?" I ask after some silence. "You liked him, didn't you?"

"Jimmy Carter was a good president and a good man. He

was from Georgia." He says this with an air of finality, as if by simply being from Georgia, Carter's place in history is forever sealed among the eminent. "Reagan is from California." He says *California* like a man would spout the name of his most bitter enemy.

"Carter was rich." I challenge.

"Yeah, he was rich, but he worked fer his money. He come by it honest, the way God intended. He didn't steal his money like a lot of these Republicans."

The great dividing line in Papaw's political philosophies is a single issue: Republicans are for the rich man, and Democrats are for the poor man. Having always been poor, it stands to reason that he has always been a Democrat.

"Well," I say, "he'll be out of there soon."

"He's gonna run us all into the pore house." He says, laying the matter to rest.

We pull onto Glades Road, and fall in line with a procession of Saturday morning tourists. They stop periodically, gazing at wonders and pulling into craft shop parking lots. The Glades Crafts Community is a seven-mile loop, with a kaleidoscope of stores selling their hand-made wares. We pass the leather shop, the glass blower, a myriad of woodworking shops, several potters, some antique stores, a bakery, the blacksmith, and various other businesses that are a homogenization of all. Some are related to me. Mine is a family of woodworkers and weavers. Seamstresses and blacksmiths. Randy Whaley, my cousin owns and operates one of the first woodworking shops in the Glades community. I glance at the differing license plates on the road ahead of us. I wonder what it is about this place that draws so many from so many different places. To me, these shops and the trees and the mountains and the fog are all commonplace. I have outgrown the magic of the place. This place depends on these yearly visitors, as does the entire city of Gatlinburg, being fed by dollars earned in factories and industrial establishments, banks and firms, far away and foreign to it. But my family is autonomous. We have existed long before they came, and we will be here when they are gone.

Papaw surveys the landscape. The rolling, green hills, the little creek along the road, the sporadic armada of shops and parking lots. "You know, at one time, I could have bought ever bit of this for twenty-five dollars an acre."

"Why didn't you buy it?" I ask.

"Cause they was asking too much for it." He says, simply. "At that time, twenty-five dollars was a lot of money, and this place here wudn't nothin but an old, worthless swamp. It'd flood three or four times a year. The kids used to float on old tractor tires down the road. They built this up, filled it in, put all these buildings on it, and now they sellin it by the square inch. Somebody really knew what they was doin when they bought all this."

"Too bad it wasn't you." I say, but he is not listening to me.

"You know, when your ancestor, Peter Nolan came over here from North Carolina, he didn't have hardly nothin to his name. Just the clothes on his back, an old covered wagon, and a wore out pair of mules. He was a true pioneer."

"What did he have when he died?" I ask.

He laughs. "Not much, just a little plot of earth six foot by four foot by six foot deep."

"I guess that's what we all wind up with." I say.

"He was a man of ideas, though." He says, with admiration.

"What brought him over here in the first place?" I ask.

He smiles. He has been waiting on me to ask that. To open the door to the story.

"Well," he says, casing into the story gracefully, "his people came over here from Scotland. They settled in North Carolina. Just over them mountains, yonder. Peter got to be perty well off. Owned quite a bit of land. He got to be a perty important man in the community, too. People came to hear what he had to say. Some folks got to talkin about runnin him for some kind of office. Well, an important man with a lot of land and a lot of friends also has a lot of enemies, and as it turned out, he got put in jail for attempted rape."

"Attempted rape?" I ask. "Don't sound to me like he was much of a man."

"They wudn't no truth in it. Peter was married with children then, and they was this woman that lived down the road from him. She used to have to walk everwhur she went. Peter got to feelin sorry for her, and if he was goin the same way as she was, he'd give her a ride in the wagon. She was right smart lookin, and not married and young, and maybe it wudn't the smartest thing for a man like him to be doin, but he went ahead and did it anyway. He was like me, he just liked to help people. Well, some of his enemies who was just lookin for a chance to do away with him paid this woman to make up this story about him, how he attacked her, and the sheriff believed it and put Peter in jail."

"How do you know she made it up?"

"Years later, when she was old and on her death bed, she got to feelin real bad about what happened, all the trouble her story caused, and she finally admitted that she made it all up."

"What happened to Peter?"

"Well, they put him in that jail, and he sat there, waitin on his trial. The circuit judge was a man who just happened to be a silent financial partner to some of Peter's enemies, and Peter knew that he didn't stand a chance for a fair trial. He figgered he's gonna be hung fer shore. Well, his wife come to see him one day in the jail. The jailer checked her out. Made shore she wudn't totin no hacksaws or hammers and chisels and sech, and then he let her on in the jail. The jailer sat outside the door, whittlin, or readin a book or somethin, and she visited with Peter a spell. She come out some time later. The jailer let her out the door. She nodded at him and went on her way. Later that evenin, the jailer opened the door to bring Peter his supper. He walked inside and dropped that plate of beans right on the floor. There was Peter's wife sittin on his bed, perty as you please, dressed in Peter's clothes. The jailer run out for the sheriff, and they looked and looked for Peter, but they couldn't find him. He was half-way across the Cumberland Gap, his skirt flappin in the wind."

"What happened after that?"

"He met him a Cherokee princess, married her, and settled right here in this part of the state. He knew he couldn't never go back to North Carolina to see his family, so he had him a whole slew of young'uns. He tried to have a go at land again, but he just couldn't seem to make it work. I guess he figgered that it was too hard with so many against you."

He sighed.

"Life shore is hard on a pore man. You know it?"

"I do." I said.

My gas gauge is flirting dangerously with the *empty* mark. I look to my right as we pass Lebanon Baptist Church, its white walls standing in stark contrast to the brown structures around it, and the spectrum of colored cars passing by it. It is stuck in its own time, pulling itself back from the now, retreating into the sweet bliss of yesterday. Just passed the church, we reach the spot where the Glades Store used to be. I remember the two gas pumps that used to sit in the front of it, and I silently curse progress. We go on past the bend, where my great-grandmother lives in a great, silver peaked white house. Built one hundred years ago. It sits atop a steep but low bluff like a perched white owl, its visage obscured by the protecting barrier of leafless tree limbs. If it were spring, or summer, the house would seldom be seen behind the canopy of fully-grown leaves, full of green life. In the Fall, the trees boast their fiery colors like a holocaust of flames, like the Children of Israel saw in the desert.

"Let's stop and check the mail." Papaw says. He doesn't have a mailbox at his own house. It has something to do with the Clique.

"Alright." I say, and turn up their driveway. We pass the apple orchard where I worked as a child. I spent many a summer and Saturday planting trees and straightening saplings. All day long, for five dollars. I worked for my uncle Henry, a lifelong bachelor and minister, who lives with my great-grandmother, Cora Morton. We park next to Henry's truck, an old Ford with a beat up camper top on the back. The bed is filled with bushels of apples. The sweet smell of almost over-ripened fruit hangs in the cold air. Henry meets us at the door. He bids us enter

silently. He has a funny way of talking. He is an old-time minister, from a time when one's worth as a preacher was accounted
by the volume, pitch and drama in one's voice. Each syllable
was selected carefully, and manipulated to catch the ear of the
back-slidden church member, and prick the heart of the long
lost sinner. When he does speak, it is usually loud and sudden,
each letter in each word enunciated. We walk through the dark
foyer, into the kitchen, where my great-grandmother stands,
stooped over a wood-burning stove, her fingers pushing a
wooden ladle into a great, steaming pot. It smells old inside the
house; wood and metal, canned vegetables, shoe polish, well
water. The olfactory sense is hinged more tightly to past memories than any other sense, and my nose pulls me backwards to a
time just beyond the horizon, just where I left it. I came here almost every Saturday as a little boy, usually to work for Uncle
Henry. My great-grandmother was always putting breakfast on
the table. My great-grandfather was there then, this was before
he died. He was always sitting at the kitchen table, drinking coffee. And Henry was always semi-reclined in the dark living
room, staring pensively at nothing. He always looked deep in
thought. He would sit in silence for several minutes, and then
suddenly, burst forth in his loud, booming grandiose voice,
seeming to rattle the very beams of the house. I would always go
into the living room, to tell him that I was ready to work, and he
would just stare, like he hadn't heard me. I would start to repeat
myself, and then he would jump out of the chair, slam his gigantic hands together in front of my face, like he was making a dramatic point from the pulpit, grab my shirt around the collar,
and hoist me three feet off the ground, (I never had a single shirt
as a child that was not stretched out of shape around the collar.)
and tell me that if I ate greens and cornbread every day, like he
did, that I might one day grow up to be as stout as him. He was
always a giant to me. My great-grandmother would come rushing in and sternly say, "Henry! Put that boy down! You might
hurt him!"

One particular Saturday morning, it was too wet to work in
the orchards, so I spent the day loafing around their old house,

exploring mysterious catacombs and unearthing imaginary se-
crets behind imaginary vaults and hidden trap doors. An old
house holds a certain magic for a child, and a child has a certain
magic for an old house. When the two get together, there is no
telling what miracles and wonders can be dreamed into existence. My great-grandfather, Verless, was outside somewhere.
Uncle Henry was in his room, studying the Bible. My great-
grandmother was out on the porch, weaving on her great, old
wooden loom. And I was a battle-weary Confederate captain,
hiding out in the attic. There was a squad of Yankee soldiers
looking for me, they were just downstairs and I had to be still as
a mouse. The old steps and floor of the attic were worn and rot-
ted, and the slightest movement of my feet caused them to
creak. I knew I wasn't supposed to be up there, but I couldn't resist. Besides, it was the best place to hide from the Blue-Bellies.
I heard footsteps on the stairs, and readied myself to leap out
onto the federal invaders. The steps were drawing nearer, almost
on me, as I crouched in the darkness, my hands clasped tightly
around my imaginary rapier. The door to the attic came open,
and I heard my great-grandmother's voice in the darkness.

"Donnie? Are you up here?"

"Shhh." I whispered. "The Yanks will hear you."

"You know you ain't supposed to be up here." She said,
sternly. "Come out of there before I call yore momma."

"Yes ma'am." I said, coming out of the darkness. Even
then I knew that great-grandmothers out-ranked captains. We
walked down the stairs together, and she told me to come out
onto the porch to help her put a new warp on the loom.

We sat at opposite ends of the big loom. I turned the crank
that pulled the thread from her hands, through the heddles, and
around the big beam at the back. She didn't say anything for a
while. Sensing she was still angry about my recent transgression,
I said, softly: "I'm sorry I went up into the attic."

She held the threads tightly, so that I couldn't turn the
beam. Then she sat back on her bench, like a sage.

"That ain't the first time you've been up there. That was
just the first time you got caught. Wudn't it?"

I nodded.

"How many times have you been told that it's dangerous to play up there?" She asked, without anger.

"I don't know." I answered, shrugging my shoulders. "A bunch, I guess."

"What do you reckon your momma would do to you if I told her."

"She'd probably cut a hickory switch." I said, cringing a little.

She said nothing for a moment, and then: "Do you know what happens to little boys and girls that don't do what their folks tell them to?"

I shrugged my shoulders again.

"Hurricane Ed gits 'em."

"Who is Hurricane Ed?"

"He's an old man that wanders around here, lookin for mean little children that don't obey their elders. He lives under folks' houses, and he's always listening, always *watching*. When he finds kids that are actin up, he comes out and gits them."

"What does he do with them?"

"He puts them in this big ole wool sack that he carries on his shoulder, and then he takes them down and throws them in the river."

"Awe." I said, not believing her. "Yore pullin my leg."

"No I ain't. Some folks say that he was a schoolteacher a long time ago. He taught third and fourth graders, and all them long years of listenin to their racket and puttin up with their mischievous ways finally drove him crazy. Some folks have seen him. He's a little, stooped over man, from having to live under folks' houses. He walks real slow, kind of shuffles. Folks have seen him carryin children to the river. They've seen that sack on his shoulder. They've seen it *move*. Like little arms ands legs squirming around inside. Some have heard voices in the sack. Little voices, cryin softly. Oh, he's real."

She got up to go inside the house to stir a pot of boiling beans. I walked over to the screened-in window and stared out into the damp Saturday afternoon. Imagine her thinkin that I still believed in stories like that, at nine years old! *Hurricane Ed.*

What, did she think I was still a kid? *He throws mean little kids into the river.* Did she think I was still eight, or something?

Then, I heard something under the porch. It was barely discernible. Soft movement, like sand sifting through a crack. *It's just the wind,* I thought, *blowing up in underneath the porch.* But then I heard another sound. This one was louder and less mysterious. A grunt. I turned to see if my great-grandmother was returning. I could hear her all the way in the kitchen, humming and stirring the pot. I looked back out through the metal screen, down at the bottom of the porch. Afraid to speak. Afraid to move. Then, I heard the unmistakable sound of shuffling feet across soft earth, and a scraping sound underneath the floor, like someone's jacket rubbing against it. *Or a wool sack,* I thought and shuddered. I leaned toward the screen, to get a closer look at the bottom of the porch. The porch was about three feet off the ground, and the space underneath was boarded up with scrap pieces of plywood, nailed haphazardly onto the support beams. I watched and listened, and the shuffling grew louder and faster, and after every few steps I would hear that scraping sound again. A sound like cloth rubbing against the underside of the floor. Then, one of the plywood boards rattled against its nails. I jumped, but I could not run away. I could not even look away. It rattled again, and then it started to pry itself away from its moorings. Then a movement caught my eye. It drew my line of vision to itself and shrunk the world into its place. It happened in slow motion, and I looked at it for a long time before I believed it.

It was a hand, old and stained, gnarled and knuckled, with dirt under the fingernails. It was perched atop the plywood, pushing it out. I heard the nails scream as they came loose from their moorings. And then the plywood fell to the ground. The hand retreated back into the darkness underneath the porch, and then I heard silence. Silence, for a minute or for a thousand years. I could not count the time. But then, the shuffling came again, and one last scraping of cloth against the floor. And then I saw a hat emerge from underneath the porch. It was an old, crumpled hat, like men used to wear a long time ago. It was cov-

ered with dirt and smudged with oil. It was like a hobo's hat. I could not see the head or the face of the one who wore it. I stopped thinking about the face when I saw the big wool sack that it had slung over its shoulder emerging from the darkness underneath the porch.

And the sack was *moving*.

I screamed, and ran up in under the loom. I curled up in a little ball, pulling my arms and legs as close to my chest as I could. I held my breath, but I couldn't stop shivering. I was no longer the brave Confederate captain, but just a scared little nine-year-old boy who believed in Hurricane Ed.

My great-grandmother came running just as fast as her eighty-year-old legs could carry her. She came in and stopped. The screen door to the porch was opening and there stood Hurricane Ed, stooped over, bearing his cargo. His wide-brimmed hat was pulled down over his eyes, obscuring his countenance. He was breathing heavily. There were soft cries coming from inside the cloth sack. His big, muddy work boots stepped across the threshold.

I came running out from under the loom, and clutched the back of my great-grandmother's dress, burrowing my face into her back. "Don't let him take me, mamaw!" I cried. "I'll be good! I promise I'll be good! Just please don't let him take me!"

"Hush, now." She soothed. "Nobody's takin you nowhere."

Then, suddenly, from somewhere, I heard my great-grandfather's voice. "What's all this racket, Cora?"

"I don't know, Verless. I was just in there fixin supper and next thing I know, Donnie was screamin like the Dickens."

"Huh. Well, I got them cats rounded up from under the house. What you reckon I ought to do with them?"

"I guess you arta take 'em down thar to the Glades Store. They'll probably be able to give 'em away to somebody."

Then I looked out from behind her dress, and suddenly, it wasn't Hurricane Ed there in the doorway. It wasn't anything scary at all. It was my great-grandfather. He was covered in mud from underneath the house, and he had a sack of stray cats slung over his shoulder.

"What's got ye so skeered, boy?" He asked.

"Nothin." I replied, breathing a sigh of relief. "I just thought I saw a snake over in the corner of the porch."

"Mmmm." He said, turning around in the doorway. "Snakes is bad this time of year."

Papaw says, "Hidey, Verless."

"Hidey, June." My great-grandfather replies, lookin up from his cup. "Set down and have ye a cup of coffee."

"Naw. Me and the boy just stopped to check the mail."

"It'll be in there on the piano. If there is any."

Papaw goes into the living room. My great-grandmother comes into the dining room from the kitchen. "How are you, Donnie?"

"I'm fine." I say.

"Set down and let me fix you somethin to eat." The food smells good, earthy, and the house is warm and she smiles in a way that makes me want to stay. There is something about that house that makes me want to stay ten years old and forever inside of it, but the road is waiting and calling for us, and we for it.

"No thank you. I 'spect papaw'll be ready to go in a minute. You know him. He can't set for too long in one place."

She laughs.

Henry comes into the room slowly, dramatically. He looks me over, up and down. We are about the same size now. Then a smile sweeps over his face, and he greets me loudly, and grabbing my shirt collar. He tries to pick me up. This time, my feet are only a few inches off the floor.

"Put that boy down!" My great-grandmother commands, sternly. "You might hurt him."

This house is full of history. These people are full of history. My people. My history. As much a part of me as my hair color. The length of my arms. The curves of my ears. Everything there is full of history. Everything there is full of time. There is an outhouse in the back. Once a bear broke in to the hog pen at the back of the house and killed a hog. Used to be an apple orchard over there. Used to raise peanuts over there. Beans and Irish potatoes over there. Used to gather chestnuts from the big

chestnut tree over there and take them to Knoxville to sell. My great-grandmother saw a black panther over there when she was a little girl. Over there in the root cellar a Confederate soldier who didn't want to kill anymore was hidden and fed. And the people, alive and deceased, as real as anything. My great-grandfather was a man who loved his family he would walk forty miles to North Carolina to hitch a ride over to New River to work in the logging camps. Once a week he'd kiss his wife goodbye and take to walking to work. Then he'd walk back on Fridays. He broke his hip, his collarbone, his arm and his ankle in the time he worked there. He got buried alive once, too. All of these stories told through the years. These are my people. These people are me.

# III

*We drive on, the shops now becoming more sporadic and quintessen-*tial. Traffic has dwindled down to a few slow moving cars whose drivers will no doubt soon stop to turn around, thinking they are lost. The road winds in dangerous curves, but we have been riding on them all of our lives, and we have no fear. A car approaches in the other lane, and when it is close enough to make out the driver, Papaw throws his hand up in a familiar gesture of greeting. The driver returns the sentiment.

"Who was that?" I ask.

"I don't know."

I laugh. "Why did you wave at him, then?"

"Well, he might've know'd who I was, and I wouldn't want him to think I was mad at him."

Papaw prides himself in the people he knows, and assumes that he knows everyone. He also expects everyone to assume the same.

We come up on Lee Ogle's farm on the left. Papaw tells me to stop and let's see old Lee for a minute or two. I pull into the driveway. His house is immense, by our standards, and holds its age well. It is a formidable structure, and boasts its girth behind a huge, green yard. There is a small patch of field fenced in next to the house. A sorrel mare grazes contentedly in it. The farm itself stretches out thinly along the road, on both sides of the house. It is a large farm, for the area and the time. Before I can park my truck, the front door opens, and then the screen door, and Lee comes out onto the front porch. He is an old man, stooped over and of a slow gait, and a bit standoffish with strangers, but his shuffle toward us is welcoming. Papaw begins his slow, exaggerated performance of getting out of the truck.

There are groans and grunts and a shaking of the truck on its springs. When he makes it out, he pulls up his pants in the front and then the back, and says, "What d'ye say thar, Lee?"

Lee looks at us with his head bent forward. His eyes squint and concentrate on us for a moment, and then recognition sweeps across his face and he says, "Hidey, June!"

"Well, hello thar, Lee!" Papaw shouts ecstatically. "What d'ye know?"

"Not as much as I did." Lee replies, laughing. "Come on up here and set a spell."

We approach the porch, and Lee suffers us to sit on his bench. The porch creaks loudly from our weight, sounding louder than normal in the cold air. Papaw says, "This here is my grandson, Donnie. He's Stella's boy. You remember her, don't ye?"

"Well, my lawz." Lee says, throwing his head back. "Shore I do. Boy, that last time I saw you, you wudn't no bigger than a June bug!"

Lee wears a long, white beard in the wintertime. I remember him in sporadic flashes, the beard, the laugh, and the childlike associations with Santa Claus. He studies me for a moment. "Yore gonna be as big as your papaw here perty soon, ain't ye?"

I laugh. The truth is, I am already bigger than him, but not yet big enough to admit it.

"He's carryin me around." Papaw interjects. "He's my chauffeur."

"Well, that's good. I shore do wish I had somebody to carry me around. You don't hire out, do ye, boy?"

I shake my head and offer an accommodating laugh.

Papaw gets down to business. "What have ye got here that's worth tradin on, Lee?"

Lee runs his fingers under his cap, and absent-mindedly scratches his head. "I don't know, June. Lemme think . . . I got an old pushmower 'at needs some work done on it. It'd be perty good fer somebody 'at likes to fool with 'em. What have *you* got to trade?"

Papaw motions toward my truck with a cigarette. "I got a hunderd dope bottles out thar. They worth ten dollars."

Lee says, "I ain't got no use for no Coke bottles."

"Well, I ain't got no use for no pushmower, really. I got more of 'em than I know what to do with at the house."

They talk of other things for a while. The weather, politics, tobacco prices, and a myriad of other small town trivialities. I listen, uninvolved, for I have nothing worthwhile to offer on such subjects. When they have had their fill of talking, Papaw rises and looks at me. "Well, you ready to go?"

I nod and rise as well. Lee says, "Don't rush off, boys."

Papaw says, "We'd better be goin. I need to run up to the courthouse and then we're goin to Newport."

Lee stands. "How many Coke bottles did ye say ye've got?"

"A hunderd. You need ye a bunch of dope bottles, Lee. They's better than money, 'cause nobody'll try and steal 'em. They too heavy. Most thieves wouldn't think twic't about taking a ten-dollar bill, but they ain't no way they'd carry off a hunderd dope bottles. If they's that willin to work, they'd have a job and wouldn't be stealin."

"Well," Lee says, scratching his head again. "Come on out here in the shed and lemme show ye this lawnmower."

We follow Lee, and I tap papaw on the shoulder. "We need them Coke bottles to get gas."

"I've got a little money." He whispers. "I didn't wont to tell ye on the phone. I think the Clique is listening in on my phone calls. I don't like to let them know I've got money."

The transaction is made neither with paperwork, nor by the shaking of hands. There is a silent agreement between the two parties, a mutual nodding of heads, and then Papaw says to me, "Run and git them bottles out of the back of the truck."

I bring the bottles and place them in the shed. Lee remarks, "Now, there shore is a stout boy."

Papaw smiles with pride. "Yep. Course, I was stout too, a'fore I got sick. When I was this boy's age, I could carry a plow over one shoulder, and tote the mule over the other."

I push the old lawnmower toward my truck, its wheels wobble and the handle sways back and forth in my hand as papaw winds down his conversation with Lee. I let the tailgate

down and go to hoist the thing into the bed. When I do the gas tank falls off of it. I tie the mower down with a piece of rope that no respectable mountain boy would be without in the bed of his truck. I keep it alongside a length of chain and an empty gas jug. After I have secured everything, I get in the truck, and Papaw is not long to follow.

Back on the move again, to where Glades Road and Byrd's Creek Road conjoin. We turn left, along the ridge and through the white mist rising up from the unseen creek below us. It swarms along the road and across it. On the corner, on our left is Charles and Ollie's place. The place rests like a Flemish painting on the endless green, in front of acres and acres of high, rolling hills, blanketed by a canopy of trees, their leaves a thousand hues of green. The house is by far the most beautiful in the county. It is tall and white and Federal in construction and it boasts its great girth atop the countryside like the master of its domain, like a great, sprawling dream. The big, posing porch in front resting easily, welcoming. The Doric columns stretching upward to the roof, standing tall and sure like the arms of Atlas. Two swings on either side, swaying, always swaying slightly with the unambitious breeze. The little creek running around and in front of it all, walled and rocked in and forced into something beautiful and serene. The whole place stays on your memory long after you've passed it, like a faint dream tattooed on your mind. We pass it, and neither of us speaks for a while. Finally, Papaw says, "Old Lee's a good 'un. I kinda hated snookerin him like I did."

Now, among traders there is a certain hierarchy of behaviors, which determines one's prowess at the art. The secret of trading is leaving with more than you came with. Some might argue however, as to whether or not you are actually leaving with more than you had. Lee Ogle was no doubt now counting his bottles and thinking, *Old June's a good 'un. I kinda hated snookerin him like I did.* If you rationalize the transaction, you figure that at .50 per bottle, papaw had spent a total of fifty dollars on them. But then, when he bought them, he didn't just get the bottles, but their contents as well. Now, one might suppose

then, that papaw gave fifty dollars for an old pushmower, but in reality, minus the ten dollars from the deposits, he gave forty dollars for fifty dollars worth of sodas and an old pushmower. This kind of rationalization is needed to be a good trader. You must convince yourself at all costs that you made the better deal. At least now we weren't carrying around a bunch of empty bottles.

"We'd better get some gas pretty soon." I say, glancing worriedly down at the gauge on the dashboard.

Papaw leans over and looks for himself, judging himself to be a better authority on the matter. "Yep. I guess we'd better stop up here at Hammerhead's. Normally, I don't like to trade there, but I guess we'll have to."

Papaw never *buys* at stores. He always trades. In his mind, commerce is brought down to this rudimentary procedure: *I'll give you this for that.* If he is in a store, he trades money for product. It is primitive in nature, and has been around since the dawn of time. The only trouble is, in today's marketplace, there is little room left for negotiation. I mean, you can't walk up to the cashier at Wal-Mart with a new car battery and say, "I see you're asking forty-five dollars for this battery. I'll tell you what, I'll give you this Barlow pocketknife and twenty-eight dollars cash money. It's got a good blade on it, and has never let me down for whittlin and cleanin out fingernails and such." The cashier would no doubt immediately summon the manager and perhaps the men in the little white coats. Now, there are two areas of capitalism, which still adhere to this ancient system of barter: The automobile trade and real estate. It is almost shamelessly promoted in these industries. *Come on down and we'll make a deal! Bring us your best offer! No offer refused!* I mean, only a fool would pay the asking price for an automobile on a lot, or for an acre of land. That is why these are two of Papaw's favorite commodities to trade. He trades on anything, but cars and land are his two loves.

We pull into Byrd's Creek Market, and stop at the pumps. Surrounding us are a myriad of pickup trucks, laden down with tools and sleepy-eyed workers who are seeking to make up for

lost work during the week. This is an agrarian society, but not in the manner of long ago. Years ago, life depended upon the land, for life was gleaned from the ground. The ground depended upon the weather, and harsh weather meant a harsh yield. The weather has always been very fickle around here, because of the mountains. It is sporadic with snow, sunshine, thunderstorms, oppressive heat, humidity and wind. It has often been said that if you don't like the weather around here, wait about fifteen minutes and it will be bound to change. The economy here is still largely dependent upon the weather, though there is very little commercial farming that goes on. The landscape is painted here and there with small, part-time farms, having the bulk of their land sold off at auction, leaving only dim reminders of what they used to be. They are little junctions to the past, set like thorns in the midst of mammoth subdivisions. It used to be that tobacco was the big cash crop around here, and a family could live on a modest sized tobacco farm, but now it seems that the only cash crop around here is houses. They are springing up everywhere, like kudzu. Roads are cut into green mountains, spilling out brown blood upon a once beautiful and virgin bosom. Bulldozers push their way through, and the man-less ground is peopled. The highest paid workers in the community now are not farmers, but skilled carpenters, plumbers, masons and electricians. But their labor, too, is contingent upon the weather, and many must work on Saturdays to make up for rained out days through the week. They do this without question. Because banks don't care about the weather.

The workers come out of the market with biscuits wrapped in paper, and Styrofoam cups of steaming coffee, to wash the sleep and the dreams from their eyes.

"How much do you want me to get?" I ask, as we exit the truck.

He reaches his hand into his pocket and pulls out a pathetic little roll of bills. He begins counting them, and then he reaches in and pulls out some change. "Get $4.63 worth." He says, and then he walks into the store.

I pump the gas carefully, as I am not sure if he has any

more money to pay for a mistake. I stop at exactly the right place. I have been pumping gas for my mother since I was old enough to reach the nozzle. I get back into the truck and wait for him. I see him inside, through the glass, laughing and talking with various people, people that he has never met before, but that he knows because they are like him. He comes out a minute later with a cup of coffee. I start to laugh because his cap is sitting ludicrously crooked on his head. He sees me laughing and smiles, kicking his legs up again, dancing his jig.

In the truck, he situates himself with his coffee and says, "Did you wont somethin from in there?"

"No." I say. "Did you know that your hat is on crooked?"

"It's alright. Some people say that my head is on crooked too."

He blows air through his lips, making them flap loudly. "It's right cold out thar."

I jump at the opportunity to use a quotation, which I had read not too long ago. "You know what Mark Twain said about the weather?"

"What's that?"

"He said that everyone complains about the weather, but nobody does anything about it."

He laughs a little. "Yep, that Mark Twain, he wuz a good 'un."

We start out back on the road again, and I can see in his eyes that he is trying to plow new conversational ground, but the soil is not turning easily, so he returns again to the weather. "We're liable to git us some snow." He says. "How would you like that?"

"I'd like it fine." I say.

Now, snow in east Tennessee is a special thing. A fine thing. It is almost magical. We don't get a lot of it here in the valley, maybe two or three good ones a year. But when it does snow, it conforms everything to its own pure magic. The county is not equipped with the machinery to clear the roads as other counties who receive more than their fair share of snow each year. We are never ready for it when it comes. The world stops.

The schools close, the stores lock their doors, even the churches cancel services. And if we are lucky, the power goes off and we are pushed into primitive times, huddled together in warm, silent masses, drawing ourselves tenaciously into the sparse, yellow light of candles and the prickling fingers of fireplace fires, darkness pushing us into a core of flickering ghosts, hinged together by the light and the heat. It really is magic. Then, when the snow is packed down tightly on the roads, travel becomes impossible without the ingenuity of children, who fashion for themselves rockets of cardboard and plastic. They fly by in a blur, blazing trails in the snow, the soft echoes of their laughter and terrified screams of joy hanging faintly in the cold air.

One year, Kip got an old mattress and made a kind of makeshift bobsled. It could hold about eight kids. We flew down on its maiden voyage. The trees passed us on both sides at mind-boggling speeds. We screamed all the way down. We came up on the curve at the bottom, and leaned into it, riding it like Cale Yarborough or Richard Petty, but we were going too fast, and piled it up in the ditch. We were flung off into the snow, drunk with exhilaration, and our small bodies lay strewn across the white snow like the aftermath of the carnage of some great battle. Our screams were screams of joy. Then, someone said it. "Who's gonna carry the sled back up?"

"Not me." Said one.

"No way." Said another.

"I'm just a girl."

"It's too heavy."

So the thing remained at the bottom, discarded in the ditch, waiting for the anxious tug of children's fingers.

# IV

*On we go, we two pilgrims, adventurers, my grandfather and J, my* headlight beams laying on the fog in light-shadows, carving a path through the white sea. A dark mule eyes us suspiciously from behind a crooked, barbed wire fence. It offers a quick, hard breath, which sends plumes of white smoke out into the crisp, cold air. "That shore is a mean lookin mule." Papaw says. "Reckon if I could wrastle him down, you could git on him and ride him?"

"I don't know." I say. "He looks pretty stout to me."

"I bleeve I could handle him. I used to wont to be a wrastler, ye know. Just like Uncle Ray."

"Who was Uncle Ray?" I ask.

"I can't believe you've never heard of the famous Ray Nolan. He was a real legend around here. He was a great big man. He used to wrastle in the ring in front of hunderds of people, back when wrastlin was real. He got himself elected sheriff of Sevier County. Made a name for himself smashin up moonshine stills. Folks really loved old Ray. Yessir, I can go into just about any bank here in the county and tell them that I am the nephew of Ray Nolan, and they'll say, 'Come right on in here and set down, Mr. Nolan, let us git you a cup of coffee and you just tell us what you need.' People shore did think a lot of Old Ray."

"Sounds like he was quite a man."

"They wuz this one time, when Ray got called out to go break up a fight at a little out of the way beer joint. Back then, if a policeman got called out, he had to go by himself, they wudn't nobody else to help him. Well, Ray didn't know what he was gettin himself into. It turned out that they wuz this crazy feller from over in Cosby there, about half drunk out of his

mind, who had run everbody out of the joint and locked himself inside with a loaded shotgun. He was hollerin and carryin
on and sayin that he was gonna shoot the first lawman that
come down there to git him. Well, somebody had called the law,
and Ray had to go out by himself.

"He got there, and everbody was outside, kind of hunkered
down behind cars and sech. Ray pulled up, got his big old self
out of the car, and pulled the bullhorn out with him. He stood
right there behind the hood of the car. Somebody said, 'Ray,
you'd better git down. That boy in there's crazy. He's liable to
shoot you.' Ray acted like he didn't even hear him. He just kept
lookin at that beer joint. He put that bullhorn up to his lips and
said, 'This here is sheriff Ray Nolan. You come on out of there
and stop this foolishness before somebody gits hurt.' He put the
bullhorn down and waited.

"Well, that feller hollered somethin back at Ray that got
his dander up. I ain't gonna tell you what he said, but it must
have been perty bad, cause the folks that was there said that they
could see Ray's face turn blood red in the moonlight, and ever
muscle on his big body kind of shook. He hollered in the bullhorn, 'Alright now, they ain't no call to be talkin thataway.
Come on outta there now I ain't gonna tell ye again.'

"That feller in the beer joint fired a shot then, and everybody ducked down except Ray. He just stood there. The shot
went wide and shattered the red strobe light on top of his car.
Ray just kind of looked at it, and then he looked back at the
beer joint. 'This is yore last chance. If you don't throw that shotgun out the winder and come outta there, I'm gonna come in
there and git you. And if I have to come in there, you'll be sorry.
They won't be but one of us walkin out.'

"That feller hollered somethin else that don't bear re-
peatin, and Ray come out from behind his car. He started
walkin toward that beer joint. Everbody there was hollerin for
him to git down, but he just kept right on walkin. He didn't
have his gun drawn. He didn't even have his hand on it. The
boy in the beer joint fired again. The shot whizzed by Ray's
head and he didn't flinch. They say he didn't even blink. He just

kept right on walkin. Starin at that beer joint. Well, that must
have skeered that boy in the beer joint a sight bad, cause he
threw the shotgun out the winder and started hollerin about
how sorry he was and how he didn't know what he was doin.
Ray hollered back that it was too late for that. When he got up
to the door, he kicked it down and kind of lunged inside. The
folks outside heard the awfullest racket for about three minutes,
and they heard that boy a' cryin and screamin. They heard
chairs crashing and glass breakin. Finally, it got real quiet. Nobody knew what was gonna come outta that door. Everbody was
kind of holdin their breath. And then Ray came out, draggin
that bloody, cryin boy behind him by the collar of his shirt. He
put him in the squad car and told everbody to go on back
home. Everbody did. Nobody said a word to Ray."

"Well, then." I say. "Maybe you've got enough of Ray
Nolan's genes in you to whip that mule after all."

"Ray never did wear jeans." He says. "I don't much keer to
wear 'em myself. These here is a sight more comfortable. And a
sight more stylish too. I look right smart, don't I? Good enough
to go to town?"

"You look pretty as a picture."

"Just think, one day all of this will be yours." And he
laughs.

"I can't wait."

"Say, speakin of mules, did I ever tell you the story about
Pappy and the mule?"

"I don't believe so." But he has. Many times. Pappy Nolan
is a legend to him. To me. He was his grandfather on his daddy's
side. He and Mammy moved over to the Smoky community
from Greenbriar many years ago. Built a log cabin out of the
wilderness there. Built a farm out of the roots and the rocks.
Had one of the prettiest spreads in the county. Mammy loved
that place. Raised their children there. Their son Oath went off
to fight the Germans in WWI. Came back with malaria. Died in
that house. After they buried him they sold the place and
moved to Clinton. Mammy said she never wanted to live in that
house again.

"Pappy went out to the barn one day, and there come his mule out of the barn, and they was a stranger sittin on it. He says to this stranger, 'What are ye doin on my mule?' And the stranger says, 'This here is my mule.' And Pappy says, 'I don't believe it is. I got a piece of paper in there in the house that says its mine.' And the stranger pulls a sawed-off double-barreled shotgun out of his coat and says, 'This right here says this mule is mine.' And Pappy says, 'You'd better put that thing down, before you get hurt.' And the stranger says, 'You the only one that's gonna git hurt, old man.' Now, Pappy must have been about seventy, and what that stranger said to him then really got him riled. He started for that stranger, and the stranger pulled them hammers back. Pappy didn't even flinch, he just kept right on comin. That stranger let loose both barrels into Pappy's chest, and he went flyin backward. The stranger turned that mule around and started off, but before he knew it, Pappy was up and had hold of his leg, tryin to pull him off of it. The mule started rearin, and the stranger was tryin to keep it still and reload his shotgun, and shake Pappy off'n his leg. That mule was rearin and spinnin and kickin and strikin, and Pappy just kept on a'holdin on to that stranger's leg. The stranger hit Pappy a couple of good licks in the head with the barrels, and reared back to hit him again, but Pappy caught the end of it, and gave it a good yank and the stranger went flyin to the ground. Pappy calmed the mule down, chunked that shotgun over into the woods and started stompin that stranger. Pappy really had his dander up. It took two or three to pull him off of him. That stranger crawled off Pappy's farm. Ain't nobody heard from him since."

"What happened to Pappy?" I ask.

"Oh, he's alright. When the doctor came to see about him, he told him he'd have to give him something to knock him out so he could dig the buckshot out. Pappy said not to worry about that. The doctor said he didn't bleeve Pappy would be able to stand it. Pappy told him he was able to stand it when it went in, he reckoned he'd be able to stand it coming out. We come from good, stout stock, you know it, boy?"

"I sure do." I say.

I notice the shapes of two men walking alongside the road ahead of us. They are dark forms beneath the fog, and then my headlight beams bring them to life. They have an odd gait, a shuffle really, and it is not until we reach them that I realize the reason for it. It is Clemmie and George, and between them, they are carrying a porcelain kitchen sink.

"Why, there's Clemmie and George!" Papaw exclaims. "Let's stop and see 'em boys a minute."

Clemmie and George are not boys. They are in their sixties, but because they are lifelong bachelors, they will always be referred to as *boys*. They are a couple of town characters. Now, by *characters,* I mean that their personalities and mannerisms are such that they stand out in an ordinarily conformist society. Their minor eccentricities are hallowed by the community, and kept as treasures, boasted of to strangers as if heralding some natural wonder or landmark. Clemmie and George are brothers, and never seen apart from each other. Most of the time, they can be seen walking alongside the road, carrying some miscellaneous items gleaned from the county dumpsters. (Before the dumpsters were fenced off with chains and Constantine wire and guarded like Buckingham Palace.) Often, they can be seen sporting a nice velvet hat or a gold wristwatch or some other thing that someone has thrown away, and they are always quick to tell of where they found them. "Would ye bleeve somebody actually threw this away?" They will say, with the special pride affixed to the statement, a pride felt only by those who can see the beauty and practicality in the things that others have discarded.

We pull ahead of them, and park on the side of the road. They approach us with some measure of trepidation, not recognizing my truck. When they reach us, Papaw leans out of his window.

"What d'ye say thar, boys?"

They stop, and still holding the sink, nod their heads in recognition.

"How are you, June?" One of them asks. I can never tell them apart.

"I'm feelin a sight bad." Papaw says. "I got this here

rheumatiz in my shoulder 'at the cold aggervates somethin awful. I ain't got no money. Reagan's in the White House, and I think I'm comin down with a touch of the gout."

"You in perty bad shape." One of them says. "Ye wont me to shoot ye?"

"I might be better off."

"We ain't got no gun, nohow." The other says.

Papaw laughs. "Shore is cold, ain't it?"

"Yep." One of them answers.

"You know what Mark Twain said about the weather, don'tchee?"

Clemmie and George look at each other.

"He said 'at everbody complains about the weather, but nobody does nothin about it."

One of them says, "Wouldn't do no good to complain about it no ways, keen't do nothin about it."

"It takes all types of weather to keep the earth on its seasonal continuum." I say, over Papaw's shoulder, and the three of them cast bewildered glances at me.

"So, whur you boys headed?" Papaw asks.

"We totin' this here sink to town. We gonna see if Carl Ownby wonts to buy it."

"Boys, it's a good five mile to town. Tho 'at thing in the back of the truck and hop on in here whur it's warm. We'll give ye a ride."

Clemmie and George look at each other again, and then one of them says, "No thank ye June. We's in kind of a hurry."

Papaw laughs lightly and then says, "Alright. I wouldn't wont to be the one to slow a man down. Carry on!"

Clemmie and George both nod. Their hands have not left the sink during the entire discourse.

"We'll see ye!" Papaw shouts, throwing his hand out the window as we pull back out onto the road, leaving the two shapes of Clemmie and George to retreat back into their silent places in the fog.

"Em's a couple of good ole boys." Papaw says to me, after some silence.

Years later, I will see George again. I will not see him on the side of the road, but in a cold and silent nursing home. I will see him for the first time alone and sitting. He will be confined to a wheelchair, bearing his one remaining leg out before him.

I will walk over to him, stoop down so he can hear me, and say: "Hello. Are you Clemmie, or George?"

He will look at me, his eyelids squinting, pushing wrinkles around his eyes. He will say: "I'm George. Clemmie died."

"Oh." I will say, awkwardly. "I don't know if you remember me or not, but my name is Donnie Lamon. I am June Nolan's grandson. I used to see you and your brother walking alongside the road."

He will smile, rising in his chair a little. "Yep, me and Clemmie used to walk everwhur together. Never had no use fer a car, me and him."

We will stare at each other, and breathe the sanitized air between us for a minute, while white-clad ushers of misplaced histories push their forgotten cargoes about the day room of the home. And then George will start to cry.

"Keen't walk nowhur now." He will say, as tears as clear and as young as virgin dew drag tracks down his old cheeks, down the crevices and the valleys, rifts plowed by the wind and by time. "They took my leg." He will pull a wadded handkerchief from his pocket, fiddle with it for a moment with his rebellious fingers, drop it once, and then pick it up to wipe his nose. "Wouldn't make no difference nohow. Ain't got nobody to walk with now."

I will shift my feet uncomfortably, and before they wheel him away, he will say to me: "You'll remember me and Clemmie?"

And I will nod my head.

"I will remember you."

# V

*The fog lifts from its late slumber before us. The gray road, speckled with* pot-holes winding into the distance, calling us home, and the truck whines out happily beneath us, our magic carpet just inches above the pavement. Once in a while, we are awakened from our trance by the jostling of the truck over a hole in the road, which keeps us from drifting completely off. This is a metaphor for life, and I am just old enough to recognize it this time.

Papaw says, "You missed a pothole back there."

And I say, "Sorry. I'll try harder next time."

Beside us is endless green, folding upon itself and ascending to heights above us, then disappearing to the other side, to secret places where other stories live. Papaw is smoking again. Cold air is rushing in through his partially lowered window, stinging our skin softly in the warm cab. Even with its escape route in plain sight, the pungent smoke from his cigarette lingers in the truck, tickling my nostrils.

"Are you ever gonna quit smoking?" I ask, brushing the air with my hand.

"I'm gonna quit as soon as I finish this one." He says.

"Just imagine how much better you'd feel if you didn't smoke."

"Lookie here." He says, "All these scientists and doctors and politicians sayin 'at smokin is bad for ye. What do they know about it? I know people who've smoked all their lives and lived to be in their nineties. Why, ole George Burns smokes a cigar everday, and he says it's why he's lived as long as he has." He pauses. "Besides, somebody's got to keep these poor 'backer farmers in business. You know me, always lookin out fer the little man."

I laugh. He has dissuaded me from my righteous indignation again. Dissuaded me from all things serious again. He finishes his cigarette, and flicks it out the window. "You reckon yore ever gonna quit growin?"

This is a joke, for at sixteen, I am already six-foot-four. He says this because he knows I like to be recognized as a man. "I don't know." I say, laughing.

"Yore already bigger'n yore daddy. You reckon you could whip him?"

"I wouldn't want to try." I say.

In our culture, a man's worth as a man is always measured in comparison with his father. It all boils down to whether or not you are bigger and better than the one who raised you. And every father looks with pride at a son he has to look up to.

Once, when I was twelve years old, I found myself walking up Shield's View Road with my sister, just having gotten off the school bus. We approached our driveway and I noticed something strange about it. At the base of the concrete, where it joins with the road, there were words scratched crudely on the surface with a piece of brown slate rock. We used to use those same rocks to draw on concrete and asphalt because its chalky point would leave light brown traces of itself. A poor man's crayon, we used to call it. We would draw pictures, play tic-tac-toe, hop-scotch, or just simply doodle. There on our driveway, however, was not the remnants of some childish game. It was something much more sinister. Someone had written a disparaging remark about my sister. I will not say what was written, but it caused my sister to cry and made a rage swell in my chest such as I had never felt before. I knew from whence the words had come. There was a boy in my school, I will call him, Freddie. As of late, Freddie had taken a notion to become my enemy.

He was fifteen years old, and still in the eighth grade. He had a harshness about him, a hard, stony countenance, like he was a man but not yet grown. He had a rage behind his eyes that even scared some of the teachers, and the principal was afraid to touch him. He was not the brightest boy, and had been placed in the ward of the *Special Education* department of our school. I

never really knew the reason for his hatred of me. It could have been the fact that I was bigger than everyone else in the school, or perhaps because I was in the *Gifted* program. I never really spoke to him, nor he to me. One day, it was just like he woke up and decided that he hated me. He started by making snide remarks at any of my comments in class. Then, he went to calling me names, calling into question my lineage in less than propitious terms. Sometimes he would wait until I wasn't looking, and then pull my coat down from its hanger and leave it lying on the floor in the bathroom. He would pull my books out of my desk and scatter them all over the place. All of these things I abided, having the maturity to select the battles that I considered worth fighting for, but when he trespassed upon my property, and insulted the dignity of my sister, he had gone too far.

My sister was crying, and this broke my heart. She ran up our driveway, and I stayed behind, boiling in my rage. I resolved to punish Freddie with impunity. A couple of minutes later, my mother came running down the driveway, her eyes fierce and fixed upon the transgression. When she reached it, she looked down at it, looked up at me, looked again at the words, then at me and said, "I'm calling the police."

As it happened, we were close friends with one of the local police detectives. Detective Dale Teague was a powerhouse of a man, intimidating and endearing at the same time. He arrived in his police car, decked out in the ceremonial garb of his profession. It was the first time I had ever seen him in his official capacity. With his notepad in hand, he listened to my mother's hysterical lamentations, and asked the basic questions: "When did you first notice it? Have you seen anyone strange hanging around here lately? Have you any enemies?" Between sobs, my mother was able to answer all three negatively.

But I knew. I had an enemy, and he had declared war on me in no uncertain terms.

Dale offered his condolences to my mother, but told her that without an eyewitness, there was really nothing that he could do about it. After all, the Gatlinburg Police Department did not have a handwriting analyst on staff in those days. My

mother finally conceded to the futility of an investigation and told me to go up to the house and bring down a bucket of water to wash it off. She thanked Dale for his time and he apologized to her again. Then he turned to me, aside from my mother where only I could hear him. "Do you know who did this?"

I nodded. Then he said it. The one simple question that thrust my manhood upon me, a question which carried with it the weight of a thousand ancestors, the multitude of ghosts and ghosts of ghosts which make up my legacy: "Are you gonna take care of it?"

I looked at him, and then I looked at the invisible mantle of manhood cast at my feet. I took it, gird it about my waist and said, "Yes. I will."

And I did.

The next day at school, during recess, I made my move. The children were scattered about the playground like gypsy ants. I saw Freddie at the jungle gym. He was an intimidating sight: faded jeans, tight and hugging his muscular legs, a white t-shirt which looked painted upon his angular torso, sleeves rolled up with veins bulging on his biceps beneath them. He wore his hair slicked back, just like the villains in the old black and white movies, and he wore a scowl on his face. The only thing missing was a cigarette dangling from his lips. His short, stocky framed leaned against the wood logs of the jungle gym. I started for him, unafraid. He looked up just when I was almost on him. Then, he did a peculiar thing. In my many hours of strategy and planning of my attack, I had not counted on this. He ran. He darted around the jungle gym with the deftness of a squirrel. I had no idea he could run so fast. I had never seen him run before. He was not really into sports. Hanging around, standing at the jungle gym, intimidating people, those were his main pastimes. He ran like a bull. Head down, shoulders squared, feet pounding on the grass. I chased him around the jungle gym, my fingers were just short of reaching his greasy, black hair when he cut to the left, away from the gym. I stumbled, caught myself, and changed direction as well. Some other children saw me chasing him, but did not really pay attention at first, figuring

that it was just a game of tag or something. Then, someone must have seen the rage in my eyes, for I heard the childish herald of "Fight!" from somewhere, and then what seemed like the patter of a thousand tiny feet behind me. I was chasing Freddie, and half the school was chasing me to see the end of the thing. Through the swing sets we went, around the seesaw, back under the jungle gym, and then toward the softball field. He cut around the back corner of the school, and for a moment, was out of my sight. I rounded the corner, blind, and he caught me across the face with the business end of an orange traffic cone. The blow sent me reeling backward onto my backside. In a flash he was on me, his rough hands nailing my shoulders to the ground, his face inches from mine, sneering and sweating. His breath smelled like coffee and cigarettes. It really did. He put his left hand on my throat and started to squeeze. I could not breath. My rage started to turn into panic. I could hear the other children coming up now. I heard someone yell: "Hurry up! Freddie is whipping Donnie!"

Laughing, Freddie reared his right hand up, ready to let me have it, when I managed to push my chin under his hand, and then out of instinct, the need to survive, I opened my mouth and took in the tender flesh between his thumb and index finger. I could taste grassy soil as I sank my teeth sank down into his skin as hard as I could bite. Freddie screamed and jumped up into the air for a moment, just long enough for me to get my hands out from beneath him. I clasped both hands together and brought them over my head, then I brought them crashing down into his nose with all my might. The blow threw him off me. We were both up in a flash, circling each other, dancing, as it were, the dance of manhood. We lunged at each other. I managed to get him into a headlock and landed a couple of nice blows into his face before he squirmed out of my grasp. Quite a crowd had gathered around us, closing on our flanks, sealing off any means of escape. Freddie's slicked back hair had come loose and was sticking up insanely and was matted with dirt and grass. His face was red and swollen, and I hoped that mine did not look as bad. He swore and came at me again. I went to kick him

in the stomach, but he caught my leg. There I stood, with one leg held in the air by my enemy, and the other hopping, trying to keep balanced as he turned me around in circles. I heard a collective hush from the crowd, and then Freddie began to laugh. This conjured up fresh rage within me, and without thinking, I jumped up as high as I could on my free leg. I brought it swinging around and kicked Freddie square in the face. My leg swung all the way around and I landed on both feet safely, just like one of those Kung Fu experts on television. I surprised myself, and the other children watching. I heard several gasps and at least one cheer. Freddie was knocked almost for a loop, and landed in a crumpled heap on the ground. I came at him again, but he was crying, holding up his hand in protest. "I quit!" He sobbed, over and over again.

"Say you're sorry about what you wrote on my driveway!" I demanded.

"I'm sorry." He whispered.

"Say you're sorry for insulting my sister!"

"I'm sorry!"

Then, I walked over to him and knelt down beside him. He cringed, but I did not touch him. I put my mouth next to his ear, so only he could hear me, and whispered: "If you ever come on my property again, I will finish this."

Then I left him there. The crowd parted for me. No one said anything to me. I tasted something salty on my lips, put my fingers to my nose and noticed that it was bleeding. Everyone was looking at me as I walked to the bathroom, wiping my nose now and then, smearing the blood around on purpose, brandishing my badge of courage like a man.

# VI

*The city of Sevierville lies like an afterthought in the bosom of the* mountains, untouched for now, by the stampeding juggernaut of progress. Its neighbors, Gatlinburg and Pigeon Forge have grown into something else, a Mecca of commerce, but Sevierville has kept its sense of itself. It must have kept its head low when the shadow the Great Bird of Time passed over. It remains untainted. Its businesses are still largely family owned. The main road through town is still two lanes. The waitresses in the diners still remember what your favorite meal is. Most of the police officers are still known by their first names. The people still wave to each other. For no reason, just to wave. It will not remain this way for long. Even the ancient mountains cannot keep a secret forever. Soon, the world will stumble on it while stopping to re-lace its boots, or to chase a butterfly off the beaten path, and all of these things will be no more.

Simms's Barber Shop sits on Main Street in downtown Sevierville. Downtown Sevierville is the oldest, most sacred part of town. Not much has changed on Main Street in the last fifty years. There is still a Dime Store. The Joe Carr Building is still open. The Odd Shop is still peddling its wares. The old Post Office has not yet become a museum and Simms' Barbershop is full.

Simms's Barber Shop remains a testament to easier and happier times. Its great storefront window is clean and clear, and through it, we can see the congregation of Saturday customers and loafers, waiting patiently for their turn in the hallowed barber's chair, or just wasting time. Many are leafing uninterestedly through last year's sports magazines while listening to gossip and tall tales. Two old men have a checkerboard between them,

and they both stare intently at the red and black pieces scattered here and there across the board. Simms himself is busy and smiling, his white frock immaculately clean and fastened tightly at the waist. He is laughing, talking, clipping, listening and combing, both hands working adroitly, and the mouth and the ears, making his particular music, the accompaniment to the multitude of voices in the room.

Papaw says, "I reckon I ought to stop and get me a haircut. My hair's gettin pretty long."

I laugh. "You ain't hardly got enough hair left to cut."

"I know," He says, "but I like to take care of the hair I got left."

I look for an empty parking space, which through the week would be an easy task, but on Saturdays everyone comes to town. The spaces are few and far between. After circling the street a couple of times, Papaw finally makes me let him out at Simms's door and I continue my diligent search. I see a spot three blocks away. I park and walk to the barbershop.

Inside, the air is hot from the mass of men. I shake the cold off me and then locate Papaw sitting with his legs crossed, like a gentleman, between two farmers, clad in overalls and grease-smeared caps. I find myself an empty seat in the corner, next to the checker players. I sit down to listen. Barbershops are good places to talk, but they are even better places to listen. At Simms's place, only three subjects are deemed worthy of discussion: University of Tennessee football, fishing, and sicknesses.

A man sits in the barber's chair. His is about thirty years old. He is receiving the typical trim. Simms is working busily behind him, and the man has his eyes closed in bliss. Simms says to him in his high pitched, slow voice: "How's yore momma, Tommy?"

The man in the chair opens his eyes slightly. "She's doin a lot better, thank ye. "At doctor in Knoxville says he thinks he got all the cancer. She able to git around perty good now. Tha other day she come over to see tha grandkids."

"I'll bet she enjoyed that." Simms says, with sincerity.

"She shore did. It'uz all she talked about since."

"You wont me to leave the sideburns?"

"That'd be fine."

Simms finishes the trim. He pours some lotion into his hands, rubs them together and smooths it out down the back of the man's neck. Then he ceremoniously removes the barber's apron and towel. The man rises, almost hesitantly, as if awakened from a sweet dream, and gazes at Simms' work in the mirror. Satisfied, he turns and pays. As he is about to leave, Simms says, "Tell yore momma we'z all thinkin about her."

"I will." The man says, and leaves.

Beside me, one of the checker players says to the other: "Are you gonna move, or not?"

And the other replies: "A already moved five minutes ago."

"Oh. Whur did you move to?"

"I forgot."

Simms cleans off the chair with a whiskbroom, and then, turning to the congregation, says loudly, "Alright, who was next?"

One of the farmers seated next to Papaw rises from his place. "I reckon I was." He says, and removes his hat. His gray hair is matted down in the perpetual outline of one whose head is seldom without cover. I have often wondered why folks who always wear hats don't just get their hair trimmed around the hat, since that is the only part of their heads that anyone ever sees. He mounts the barber's chair slowly, relishing the moment in the spotlight. He places his hat on his knee and Simms covers him.

The trim is underway, and the farmer turns slightly to say, "When do ye reckon they are gonna ride Johnny Majors out on a rail?"

Simms laughs his high-pitched laugh. "Somebody shore needs to do somethin with him. He ain't doin much good whur he's at."

"You goin to tha game this evenin?"

"I guess I will. I already got tickets, and I hate for 'em to go to waste."

Simms closes his barbershop every Saturday at noon. He never misses a home game.

"Maybe you arta go down on the field and tell Majors to stand aside and let a man coach what knows what he's doin. You probably know more about that football team than he does." The farmer cackles loudly, and slaps his knee under the apron. A couple of other men join him in laughter.

Simms smiles. "I don't know. I might make a bigger mess of things than him."

Papaw is talking to another farmer. Their voices are mingled in together with the others. The checker players are arguing over whose move it is, and Simms and his customer go on and on lamenting over Tennessee football. The scissors clip through hair and in the air and it all blends together harmoniously, the sounds floating in the hot air of the shop, pushing my thoughts deeper and deeper into oblivion. I drift away to the melody of earnest voices and the steady clipping of stainless steel scissors. Before I know it, the lullaby has carried me off to sleep.

A dream comes to me in vague whispers, like fog rolling across the hillsides. It is of another time, when I was younger, in another barbershop long since forgotten by most. It was Hugh Ogle's place, nestled between metropolises of modern commerce. It sat in quiet modesty with its barber's pole turning like a lathe of time. Hugh's was the only barbershop in Gatlinburg at that time. The age of pre-fab, national salon franchises had already dawned. People were growing fond of being ushered through sanitary, scentless salons then. They liked the impersonal attendance, the quiet waiting rooms. But my father and I, we understood that there was an art to cutting hair. We knew that the cutting of hair was only a small part of the occupation. A skilled barber was a master conversationalist. His art was words. He had quick, deft fingers and a keen ear. He sculpted stories out of thin air. He drew stories out of your own mouth. Stories that you didn't even know that you knew. And he gave you a pretty decent haircut in the process.

Hugh Ogle was as masterful a sculptor as ever drew breath. It seemed like he had been working his art for a thousand years.

Though he rarely had a new customer, he managed to stay in business in the middle of downtown Gatlinburg by retaining a small cult of devoted followers, of whom, my father and I were members. Most of us went to Hugh's place every Saturday, whether we needed a haircut or not. In my father's mind, to go anyplace else would be akin to blasphemy. He would rather take a beating than be seen in a beauty salon.

My father and I walked up the deserted sidewalk toward Hugh's place one Saturday morning. The streets were empty. The t-shirt shops and junk stores had not yet opened. Most of the tourists were still sleeping away the remnants of yesterday's adventures. They knew not the significance of this day. Today was the day of my first professional haircut.

We walked together, my small legs trying to keep up with his stride, the words of the song, *Daddy, Don't You Walk So Fast*, which my mother had often sung to me, echoing softly in my head. The town was waking around us. Door locks were clicking open, shades drawing up, busy feet hurrying to their cars. Storefronts were slowly being decorated with tables and sidewalk sales. The sun, awakened by God, pushed the street awake with its own silent goading. Cars began to appear, and by the time we reached the intersection of our destination, the parkway was alive with carbureted life. Daddy stopped me at the crosswalk, and looked up and down the street. Then, he took my tiny hand in his burly, rough one. His hand, which had known wood and tools and toil all of its life, clasped the tender skin of my unblemished one. He looked down at me and said, "Whatever you do, don't let go of my hand."

"I won't." I said.

We started across the street when the coast was clear. Our feet had just stepped out onto the blacktop, when a car pulled out of a driveway and headed toward us. The driver was half-asleep, or putting on her make-up, or fiddling with the radio, or anything. She slammed on her brakes inches from us. Before she could hit her brakes, however, my father, like the Artful Dodger, clamped his sure hand around mine and stole me out of death's pocket like a gold wristwatch, pulling me into the air

and carrying me to the other side of the road by my hand. When we were safe on the other side, I looked up at him and said, "See, I told you I wouldn't let go."

"You did a good job." He said. Then, pointing at the twirling barber's pole on Hugh Ogle's door, "There it is."

I looked at the red and white pole, transfixed by the stripes, how they appeared from out of nowhere at the bottom, traveled up the white pole, and then disappeared into the top.

"Where do the stripes go?" I asked.

My father, knowing the fierceness of my curiosity, having known for some time that my inquisitions were sometimes out of the ordinary, told me that they go to Heaven.

Scratching my head, I asked, "How do they come back?"

"Let's go inside." He said, quickly, and ushered me through the door.

Hugh's door has a bell on it, and it rings when we open it, welcoming us. There is a small, dark hallway ahead of us, and we walk toward the dim light at the end of it. Along the walls are scores of pictures, plaques and mounted fish. Pictures of Gatlinburg before it became Gatlinburg, of men whose strong, silent stories are frozen in black and white, behind glass, trapped forever there between the panes, forgotten by all, but not by Hugh Ogle. And not by us, because we were there, and we looked. There are fishing awards, thank-you, commendations, a military award from somewhere, a city business license, and at the end, behind dirty and cracked glass, is Hugh Ogle's diploma from barber's school.

Inside the barbershop proper, I see old vinyl chairs lining the walls, and the chairs are filled with the slumped shapes of old men, and some younger men, whose postures have not yet conformed to the lethargy of age. The place smells of Old Spice, tobacco spit, hair oil, and old men. Some are talking to each other. Others are reading ancient magazines. They all stop their actions to watch our entrance. When they recognize us, they return to their activities. We have been accepted. Hugh Ogle is cutting hair, and he says to us in his calm, raspy voice, "Well, if it ain't Pete and Little Pete!"

My father smiles with pride. This is no exaggeration. True pride is easily recognizable. His is proud because I have been recognized as his son. I have been officially associated with him by his peers, who have bestowed upon me the mantle of transference. I am Little Pete to them, or The Next Pete. He sees this, and he is proud. It is a very gratifying feeling to know that you have given pride to someone else just by being born.

One of the old men sitting along the wall says, "That boy's gettin pretty big now, Pete. Yore gonna have to lay a cinder block on his head a'fore long, or he is gonna be bigger than you!"

"Yep." My father replies. "He's already growin so fast 'at we have to make two trips to the Wal-Mart every time we go. We buy him clothes and by the time we get home he's already outgrow'd 'em."

"I reckon he's about big enough for his first haircut." Hugh says.

"I guess so. His momma's been cuttin his hair 'til now. She tries hard, but she don't know how to do a man's haircut." Then, looking at me, he says, "Yore wontin a man's haircut, right?"

Smiling, and looking up, I say, "I shore am."

"Well, you boys grab you'unz a seat somewhur and I'll git to ye in a little while." Hugh says, returning to his work. The man in the barber's chair has not stirred through any of this. His eyes have been closed the entire time. I think that he is asleep.

We sit down. My father talks to the other men. They speak of the weather, politics, the economy, and a myriad of other things, which do not interest me. I turn my attention to a ten-year-old copy of *Field and Stream* lying on the seat next to me. There is a picture of a Rainbow Trout flailing above a clear stream on its front cover. A multicolored lure hangs from its mouth. The fishing line trails from the lure off the cover to invisible, joyous hands. One of the men sees me looking at it and asks me: "You like to fish do ye, boy?"

I look up at my father and he says, "Go on and answer him."

I nod my head.

"What kind of fishin do ye like to do?"

"Trout fishing." I say.

He laughs. "I didn't know there was any other kind.

Hugh wakes the man in the barber's chair, removes the apron, and suffers him to get up to let someone else have a turn.

"Who wuz next?" Hugh asks, sweeping hair from the seat and off onto the floor. An old man raises his hand slightly and says, "I bleeve I wuz, but I wont to give my turn to this boy here. It ain't everday a feller gits his first real haircut."

My father goads me onward, whispering into my ear, "Tell him 'thank you.' "

I do, and the old man nods slightly, smiling.

The barber's chair seems mammoth to me. It is a great, brown vinyl thing, with three levers just below the seat, like a dentist's chair or something. Somehow, it makes me think of some medieval torture device. Everything in the barbershop is brown it seems. The tile floor, the paneled walls, the wood ceiling, but this chair seems even browner than brown. Altogether, it is not a welcoming sight, but I have already risen and started walking toward it, and it is too late to turn back now. There is a silver step at the front. It is grated like a storm drain. Sticking up from that is a footrest. I know that it is a footrest because it is shaped like a shoe. It was probably originally intended for shoeshines, but not too many people in Gatlinburg have enough money to get their shoes shined. Not many people in Gatlinburg own a pair of shoes worth shining. I mount the step, and then start the arduous climb up into the seat. I am finally able to put one knee up on it, and after some effort, pull the rest of my small body into it. It seems to swallow me whole. The armrests are just scarcely below my chin and the back of the chair dwarfs my sitting body.

"We're gonna have to do somethin about this." Hugh says and shuffles over to the corner of the room. He returns a moment later with a small board, about eight inches wide and two feet long. He tells me to get up for a second, which I do, and then he lays the board across the two arms of the chair.

"Set down there." He says. "I bleeve that'll work."

It does. Hugh fastens a small napkin around my neck, and then ceremoniously drapes the apron over me. I glance at myself in the mirror. I am a tiny head sticking out of a bulbous pinstriped tent. Hugh gently tilts my head from side to side, and then forward, and then back. Inspecting it. "How do you wont it cut, Pete?"

"Just trim it up perty good." He says. "Like you do mine."

"Alright, then." And then Hugh goes to work, a black comb in one hand and his scissors in the other. Combing and clipping, tilting the head, side-to-side, combing and clipping. The scissors clip all the time, whether they are cutting hair or just dancing in the air behind my head. It is a very soothing sound, the clean snipping of well oiled, sharpened blades. He works quickly, cutting and talking, telling stories. And I listen to the cutting and the telling, the ancient symphony of contented labor.

"They wuz these two old folks," Hugh says, to anyone who is listening, "who went to bed one night. The old man got up out of bed and said, 'I bleeve I'll go down and fix me a bowl of ice cream, you wont one?' The old woman said, 'That sounds perty good. Bring me one up, but pour a little chocolate on mine.' The old man told her that he would. Just as he wuz about to go out tha bedroom door, the old woman said to him, 'You better write it down. You'll forget.' The old man looked at her, 'Woman, I don't need to write it down. I ain't that old yit. Is 'at all you wont on it?' The old woman thought for a moment, and then said, 'No, sprinkle me some nuts on tha chocolate, but you'd better write it down.' The old man flung the door open. 'I don't need to write it down. I won't forget. What else you wont?' The old woman told him to put some Cool-Whip on it, but to write it down so he wouldn't forget. The old man stormed through the door. 'I won't forget, for goodness sakes!' Then he slammed the door behind him. The old woman sat in the bed and waited for her ice cream. Fifteen minutes passed, and she could hear pots and pans bangin around downstairs, the old man swearing in the darkness, water running. Thirty more

minutes passed and the old woman wuz startin to worry. Finally, the old man came back into the bedroom, carryin two plates of scrambled eggs and toast. The old woman rolled her eyes. 'See,' she said, 'I tole you to write it down. You done went and forgot my bacon.'"

Everyone in the room laughs at Hugh's joke. Somebody says, "Tha'z a good 'un!"

He works on, and I am beginning to feel hypnotized by the music that he is making. It is like being in a waking dream, my extremities being tickled slightly underneath the apron by invisible fingers, goading me into submission, my head drifting off on a cloud of incoherent thoughts. Whispers of dreams not yet dreamed. I can hardly feel the light sweeping of the apron as it is removed, and I can barely hear Hugh say, "Alright, Little Pete. That's it." I look at myself in the mirror. My hair looks good, as far as I am concerned, which is not very far.

"What do ye think?" Hugh says, dropping the comb into a great jar of neon blue liquid. "Z'at suit you all right?"

"It looks alright to me."

"How 'bout it, Pete?" Hugh says, seeking the final authority from the one who will be paying for it.

"He looks like a young man, now." My father says, smiling. He rises and pulls out his billfold. He leafs through it for a moment, and finally brings out three dollars. He hands them to me as Hugh releases me from the chair. "Give this to Hugh," he says, "and tell him thank you."

I do, and then we say our short goodbyes to the other customers. As we start toward the door, one of them says, "He's a right smart lookin boy thar, Pete."

My father turns around. "I know, he takes after his momma."

We leave the sounds of their laughter behind us as we exit the shop and walk out into the busy Saturday morning street, leaving Hugh Ogle's time behind us, where it will steadily slow over the years, like an old grandfather clock winding down, the momentum of its great pendulum dying a little a decade at a time. Eventually, time will stop for Hugh's place altogether.

Hugh will die and his place will sit empty for a year or two. The barber's pole will remain, unmoving, and his old customers, those who are still alive, will pass it and wonder when the old thing will spin again. I will wonder if old barbers go to Heaven when they die, like the stripes on the pole. Or if they just appear out of nowhere for awhile, and then disappear at the top. I will wonder if they ever come back again. I will wait, and then one day, the pole will be gone.

"You ready to go, John?"

I open my eyes in Simms' Barber Shop, stirred out of my slumber. Papaw is looking down at me, standing above me.

"Huh?" I ask groggily.

"Let's go John, er . . . Paul . . . er, Kip . . . what is yore name, anyway?" Sometimes he gets the names of his children and grandchildren confused.

"It's Little Pete." I say, rising.

We leave Simms' Place. Before papaw can put his hat back on his head, I look at him and say, "I can't even tell that you've had a haircut."

"That's the mark of a good haircut." He says, returning his old, wrinkled cap to his head, then smoothing out the bill like some gentleman with a fancy derby. He taps his walking stick on the sidewalk like Fred Astaire. And I stand there, loving him. We walk toward the truck, and he says, "I reckon we arta run up to tha courthouse and see who's thar."

I agree.

He scratches his head with the tip of his stick. "We might arta go check on that lawnmower in the back of yore truck first. Somebody might decide to steal 'at fine machine."

"What if somebody has stolen it?" I ask, with a wry grin. "What will we do?"

"Well, I got my trusty stick here. You can chase 'em down and hold 'em till I git thar."

The old lawnmower is still safe where we left it. We start walking toward the courthouse.

On Main Street we meet the shuffling, stooped over, blue-suited figure of Joe Carr. Joe is a bona fide businessman. I know

it's him, because he is smiling Joe Carr's smile. Joe is always smiling.

"Well, hidey Joe!" Papaw says, tipping his cap. "Don't you look right smart today!"

Joe's smile widens. "June Nolan." He says, "They lettin you come to town now?"

Papaw laughs. "I git out ever now and again, when they ain't lookin."

"That's good. I'za tellin somebody tha other day how I ain't seen June Nolan in a coon's age."

Papaw leans on his walking stick. "I'm surprised to see you, Joe. I figured you'd be off somewhur countin your money."

"I've got a feller paid ta count it fer me." Joe says. "When he's done, I'll send him over to yore place to count yor'n."

Papaw laughs. "That'd be mighty short work."

"Aaw June, we all know yore the richest man in Gatlinburg."

"Huh?" Papaw says, "Joe, if I had yore money, I'd tho minc away."

They go on and on like this for several minutes. Arguing over who had the most money. Both of them knowing the truth. I stand by, watching, and then Joe sees me for the first time.

"Who's this ye got here with ye?" Joe asks, reaching up to pat me on the head.

"Papaw's eyes dart as if he doesn't know what Joe is talking about, and then he remembers that I am with him. "Oh, this here is my grandson, Donnie. He's Stella's boy."

Joe grins widely, nodding his head up and down. "Well, Lord have mercy!" He pokes me in the ribs. "I ain't seen you since you was knee-high to a grasshopper!"

"He's grow'd up to be tall and handsome, just like his papaw."

"I used to be tall and handsome, too." Joe says, poking me in the ribs again. "But that was back before I got married."

They both laugh and talk some more, and then Papaw decides to move on. "Well, we'll see ye, Joe. We's goin up her ta

that courthouse and then goin ta see a man in Newport about a tractor."

"Wait a minute, here." Joe says, reaching his hand into his pocket. He digs around for a while and then produces a shiny quarter. He gives it to me. "Here, boy." He says. "Take ye some carryin around money."

Joe Carr has been giving me quarters since I was six years old.

He says goodbye, and shuffles down Main Street. He is but a few feet away, when he turns and calls out: "You watch him, boy! Don't let him get in no trouble!"

I nod, and Joe waves wildly, shuffling, shaking his head, laughing and laughing and laughing, talking to himself, to wherever it is that he is going.

We start again for the courthouse, and Papaw says, with admiration, " 'At Joe Carr . . . he ain't got no more sense than a sack 'a hair, and he's got more money'n he knows what to do with."

# VII

*The courthouse is a mammoth thing, for such a small town. It stands* in the middle of town, like the hub of a great wagon wheel. Its peak stands out beneath the eldritch mountains, which surround it. It is spread out to about two city blocks, but it culminates into its steeple, the most prominent feature in the city. Any place you need to get to, can be found in relation to the courthouse.

The entrance to the building is a series of steps, a half circle, with stairs on each side, *the open arms of the South,* they used to call them, bounded on each side by red bricks mortared and laid by hands long laid to rest. We pass a few people on our way up. A couple, bearing their love between them on a signed parchment of official government script, their eyes washed blind by a litany of dreams. They will find a preacher somewhere, and a church. They will utter their sacred oaths, kiss and walk together into the unknown. Unknown, only to them, for their eyes have been washed blind by love. All others see their fates. They will get in their old car, which will crank on the third try, and head for Pigeon Forge. The motel rooms will be cheap this time of year, and they will pay in advance for two nights. They have a little money the girl's father gave them. The girl's father got the money from a pawnshop. They will consecrate their love for two nights. Later, the boy will find a job washing dishes in some restaurant, he will come home excited, saying that in a few years, he could work his way up to cook. The girl will wait tables, or clean motel rooms. They will buy themselves a brand new mobile home, secure a nice spot in a trailer park to rest their dreams, and settle into the life before them. Because they are lucky, he will not drink, and they will be spared the

bruises and the curses, the nights in jail and the uncomfortable stares from their neighbors. He will be a cook, they will have two car payments, because if they can't buy a house, they might as well have a couple of nice cars to ride around in. They will have two or three children, who will go to school, grow up, and one day mount the courthouse steps, find a preacher, and have two nights of bliss in Pigeon Forge, secured by a high interest loan secured from Check into Cash by the boy. The original couple, now old, will look on with a bitter pride. Their eyes are no longer washed blind. But once in a while, you will hear them talking about their two nights in Pigeon Forge, where they lived out their love in a clean room, with fresh towels and a television set that got thirteen channels. Thirteen channels.

Inside the courthouse, the air is washed with artificial heat, and the floors are shiny. The place is all but deserted, for few offices are open on Saturdays. Our feet resound in the silence of the great hall. We pass the various windows, most of which front drawn plastic curtains, with a little sign reading, "Will open at 9:00 A.M. on Monday." We are heading for the main lobby, where a group of Saturday regulars is congregated on two benches.

They are old men, mostly clad in overalls. A few are wearing ragged suits, the kind one might find at the Salvation Army. Crumpled hats cover their heads, the brimmed kind, with the little velvet rings around the top. They are talking and laughing, and fishing things out of their pockets. They are from farms and little houses all over the county. They come to the courthouse on Saturdays to catch up on gossip, and to trade knives. They are the knife traders, and the keepers of the sacred lore. You can find out anything you need to know from them. Who is getting married, who is getting divorced, who died, who is sick, what to plant next year, when to plant it, how the elections will go, who went to jail, why they went, when the end of the world will occur.

We stand before them, these seers and hearers of things. They grant us access to their world. One welcomes us with the familiar nodding of the head and a slight winking of the eye. There is no room for us to sit, and we would not sit anyway, not

unless we were invited to. These were men whose stature in the town has so long been established, that it would be an extreme breach of etiquette to just sit down as if we were one of them.

"Hidey, fellers." Papaw says, tipping his hat.

They nod in unison. One old man has a great wad of tobacco resting in his right cheek, and he switches it to the other side of his mouth with the adroitness of a squirrel. He leans over and spits into a plastic cup sitting between his legs. He does this without looking at the cup and to my amazement, he does not spill a drop. "How you doin,' June?" he says, wiping his mouth with the corner of his hand.

"If I'z doin' any better, I'd need two of me jest to keep up with myself." Papaw says, and there is some light laughter from some of the men.

Another fellow is shaving slivers of wood from a stick with his pocketknife. The pieces float down into a crumpled paper sack at his feet. He pushes the brim of his hat up with his knife and says, "What you two boys up to?"

"We ain't up to much. We goin' to Newport."

The tobacco chewer says, "Whose 'is boy ye got here with ye?"

Papaw smiles, "Oh, this here is. . . . is, um . . ." he clears his throat and looks at me, "what is yore name, anyway."

I tell him, again.

"This is Stella's boy." Papaw says, laying his great hand upon my shoulder, "I got so many young'uns and grandkids 'at I keen't hardly keep 'em all straight."

Another man is sleeping with his chin pressed against his chest. At least, I think that he is sleeping, but he abruptly raises his head and says, "I keen't bleeve Stella's already got a boy this big."

"Yep." Papaw says, smiling proudly, "She's got another little girl, too."

" 'At's a right smart lookin' boy." The whittler says. Then, looking at me, "You a trader, like yore papaw?"

"I try." I say, "but I ain't hardly as good as he is."

I have seen these men off and on my entire life. I

remember them all, but the recollection of my face only comes to them in bits and pieces. I was one of the many children who came here with fathers and grandfathers. Seeking to see the seers. Seeking to hear what they have seen, and sometimes, to see what they have seen.

I was fortunate to have seen it as a child, coming here to the Courthouse on Saturdays, my mind swimming in the endless optimism of one whose blinders have not yet been put in place, one whose hands have not yet been lashed to the plow. I heard their tales, and saw the images in my mind. I saw the stills, and the supped up hotrods, their back ends almost dragging the ground, loaded down with bootleg whiskey, blazing a trail of outlaw dust along country roads, radios blaring out old country music: Hank Williams, Bill Monroe, Johnny Cash, Porter Wagner and the like. I could see the lazy eyed driver, somebody's cousin, one hand perched atop the steering wheel, and the other running a comb through slicked black hair, a cigarette dangling like a hanged man from his lips. Driving at break-neck speeds, he sits leaning in the seat, as if he were out for a Sunday drive. They would tell it, and I would see it, like a movie in my mind. The sirens in the distance, the flashing strobes atop the police cars washing the wall of trees with blue light, down into a holler where the sun doesn't even shine at noon. Down they went, chasing the bootlegger, their own powerhouse V-8's growling hungrily, like hound dogs after a coon. The bootlegger glances in the mirror at them, but he is not worried, nothing worries him, for he is young and invincible. He pulls his youth about him like a magical cloak, and eases his foot down on the accelerator, pushing it all the way to the floor, and through it, down into the block itself, and his hotrod shudders with excitement, doing what it was born to do, as he is. Along ridges and through tree tunnels, the lightning quick caravan speeds, up mountains and across narrow bridges. The bootlegger comes up on a sharp curve, he lets up on the accelerator going in, and then just at the right time he floors it again, his car reeling to the edge of the precipice, flirting with it, taunting it, and then the wheels are pulled by gravity back to the other side, and down the strait he

goes, his speedometer topping out at 100 m.p.h. He glances in his mirror, the police are still behind him. They have had as much practice at this as he has. He knows he can't shake them, and he can't pick up any more speed with this weight on, so he flicks his cigarette out the window, and flips a switch just beneath the radio, emptying out one of the whiskey tanks. The clear liquid splashes out on the road behind him, little wisps of steam rising from it. His car lurches forward, it's conscription lightened, it gives him more speed, and he starts to pull away from his pursuers. Then like a rifle report the front tire explodes and the car weaves back and forth across the road. He throws both hands to the steering wheel, and watches his youth disappear decades at a time. The car runs off into a ditch to the right, bobbles back and forth in it, and then jumps back out. It lands hard on the road, striking up sparks with its rear bumper, as its rear is still overloaded. It starts for the edge of the ridge, he tries to right it, but it is too late. He and his car go down the side of the bluff, leaving a trail of burning liquor behind them. The police cars pull up to the spot where the flames fall down off the road. They watch the burning trail and the consumed car that it leads to, shaking their heads, as blue lights spread their cold fingers across their faces. Down at the bottom of the holler, car and driver lay together, burnt beyond redemption, forever fused together in the darkness of their spent infinity.

I see a ragged family, huddled in the sputtering light of a dying campfire. Their bodies are thin and bony, and their eyes sunk deep into rigid sockets in their faces. They are clothed through the benevolence of some unmanned dumpster, wrapping themselves in the rags that others have thrown away, staving off the cold however they can. Two empty cans of pork and beans lay on the ground next to the fire, and the four of them look at them wistfully, remembering the Sunday School story of Elisha and the Widow, and the jar that never emptied. They are people of faith, as are most people who have nothing left to call their own, but none of them are brave enough to check the cans, none of them want the disappointment. The two children sit next to the mother. They are playing with sticks and

trying to forget how hungry they are. The mother sits wrapped in a dirty shawl, her belly aching from hunger, looking longingly at the children, hopelessly at them, she can look at nothing else. She can see nothing else but the slow death of her children. The father is an empty shell, his manhood stripped from him by forces he has never seen. Forcing him to pull the blame deep inside of himself, where only he can see it, and hate it with a passion reserved only for the most deplorable, the most hideous of creatures on the earth: A man who cannot provide for his family. They sit around the campfire until it dies, and the night comes over them like a burial shroud.

I see floods and fires, 10 lb. basses and 12-point bucks. I see tobacco stalks fatter and heavier than any ever grown before. I see tent revivals and river baptisms, covered wagons and Indian wars. I see hound dogs and pocketknives, 4,000 lb. bulls and 20 hands-tall horses. I see weddings and funerals and wakes and babies. I see it all. I see everything they tell me.

And I see the huddled masses of olive drab bodies, pulling themselves closer to each other without moving, willing themselves closer together as cannons rock the earth like some giant treading upon the ground. The relentless pounding of giant feet, stepping carelessly upon and crushing worlds too small for the giant to see. They huddle in their silent masses, afraid to open their eyes, afraid to see their own selves laid waste. They dream of home. They place their homes safely in their dreams where no giant's feet or falling shrapnel or sniper's bullet can harm them. They go to those dreams whenever they can, where their worlds are, their wives praying at the altar of some small country church, their children making little American flags with their names on them in classrooms, mommas and daddies clutching tarnished photographs of them, running their fingers over the flat faces, trying to pull them out of the pictures. I hear their silent prayers, offered up through the smoke and the haze of war, wafting up through the chaos like incense and into the sky, far above the planes and the falling bombs, where the air is still and silent. They do not pray for victory, not in so many words. They pray to go home. To see the faces, which have painted

their dreams over the harsh years, to touch the untarnished ground, to breathe unvanquished air. They want to go home, and some will. Some will come home and live, and tell stories to young boys in courthouse lobbies.

"What kind of knife are ye carryin'?" One of the old men asks me.

I push my hand into my pocket, navigate through a battlefield of loose change and pocket lint, and pull out my pocketknife, something no southern man would ever find himself without. It is an Old Timer, with three blades. The blades are black mostly, but shiny silver along their edges, as I learned how to put an edge on a knife shortly after I learned how to walk. I hand the knife over to him for his inspection and verdict. He eyes it suspiciously, turning it over and over in his hands, feeling the weight of it against his palm. He works each blade back and forth. He listens to it. The knife speaks to him, tells him its story.

He lays my knife on his knee and produces his own knife, a worn and tarnished one-bladed Barlow. He hands it to me. I look at it, try to read it, try to hear it, but I cannot.

"What do ye say?" He asks, hopefully.

"That'll do." I say, and place the knife in my pocket.

No one comes to these seers without bringing something to trade, just like when the Indians used to go see a Medicine Man. I have been doing it since I was a child, sometimes trading for the same knife four or five times. But I have always liked to do it. Especially when I was very young, when I would always leave the courthouse feeling like one of their peers. Feeling like a man.

We talk some more, but mostly, we listen. And then we leave their smiling contended faces behind us and head for Newport.

Years later, I will visit the courthouse again, and go to the lobby where I saw so much. I will find the benches gone, and the space littered with milling people, going here and there hurriedly, hearing and seeing nothing. I will go to the spot where they sat, as the frenzied mob thrashes by me. There will be a

sign hung there on the wall, just above their place. It will be an
official looking sign, professionally done and sanitary in it au-
thenticity. It will say, NO LOITERING. I will read it and know
that this is what the world has become: A world moving so fast
that it has little time or room for loitering. A world with no time
for the past, holding it as irrelevant, relegating it to libraries and
archives, no time for living archives, for seers and sayers, but for
concrete walls and hallways and quiet filing cabinets. A world
with no time for old men who like to trade knives and tell stories. A world with no time to make a child's day.

# VIII

*Back down Main Street, onto the Parkway, we pass Atchley's* Funeral Home. There are a lot of cars there. A funeral is in progress. There are always a lot of cars at the funerals around here. Everyone knows everyone. Nobody wants to be the one who didn't come, the one who didn't sign the little book, the one who didn't bring flowers or food.

"Wonder who died?" Papaw says, almost to himself. No one can pass a funeral without asking this.

"Why do you want to know?"

"I just wanted to make sure it wasn't me." He answers, lighting another smoke.

We drive up the Parkway, and then on to Old Newport Highway. We stop at a store. The name on the sign says, McCarter's, but for some reason, Papaw always calls it, The Commodore's Place. We pull in and park in front of the store. It is midmorning now, and there are still a few late risers parked alongside us, their owners no doubt inside, checking to see if the breakfast grill has already been shut down.

Papaw turns to me, "You wont anything from in here?"

My stomach is not empty, but it is not full either. It is non-committed. I tell him that I would like a Snickers Bar and a Mountain Dew.

"A Snickers Bar and a Mountain Dew." He repeats, exiting the truck. "Alright, then."

A sports car pulls up beside me. It is a blue Camaro, with chrome mag wheels and a partially tinted front and rear wind-shield. The tint is bubbling up and tearing loose on the rear, like a leprous, shadowy curtain. The windows are free of tint, and through them I can see the forms of two giggling, teenage girls.

The driver gets out. She is my age, maybe a little older, with a *Member's Only* jacket on and tight, faded jeans. Her hair is long and curly and hangs in thick, blonde bunches. She turns and looks at me. She smiles, her pale face gleaming in the cold air. I try to return her smile. I try to do what I am supposed to do, but I feel awkward and glance down at my motionless hands instead. The other girl rolls down her window, lights a cigarette with her right hand, takes a deep draw from it, and then hangs it out the window with the ease and nonchalance of a seasoned smoker. She notices me, and stares for a second. I watch her watching me out of the corner of my eye. I have seen her before I think, somewhere, at school, at some church. Maybe I saw her at Wal-Mart, but I can't place her name. She is very pretty, not beautiful, but pretty. And I have always thought pretty was much better, anyway. She has long, dark hair. It is straight and hangs down over her shoulders and chest. It is parted in the middle, and reveals a round, rosy face, big brown eyes and full lips. She sees me trying not to see her, and then she smiles. I don't know if she is smiling because she is flattered, or because she thinks I am an idiot. I am not the most perceptive person at such things. I feel awkward and self-conscious, not knowing whether to fully look at her, or to avert my eyes altogether. She is so pretty, and seems to be genuinely interested in me, but I am torn by indecision. Sometimes I wish that I could somehow be with a girl without actually having to be with her. To talk to her without actually having to talk to her. Sometimes I just wish they could read my mind. It would be a lot easier. A cloud's shadow passes over us, darkening the parking lot, and I decide to give it a try. She is still looking at me, and still smiling, and I turn my head to face her, painfully aware of my negligence in getting ready this morning. I hadn't even brushed my teeth. We look at each other for a moment, she smiling and I smiling without opening my mouth. She makes a motion with her other hand for me to roll down my window, and my heart stops. It had taken all of the fortitude in my soul just to look at her and smile, could I really be expected to talk to her? I make like I don't understand what she is trying to say, and she mouths the words, "Roll down your window." Then she winks at

me. I glance quickly at my slipshod appearance in the mirror. There is nothing I can do about it now. I screw my courage to the sticking post. My trembling finger reaches for the window button, and lunging blindly into the void, I roll down the window. The door panel swallows up the glass and I hear the passenger door of my truck open. Papaw is standing there, handing a small paper sack to me. He starts to get in, then stops and says, loudly, as he never worries who can hear him: "Hold on a minute, I forgot to get some suppositories for my hind end."

The girl starts to laugh. It is a cruel laugh. Not as I would laugh at him saying something unpropitious. She is laughing *at* him, and not with him, or for him, as I do. I cannot tolerate this. I look at her laughing there in the car, her cigarette hanging just outside the door. Her friend returns to the car, and the two whisper for a moment, looking occasionally in my direction. I roll up my window, hating them for their ugliness.

I look down at the paper sack on the seat next to me. I open it, and find two glass bottles of Royal Crown soda and two vanilla Moon Pies. No Mountain Dew or Snickers bar. I take one of each and then Papaw returns. I look at him.

"Is 'at not what you wonted?" He asks, digging into the sack.

I smile. "Yeah, it is. Did you get your medicine?"

He patted his shirt pocket to assure me that he had. I got Gerald some smokin, too. I thought he's gonna have a spell this mornin."

On we go, passing fields of rolling green and dead, aching trees, their bare limbs stretched to the heavens as if perpetually frozen in the act of beseeching God. There are crops of mobile homes planted along the highway, coming up and out of the ground in sporadic rows. Some are old and uneven looking, their underpinning loose and scattered underneath, weeds pushing their greedy fingers up around the bottoms of the homes, as if holding them aloft. Warped screen doors hang from the doorways, their black screens mashed and torn. The manufactured vinyl siding, sadly made to look like wood, is dented and stained with ancient, unknown stains. Their front porches are

stacks of gray cinder blocks, leaning lazily on top of each other. But these are not the saddest homes along the road. The saddest are the new mobile homes, resting beside the older ones in brackish glory, blind to their inevitable outcomes: Their brother homes dying about them. The windows are curtained and clean. Their porches are professionally made. They are landscaped and clean. For now.

We pass these things, and I think on these things, and Papaw thinks his own silent thoughts in the seat next to me. I glance at him, and he seems pensive, an urgency in his eyes, as if his mind is reaching into a gopher hole, its fingers struggling in the nothingness, trying to pull something out. After a few moments, I see a glimmer in his eyes, and then his mouth works its magic: There was this one time, when Kippy was young, about fifteen years old and just learning to drive, when he and papaw were off on some errand, driving to Knoxville, or some such thing. They spied a pizza restaurant on the side of the road. Neither of them had ever heard of or seen a pizza before, so they decided to pull over and give it a try. They parked their old car in the parking lot and ambled inside. They walked up to the counter and were greeted by a wide-toothed, smiling teenage girl. Papaw gave Kippy some money, told him to order, and then went to find the restroom. Kippy, bashful and grinning, promptly told the girl that he would like a pizza, to go.

"What size do you wont?" The girl asked.

"I reckon we'll need us a big one." Kippy replied, shuffling his feet.

"Large?"

"That'd be alright."

The girl punched some keys into the cash register, and then asked Kippy what he would like on the pizza. He didn't know what ordinarily came on a pizza, but he didn't want to seem ignorant in the presence of this aproned beauty, so he just said, "Everything."

"Pepperoni?" The girl asked, making sure.

Kippy nodded his head, sheepishly.

"Sausage."

"Yep."

"Onions?"

"Uh huh."

"Black olives?"

"Yeah."

"Mushrooms?"

"Yep."

"Jalapenos?"

"Uh huh."

"Anchovies?"

"Sure."

The girl rang up the sale and Kippy paid her. He got the pizza and she gave him another quick smile as he took it out to the car to wait for Papaw to come out. A few minutes later, they were driving down the road, Kippy at the wheel, Papaw trying to figure out how to open the pizza box. When he finally got it opened, he saw ten perfect slices of pizza, loaded down with everything. He pulled off a slice and handed it to Kippy, then he took one for himself. They each took a bite, and then promptly threw the entire thing out the window. It was the nastiest tasting thing they had ever put in their mouths. Papaw has not eaten a pizza since.

Then there was another time, when the family lived over on Grassy Branch: They had this old hound dog, which was about the dumbest thing God ever stretched a patch of skin over. It was hardheaded, and papaw often said that it must have been a Democrat. It was a coon dog but it would not hunt. It would loll around the front yard all day long. It was sluggish and panted at every step. It spent most of its days lying in the shade. One morning, the family was awakened by the awfullest sound they had ever heard. It was a frantic barking, somewhat muffled and panicked. They went out onto the porch to see this old dog loping all over the yard, dragging his head on the ground and pawing at his mouth.

"Reckon what's got into that dog?" Someone wondered.

"Don't know." Said someone else. "I bleeve he's havin a spell, or somethin."

A closer inspection revealed that the dog had somehow wedged a brick long ways in his mouth. He couldn't close it, nor could he open it any further to let the brick fall out. The poor dog was drooling uncontrollably, and whining pathetically.

"Go bring me a hammer." Papaw said, to one of the kids.

"You ain't gonna kill it, are ye?" One of the children cried.

"No, I ain't gonna kill it."

A few minutes later, two of the boys were sitting on the dog, holding its head still, and Papaw was poised over the trio with the hammer in hand, ready to strike. The dog struggled and whined beneath the two boys. When he saw his opportunity, he swung the hammer hard, and knocked the brick out of the dog's mouth. It fell into two brown pieces on the ground, along with two front teeth. That dog never was the same after that.

Down the road a piece and a car approaches us. It is an old beat-up, late model Chevy Sedan. Its front end is tilted down on the right, because the front wheel is a size bigger than the other three. The hood and roof are splotched with auburn rust, like wounds on the breastplates of a slain warrior. There is a large shattered spot on the windshield. Cracks run like spider legs from the top corner to the bottom. The driver's side mirror dangles from the door, held in place by a single, stubborn wire. The car is trailed by a large billow of white smoke rushing out of its tailpipe and sending its banner up into the air. When it passes us, I glance at the driver. His face is pressed almost against the glass of the windshield, trying to peer out through the cracks as he drives. I laugh and say, "What a sight!"

Papaw is stern as he glances at me. There is a look of deliberation and quiet sadness on his face. He says, "Don't never laugh at a pore man's car. At least he come by it honest."

I will remember this, some years later, when I will find myself driving down another road. I will be driving an old Chevrolet pick up. It will be dented here and there, bearing its bruises meekly on its white body. There will be a mashed-in place on the front fender, making it appear tilted. It will smoke intolerably, and the passenger side door will be tied shut with an old fishing stringer. In this truck, I will pull up to a stoplight. There

will be a giant brand-new SUV to my right, with the driver's side window down, and a young, tanned arm hanging out of it. I will glance through the window and see a young face, smiling, mouthing the incoherent words of the thumping music, which will emanate from somewhere deep inside the bowels of the vehicle. He will glance over at me and my truck. He will see its disheveled state. He will take particular note of my passenger's side door, where it will be jutting out about two inches from the edge of the frame, held in place by the florescent fishing string.

I will watch him laugh and shake his head in disgust. I will watch him drive away in the vehicle his mother and father bought for him. But I will not be angry, or embarrassed. I will know that he doesn't know not to laugh at a poor man's car.

I will know that he doesn't know any better.

And I will drive on when the light changes.

# IX

*We cut across Crossover Road, aptly named because it serves as a* crossover point between Old Newport Highway and Newport Highway proper. Crossover Road is mostly lined by open, rolling fields, but it is dotted here and there with small farm-houses. Some would say the area is not developed yet. One feels a kind of nervous apprehension from the land, as if it knows that its doom is eminent. It seems to cringe at the shadows of the greedy fingers, which are poised invisibly over it. The raven-ous clattering of bulldozer teeth, the hiss of chainsaw blades and the shuffling of documents can almost be heard above the serene silence of the land. Soon, the hills will be flattened, and the wild grass torn asunder. The small houses will be demol-ished and the refuse hauled away to the landfill, or burnt and plowed into the ground for the new grass, the ashes of former dreams to commune with the ground and lay in silence beneath the pillars of Development.

But for now, the houses remain, and the green fields and the little road that cuts through it all. There is one house in par-ticular which catches our attention. It is really a shell of a house, its bowels burnt out several years ago. It is a little, two-bedroom block house, with a widely pitched roof and a leaning carport. Every time we pass this house, Papaw tells me the story. I must have heard it a hundred times, but I can always hear it again. Soon, there might be no one left to tell it. *Gather ye rosebuds while ye may,* and hear stories while they are told.

There was an old couple that used to live in the house. They were in their eighties, and they lived contentedly in the poverty ascribed to them from their birth. They owned several acres of prime farmland around the house, and once had hopes

of it thriving. In the old man's youth, he had made a decent living raising tobacco. He schooled his children in the art, told them everything they needed to know to take it over. But the children grew, and their eyes were turned away from the family farm by promises and dreams born outside these mountains. They went their own ways, raised their own families, and forgot the agrarian life of their youths. The old couple was forced to watch the slow deterioration of their own dreams, bound by age and sickness. Their worlds slipped down into the circling entropy beneath them. The farm fell into disrepair, and they spent most of their days sitting on the porch, trying to remember a dream, counting the days until the grandchildren and great-grandchildren would come and visit them. They would count the cars that passed. And they would count the tobacco stalks as they died in the fields.

One night, the old couple was watching their youngest great-grandchild, a little girl of about four years of age. They had all laid down to sleep that night, the couple in their bed and the little girl in hers. It was cold that night, and the old man decided to lay another couple of sticks of stove wood on the fire before they went to bed. He did so, and the three of them fell into silent sleep in the old house.

It was the old man who woke up first, with the smell of smoke burning his nostrils. He coughed and opened his eyes to see the wisps of black and gray swirling around the room like blind ghosts. He heard the house burning in the other room. He shook his wife awake. "I'll go git the baby!" He shouted in the poisoned darkness. "You git on outta here!"

The old man started out the bedroom door and into the orange glow, toward the little girl's room. The old woman ran toward the front door, and was almost out when she heard a slight whimpering to her right. She felt her way toward the sound, and discovered its source hidden snugly behind the couch. The little girl looked up at her, her face smeared with soot and glowing from the heat. She held up her hands. The old woman gathered her up with the quickness and dexterity of a mother hen and rushed her out the door.

By this time, there were several neighbors gathered around the house, wondering what to do. They saw the old woman crash through the front door with the girl in her arms. At first, they didn't notice that the old woman's nightgown was on fire. She put the girl on the ground, patted her nightgown until the fires were all but extinguished, and then charged back into the house, going after her husband.

Neither of them came back out.

Soon, the bulldozers will make short work of this house, and its story. The contractors and lawyers and bankers will know nothing of what lies beneath the bulldozer's tracks. What dreams and ashes are buried there. What love still smolders there.

We pull off the chipped and shot surface of Crossover Road onto the new, smooth pavement of Newport Highway. Papaw says, "Let's stop and look at my land."

He owns five acres of lakefront land, and he is as proud of it as he is of anything. He bought it a year ago, at next to nothing, for the land is far removed from the town and undefeated. To get to it, you have to turn off Newport Highway onto a gravel, county road. The little road winds and spins along ridges, it rises and dips and narrows in places where only one car can pass at a time. A lush, green canopy of trees smothers the road, shielding it from the sky, and allows only small slivers of ambitious sunlight to peek through. There are only five houses on this four-mile stretch of road. You pass Hack Lafollette's farm, and then up and down and around in the darkness until you reach the end of the county road. It is easy to tell where this happens, because the county road ends where the gravels do. You remove a chain from between two iron posts driven into the ground. The chain has a *Private Property* sign hung from it with bailing wire. You drive through the gate and then put the chain back up. Then, from where the county road ends, you drive about another mile and you are there.

We sit in my truck on the upper lot, looking down into the valley beneath us. The sun shines on us now, magnanimously. Papaw looks on, mesmerized, intoxicated by the euphoria, that unique feeling that can only be acquired by owning something

that God himself made with his own hands. His eyes search the slopes, the brushy undergrowth and the dark, secret places. The lake, peeking out from between trees in the distance, shimmering in the sunlight, winking at him. He counts the trees, and the limbs and the leaves and the universe of inhabitants in them. They are his tenants. He is working plans out in his head. A house over there, a barn at the bottom, some cows grazing lazily in the sun, some pigs in the mud, a strutting rooster, two hound dogs on the porch, grandchildren chasing butterflies, and off to itself, in the shade of the barn, sits an old farm tractor. He sees it all, like it is already there.

"You remember the first time I brung you out here?" He asks me, dreamily.

I do. We all came out to see it. All of the males in the family, that is. It was him, Kippy, Gerald, my cousins Paul and John, and myself. We loaded down Kippy's old Nova with camping equipment. There were tents, sleeping bags, a lantern, various cooking paraphernalia, and a frozen roast given to us by a local cattle farmer. Our plan that Saturday was to go out and cut trees, burn brush, and then camp there that night.

It was cold that day, but the work warmed us. We had cleared away several trees and amassed quite a pile of brush. We threw a couple of old tires we had found in the woods up on top of the pile, and then set it alight. The crackling fire grew and threw soothing heat out at us, paralyzing us with warmth. Black smoke from the fire rose up to the sky like an ill-wrought sacrifice, and then when the rubber was consumed, the smoke turned to white. We watched it until dark, when the fire began to slowly smolder out.

We set up camp, built our campfire, and settled in around it. We were quite hungry by this time, and could hardly wait to get supper going. When the fire was hot enough, we filled a large pot with water, waited until it began to boil, and then dropped in the roast. John and I peeled and sliced up some vegetables, carrots, turnips and potatoes, and slipped them into the stew. We piddled around in the woods while there was still enough light. We explored the realm of Papaw's new kingdom,

testing its borders and sampling its bounty. John found an old tractor tire, and immediately hollered for me to come and help him roll it to camp. After much heaving and tugging, we finally got the tire upright, and started rolling it out of the woods. We brought it to the others as if we had found the treasures of Tutenkamen.

"What in the world are you'unz doin with that old tire?" Someone asked.

John and I looked at each other. "We don't know."

"Well, don't bring it around us. It's liable to have a snake in it."

John and I shrugged our shoulders, and with a heave, sent the tire rolling down into the holler, where the remnants of the brush fire lay smoldering. It crashed into the brush pile and sent a wave of sparks and fresh smoke shooting up at the sky.

"Don't burn the woods down." Papaw said.

We waited in the sparse light of the campfire. Our stomachs were growling angrily. An old Coleman lantern was suspended from a low hanging branch, but it did little to fight off the darkness. We were warm around the fire, but only around the fire. Whenever someone had to go off into the woods to relieve himself, we could hear him screaming, "Man, it's cold out here!" We then saw his shivering, hopping figure dancing back toward the campfire.

We let the stew simmer for about five hours. None of us were especially proficient at kitchen cooking, much less cooking outside, over an open fire. We could not see down into the pot, and so we could not tell if the stew was done or not. We had unofficially elected Kippy as the cook, and he would poke a wooden spoon down into the concoction periodically, and mumble, "Just about right," to himself as if he knew exactly what he was doing. It was just about right at least six times over the course of the night. When we could stand the hunger no longer, we decided to eat the stew whether it was done or not.

Kippy was the first. He poured a ladle full into his bowl, and paddled his spoon around in the stew for a minute.

Paul said: "Let me go git the lantern and shine it down into yore bowl."

"That's alright." Kippy said, smiling nervously in the firelight. "I don't want to see down in it."

He spooned himself out a mouthful, and then, after taking a deep breath, he ate it. We all watched him in silence, our mouths agape, waiting for him to retch, or pass out, or die. He just chewed for a moment, his face expressionless. Finally, someone asked, "Well, how is it?"

He swallowed. "John, did you and Donnie put anything crunchy in this stew?"

We both looked at each other and shook our heads. "Why?"

"Never mind. Well, dig in, boys!"

We all ate. All, except for Gerald, who took one look at us forcing the stew down and said, "I bleeve I'll just eat me some white bread."

The vegetables were still crunchy and the meat was half raw, but we ate it all. Such was the ferocity of our hunger, and the resolve of our courage.

When we had our fill of eating, we sprawled lethargically around the fire, too full to speak or move, having only enough energy to *be*. We were frozen shapes in the darkness, paralyzed by the warmth of the fire, pulled into it from out of the cold. We had not been like this long when we first heard the dogs.

It was a loud, baying sound, coming from down deep in the woods, where neither the yellow light from our lantern, nor the yellow moonbeams from the sky could penetrate. We heard two or three to begin with, and then their one syllabled voices intermingled with others. We knew that there were wolves in this part of the county. We had seen one dart across the road on the way out there.

"You reckon 'at's a pack 'a wolves?" Gerald asked.

None of us answered. We sat in silence, listening to the aboriginal symphony below us. We drew a little closer to the fire, and the baying became louder. We all looked at Kippy, even Papaw did. We all waited for him to be afraid. A shadow of

firelight blew over his face, and then we saw it there. His fear. And then we were afraid.

"What are we gonna do?" Someone asked. "We ain't got no gun or nothin."

Kippy was silent. He was thinking.

"What if 'em dogs come up here? They'll go after the littlest ones first." John said, who was the smallest.

The sound grew louder. Closer.

We all looked for bravery in each other's faces, but found none. The dark grew suddenly darker, and the cold suddenly colder. A crisp breeze whisked its way over us, and we were just on the verge of panic when Kippy stood up and took charge.

"John, go git 'em dope bottles out of the trunk of my car." (We never went anywhere without dope bottles in those days.) He turned to me, "Go find us some rags and rip 'em up into strips."

He went to the spot where we had placed our wood cutting equipment and brought back a gallon milk jug full of gasoline. John brought him a dozen bottles, and I gave him the strips of cloth. He proceeded to make an arsenal of Molotov Cocktails. When he had them made, he rationed them out, and we stood, fortified around the fire, waiting for our foes to come charging out of the darkness. The howling grew louder still, hanging in the darkness like echoes in a canyon. Then, suddenly, they stopped. The mountainside was flooded with eerie silence. The breeze ceased and the myriad of singing night creatures retired their ancient instruments. It seemed like the proverbial calm before the storm. We looked into the dark woods, and then at each other, and then into the darkness again.

There was a rustling somewhere in the darkness, and the sound of labored breathing. Shuffling feet were coming our way, and making no secret of their coming. We looked, not breathing, not moving, holding our weapons at the ready. Then we saw the unmistakable reflections of eyes in the woods, eyes pulling down moonlight out of the sky and shining in the darkness. We waited to see our enemies, to smite them with our weapons, and then we saw them.

Richard and David Ownby came strolling up out of the

woods, shotguns slung over their shoulders, leaning forward as they climbed the hill toward us.

"You'unz ain't seen our dogs around here, have ye?"

None of us spoke. We just looked at each other dumbly over the fire. Finally, Papaw said, "We ain't seen 'em, but we shore heard 'em. Come on up here by the fire and have ye a cup of coffee."

David is my uncle, on my daddy's side, and Richard is his son. They love to hunt and fish about as much as they love to breathe. They told us that they had been hunting in these parts for some years, and were unaware that Papaw now owned the land. Their dogs had gone after a coon some time ago, and they had lost them somewhere in the darkness.

"Ye arta try usin one of 'em shock collars on 'em." Kippy said.

David said, "I don't know if I'd use one of 'em or not. Not after what happened to Bobby Delozier."

"What happened?"

They told us the story.

Bobby Delozier bought a coon dog from a man in Jamestown. He paid twelve hundred dollars for it, but this was no ordinary dog. Her parents were nationally renowned hunters, and he was sure that she would live up to her heredity. He named her, Belle. She was a Black and Tan, and ran like a streaking bullet. She could smell a coon from a mile away, and would not lose it until she treed it. Bobby had one problem with her though, he kept losing her. No matter how much he hollered or whistled or cooed, she would not come to him. He was growing tired of owning a twelve hundred dollar dog that he couldn't take hunting, so he decided to try a shock collar on her.

A shock collar sounds worse than it is. It doesn't hurt the dog, it just gives it a mild shock to get its attention. It is what is known in psychological circles as *positive reinforcement*. It comes in two parts: The collar, and the remote control. There is a shock button on the control, and a dial to adjust the voltage.

The idea was this: If Belle didn't come when he called her, he would give her a light shock. Eventually, she would learn to

associate the shock with her disobedience, and he would condition her to come when he called, even without the collar. Pavlov would have been proud. He worked with her in the yard for a couple of weeks, and then decided to try it in the woods.

It was David and Richard Ownby, their dogs, and Bobby and Belle. They turned the dogs loose at dusk, and watched them disappear into the underbrush. The dogs ran a couple of coons, but they didn't tree, and at 11:30, they decided to go home. David and Richard called for their dogs, and they came running. Bobby called for Belle, but she was nowhere to be seen.

"How much did you give for that dog, again?" David asked, laughing.

"She'll come." Bobby said, pulling out the little black box with the buttons and the dial. He hollered again, but Belle wouldn't answer, so he gave her a shock. This was followed by a long, mournful baying sound down deep in the woods.

"What's 'a matter with 'at dog?" Bobby asked himself, and then he shocked her twice. The baying came again. Bobby turned up the voltage a little, and then he shocked her again. This time, the sound was louder and longer from down deep in the woods. Three more times he shocked her, increasing the voltage every time, and three more times he was answered by that sad sounding refrain.

"Maybe we arta go look fer her." Richard said.

Bobby looked into the woods with utter despondency, and nodded his head. They secured David and Richard's dogs in the truck box, and went after Belle. Bobby would shock her intermittently, and they would follow the sound of the baying. They followed it deep down into a hollow, where the trees receded from around an old pond. Bobby hit the button again, and the howling was louder than before.

"Sounds like we're right on top of her." David said, "Do it again, Bobby."

He did, and then David saw the dog. It had fallen down into the pond, and was clawing frantically at the muddy slopes, her front feet on the bank, and her rear legs down in the water.

Every time Bobby would shock her, she would fall back into the water. Then, being in the water when Bobby shocked her, well, that's where that horrible sound came from. When Bobby saw this, he threw down the remote like it was on fire, and ran, weeping, to his dog. He was knee-deep in the pond, gathering her up like Moses from the Nile.

Later on, he tried to train her again without the collar. He couldn't use it, because every time Belle saw it, she ran off. His efforts were in vain. Belle just wouldn't listen to reason. She didn't do too much after that. She didn't hunt. She just mostly sat on the front porch, kind of staring off into space.

We sat around the campfire for a while longer, but the night was growing colder, and the fire dimmer, so David and Richard went off to look for their dogs. Silence followed, no sound except for the death throes of the dying fire. We decided to go to sleep. The six of us climbed into a three-man tent, struggled with our sleeping bags and blankets for a while, and then got situated. It was two hours later when someone said, "I bleeve it's too cold to sleep."

"It shore is." Someone else said.

"Yep." Agreed another.

And it *was* too cold to sleep. It was a deep, deadly cold, which kills you in bits and pieces. It is like some almost invisible sadist, settling in around you like a friend, and then torturing you slowly. It would not let us go. It shook us and rattled us, jarring our bones and driving us down into nothing.

We lay there in the cold silence for a moment, and then Kippy said, "Where's daddy?"

We couldn't find him in the tent. We looked everywhere, under blankets and sleeping bags, under ourselves. Finally, someone said, "He ain't in here."

We went outside the tent, and were smote anew by the bitter cold.

"Wonder whur he's at?" Someone asked.

"Maybe he's up yonder in the woods," Gerald said, hopefully. "Seein a man about a dog."

We went into the woods, holding small flashlights and

candles. We hollered and called, but we could not find him. We came back out of the woods into camp, more than a little worried. Someone noticed that Kippy's car was running, and we all went to it to find Papaw sprawled out on the front seat, wrapped up snugly in his sleeping bag, the air from the heater on the dash throwing wisps of his hair up around his forehead. He was snoring peacefully. Kippy tried to open the door but it was locked. We banged on the windows, trying to get his attention, but he would not hearken. We thumped on the roof, yelled and whistled, but still no answer. Finally, Paul, the largest of us, began bouncing up and down on the bumper, jarring the car violently up and down, and then Papaw woke. He opened the door groggily, and asked what we were doing. We told him that we were trying to get warm. He laughed and scooted over in the car. The six of us slept in Kippy's Nova that night, our little tent sitting alone in the darkness like an abandoned child.

"I keen't wait to git moved out here." Papaw says, "I keen't hardly stand livin in that house in Gatlinburg."

"What' got you so tore up about it?" I ask.

"It's 'em neighbors next door. They up all hours of the night, drinkin and carryin on."

Now, to my grandfather, there are two monumental sins, which no man should commit, and they are seldom found apart from each other. These two sins are drinking and carrying on. He can abide neither of them.

"Why don't you just call the Law on 'em?"

Papaw sighs. "The Law won't do nothin about it. The Law is in with That Old Clique. But it ain't just that. A man needs a house and some land that he can call his own."

I agree, silently, and we sit looking at his land for a little while longer.

Back on the highway again, headed toward Newport. Papaw is smoking and tapping his feet to music in his head. I am driving and trying to hear it. The sun is now a giant, burning ember in the sky, throwing its mischievous fingers down upon the land, fooling the world into thinking it is summertime.

"It's a perty day." I remark.

"Yep. If yore lookin at it through a winder."

We pass two state dump trucks on the shoulder. Papaw says, "Ye know, I used to work for tha state. Helped build most of these roads."

"You did?"

"Shore did. They even made me a supervisor."

"I guess that's why you're so good at it now." I say, but he doesn't hear me.

"Had my own crew of four men. One morning, I sent them out to the job site while I finished up some paperwork back at the office. A little while after they left, one of 'em called me on the radio, sayin they had left the shovels back at the shop. I told them not to worry, that I would bring them down in a few minutes. Then, the worker asked, 'Well, what do you wont us to do 'till then?' I told 'em just to lean on each other 'till I git there."

"That was smart thinking."

"Yep. I don't know what they would've done without me."

On up the road, a funeral procession approaches us. I pull off onto the shoulder. We both remove our hats, as is our custom. We sit in solemn silence as they pass. When they have gone, Papaw says: "Wonder who died?"

# X

*The road to Newport is curvy and steep and fraught with perils.* The ghosts of ridge runners and outlaws haunt the road. They float up from the hollows and through the trees, born in mist, making their presence known, telling all that they have not yet turned this place loose. It is still Newport Highway, but where the highway goes down from four lanes to two and cuts into the side of the mountain, the road takes on a more aboriginal nature. There are homes and farms scattered sporadically along the road, and for now, it is still a green place. Green, the color of life, throwing its beauty at the jealous sky. But it will not remain. I know this as I pass, looking. Frost said that nothing gold can stay, but he was wrong, for as long as there is the sun, there will be gold. The sun washes everything with its flaxen vanity, conforming everything to its image. But green will go. It is as mutable as a feather in the wind. This green will be pushed down into the earth. But some of it may escape, and retreat and find sanctity in the only place that will grant it refuge. It will fall back into cemeteries, and flourish there, beneath the faceless slabs of watching stone, above the volumes of lives below it.

We pass Clevenger's place on the right, but he is not home. We know that he is not there because he is not sitting out in front of his camper, waving. We ride on down, around a steep curve and down into the valley, past Bush's Canning Factory, where a few of the lucky ones are working Saturday overtime. Up ahead of us, on the right, its rear bumper barely out of the road, sits an old Dodge car. An old man is shuffling around to the trunk, and trying to wrestle a spare tire from its mouth. I pull up behind him and stop without being told to, without even thinking about it. We get out, but the old man doesn't hear

us. He is stooped over the trunk, his maligned back hunched and stretched out cruelly, his old shoulder blades working harder than they should, his head disappearing into the darkness of the space beneath him.

"Here, sir." I say, softly, trying not to startle him. "Let me help you with that."

He straightens up as far as his monarchial back will allow him, and pulls a red handkerchief from his back pocket. He wipes it across his wrinkled and ancient forehead.

"Thank ye, son." He says, stepping aside.

"Did you have a flat?" I ask, because I do not mind stating the obvious.

He clears his throat and spits. It is a thing of beauty, really. Almost artistic. He gathers it up and corrals it on his tongue, rolling it into a manageable ball. He curls his tongue into a channel, holding the concoction there for a moment, and then, opening his mouth, he blows it out, like a cannonball, and it arcs through the air, catches a sliver of sunlight and falls like a drop of rain to the ground. He spits, and then starts talking again. Like it is nothing. Like it is all part of talking. "I reckon I run over somethin back thar sommers."

Papaw says, "Go on and change 'at tar fer this pore feller. I'll stand back here and supervise."

I go to work, placing the antique, one-piece jack beneath the rear bumper, and slowly cranking the mammoth car upward. As I loosen the rusty lug nuts on the flat tire, I can hear Papaw and the old man talking.

"Zat yore boy?" The old man asks him.

"He's my grandson."

"He's a right stout lookin boy. Reckon yore right proud to have him."

"He eats a lot of cornbread and taters." Papaw says, laughing. "At's what made him grow so big. He's my youngest grandson. I got another'n at'd make two of him. This'n here carries me to town when I ask him to."

The old man sounds sad. "I got me some grandkids up in Michigan sommers. Ain't seen 'em since they's babies, though.

Me and my wife, we didn't have but one young'un, 'at lived, and he took a wife 'at didn't hardly like livin down here. I kindly thought he'd wont to take over tha farm, but she wouldn't here none of it. She was convinced they arta move on up to Detroit, whur he could find work puttin cars together. They's more money up thar, ye know it?"

I can hear papaw grunt in agreement.

"I keen't hardly blame him, though. A feller's got to do what's best fer him and his. I guess I jest always figgered he'd always be here with me. They don't come down here to see us much, and me and my wife ain't got the money to be going up thar."

"Ain't ye got no kin around her 'at kin hep ye?"

"I got a brother over in White Pine, but he's worse off than we are."

They are awkwardly silent for a moment. The old man is embarrassed at having told his troubles, and Papaw is embarrassed for having heard them. I finish changing the tire. I put the wounded tire back in the trunk along with the jack. I brush my hands off on my pants, and the old man comes over to me and says: "How much do I owe ye?"

I throw my hands up in protest. "You don't owe me anything, sir."

"Ye arta let me give ye somethin."

"No sir." I say, with resolve. "That ain't my way."

"God bless ye, son." The old man says, extending his hand. I take it, his worn fingers cross my palm and clasp it firmly. He gets back into his car, and we get back into my truck. We wait for him to pull out. We watch him go up the road some distance, and then we pull out as well.

Papaw says, "I wish I had some money to give 'at pore feller."

I look at him. "Let me ask you something, how are you planning to buy this tractor, if you ain't got no money?"

He just gives me a kind of wry grin, and winks. "We'll see what happens."

On past the farms and the villages of mobile homes, past

the sleeping dogs, chasing spring down with darting eyes behind closed lids. Past the litters of dirty-faced children, playing in puddles of unquenchable depressions in half-sown yards. Past lines of clothing strung out and hung in the cold air, flapping seriously with a flippant wind, like vagabonds on a telephone wire. Past the empty-eyed stares of the vanquished through unwashed windows. Passed this world and into the next we venture, our unambitious determination bearing us forward. The road forks, and we go to the right, where the city of Newport awaits. Our destination.

The city of Newport was established in 1797, and named Olde Towne New Porte. Its sits along the French Broad River, and when exploration and settling were popular endeavors, the town was a thriving port community. The French Broad River is the third oldest river in the world, outlived only by the New River in North Carolina, and the Nile in Africa. It is older than the mountains through which it runs. It carved the mountains out of heaps of unmanageable stone. It was visited and trekked by Hernando de Soto in 1540, on his ambitious quest for gold.

In places, the French Broad River lays like a great floating corpse in the Tennessee Valley. It is stagnant, and no amount of wind or gravity can stir it into life. Trees line the river like brooding mourners of its passing, spreading their tepid branches out over the expanse as if to goad the river into animation. Even the sun shields its eyes from this unmoving trickle. Dark shadows of clouds pass over the water, and dark shadows of unseen things pass beneath. The water licks the muddy banks hungrily, as if ravenously seeking to consume the borders of its own grave. It is an eerie river, blanketed by a thick shroud of fog, its mysteries born slowly beneath it. There is a thick blanket of fog over the river, like a morose burial shroud. This is nothing unusual, airplane pilots have often passed over certain stretches of the river and remarked that it looks like a swirling mist, like white lava flowing out of the mountains. This phenomena elicits strange tales, as one would imagine, from the simple folk in the vicinity. Stories of "haints" and "boogers" and sometimes even of the baneful Banshee from some of the older inhabitants, who say

that her cry can always be heard the day before the church bell rings out the call of the dead. The river crawls in a northward semi-circle, causing the water to flow backward, *when* it flows. Most of its two hundred and ten mile expanse is topographically level. The river was once the main route into Tennessee from the east coast, and it carried many a hungry-eyed settler to better and bitter places. Many a dream was lashed to rafts and canoes to ride the unambitious course of the French Broad River. Because so many braved this route, Olde Towne New Porte became a popular place to stop along the way. The town grew as more and more settlers decided to plant their dreams here instead of westward.

All of that changed when the railroad came. People found it a much faster and easier way to travel, and the river was forsaken to die the death that it had wanted to die for the length of its archaic life. The port became more and more a novelty, and when people forgot about it altogether, they changed the name to Newport, and ushered in the age of the black rail and the dark, looming smoke. The town is now an industrialized place, with plants and factories and rail yards, high schools and incinerators, apartment complexes and liquor stores, bars and ghettos.

We pass the old Newport Drive-In, where I first saw the movies, *Herby the Love Bug*, and *Hang 'Em High*. It is now a field of brown weeds and sickly brush. It is lined by an army of gray posts sticking up out of the decay, like drowning men, confederate soldiers swallowed up a decade at a time. Above this stands the old movie screen, its white panels falling off one at a time, leaving it looking like a half-attempted jigsaw puzzle with no pictures on the pieces.

Then, on up the road, there is Rose's Department Store. It has been out of business for the last ten years, but on Friday and Saturday nights, the parking lot is the busiest place in town. Scores of high school kids, and young men who wished they were still in high school, cruise the parking lot in their cars, traveling in circles, staring at each other as they pass, each face filled with the quiet, unquenchable optimism of youth. Now, the

parking lot is empty, for the afternoon is still young. For now, the department store looks on with its empty, embryonic stare, anticipating the night like a hungry vampire, when it can feed on the misplaced hopes of the misanthropic.

Down the road, beyond where the new Wal-Mart was erected, an event which elicited many an excited whisper among the locals—the biggest thing since De Soto himself arrived here. We go into the oldest part of the town, the historic district, as it were. We pass the hardware stores, florists, thrift shops, furniture stores, check advance establishments, pawn shops, and a bonafide cobbler. An old Negro man shuffles along the sidewalk with a little, yellow plastic bag swinging from his hand. He waves at us hopelessly and we wave back.

We go along the road that takes us out of town, where people live who don't live in town. Where the man with the tractor lives.

# XI

*"Where is this place we're going to, anyway?"* I ask, scanning the road ahead of us.

"It's jest up tha road aways." Papaw says. Every place is just up the road a ways to him. This too is a metaphor for life, and I find it, somehow. The road is darkened by the shadows of trees, pushing their dark shadows out across the pavement for us to trample upon. A ditch lines the road on our right, and it is littered with debris, cans and empty beer cases, an old bicycle wheel, a muffler from some car, hubcaps from the last fifty years, paper cups, candy wrappers, and then, a sign sticking up out of the ditch, oblivious, like the preacher outside the gates of Sodom and Gomorrah. The sign reads: *Help Keep Newport Clean.* We round a curve, and see an old man limping along the ditch, a sharpened stick in one hand, and a black garbage bag in the other. He is fishing cans out of the ditch with the stick, and depositing them in his sack. I slow down and hug the center line as we pass him. He waves without looking at us.

Papaw is thinking as we pass him, and after some silence, he says, *"Verily I say unto thee, that it is easier for a camel to pass through the eye of a needle than for a rich man to enter into the Kingdom of Heaven.* You ever heerd that?"

"Seems like I've heard it somewhere before."

"That was what Jesus said." He is smiling when he says this. In his estimation, three people are the most revered in the world: Jesus Christ, Franklin D. Roosevelt, and John F. Kennedy, in that order. The latter two because they were the most famous Democratic presidents of his lifetime, the first because he was poor. This was the main thing that caused Papaw to believe in him, not only that he was good, and that he died for the

sins of the world, but mainly because he was poor, just like himself. Papaw had come to the staunch and immutable conclusion
that had there been Democrats during Jesus' time, he would
most assuredly have been one himself.

"Slow down up here." He says.

"Is this it?"

He looks for a moment. "No, they's a car up here fer sale.
Let's stop and take a look at her."

We pull off the road onto a gravel driveway. The house is
a brick rancher, and its roof is strewn upon by leaves, the dead
soldiers of Autumn, their colors evaporated into the sun-
drenched winter wind, leaving them dull and brown and brittle,
waiting to be blown away. The yard is splotched here and there
with struggling brown grass, fighting off winter and the mud
and the rocks. In the middle of the yard, ahead of two tire tracks
cut into the muddy yard, sits an old Dodge Comet. Its colors
are primer and bondo, and it clings stubbornly to its place in
this world. There are no hubcaps on the tires, and the hood is
warped. In its smudged, smeared windshield, there leans a piece
of cardboard. Words are written on it with a black magic marker:
*FOR SALE.*

"It don't look like much." I say, putting my gearshift in
neutral and pulling up the parking brake, just in front of the
house.

"I don't look like much either." Papaw says. "But that
don't mean that I ain't good for somethin." He starts to get out,
and then two growling, mongrel dogs come running out from
underneath the porch, defending their home like Hector. They
come right up to the doors of my truck, issuing their strong re-
joinders from salivating mouths and teeth and tongues.

"Maybe ye arta just blow yore horn." Papaw says, inching
away from his door.

"I ain't blowing my horn. That's rude."

"Just blow it. Whoever's home will come to the door."

"We don't even know these people." I say, but my hand is
already reaching for the horn button on my steering wheel.
Whenever you try to argue with him, you feel yourself losing be-

fore you even open your mouth. I give the horn two quick taps, hoping that the noise will scare the dogs away, but they do not move. They are vigilant, sober sentinels. I tap the horn again, longer this time, and we see a curtain fold away, and a curious face pressed against the glass.

"He's seen us." Papaw says, and we wait until the front door opens.

A man appears on the front porch, his hair a tangled mess upon his head, clad in faded overalls, one strap hanging lethargically from his back. He scratches his backside and peers at us through squinted, sleep-washed eyes. "Hep ye?" He shouts under the canopy of his cupped hand on his brow.

Papaw rolls his window down a few inches, keeping a careful eye on the dog beneath him. He shouts through the breach, "We'z kindly wontin to take a look at yer car!"

"Wait a minute and let me git my shoes on first!" The man shouts back, retreating into the house. We sit in the truck for a few moments, and then the man returns to the porch and descends the precarious steps to the ground.

Papaw shouts, "Kin ye do somethin with these dogs?"

"Oh, they alright." The man says, approaching the truck. "They won't hurt ye as long as I'm out here."

Papaw cautiously opens his door, and slowly places a tepid foot on the ground. The dog backs away carefully, giving him space, but it never takes its eyes off of him.

Papaw turns to me, "Come on and git out. He says they alright."

I get out, but the dog charged with my care does not back away. It inches ever closer to me.

"Hey!" The man shouts at the dog, "Git away from him, Jupiter!" Then, to me, he says, "He won't hurt ye son. He's just wontin to play."

The dog retreats backs away from me, but keeps growling. I cast a nervous glance at the owner. "Yore shore he won't bite?"

The man nods his head, so I close my door behind me and start toward the front of the truck. The dog bites me on the leg. I am able to get my foot back before he can latch onto skin, but

he attacks my pants leg as if it were Lucifer himself. I shake my leg viciously, twisting and throwing the dog's head about. I turn to look at papaw, but he is back in the truck, with the glass rolled safely up, with his walking stick born at the ready before him like a sacred scepter.

"He's just playin with ye." The man laughs. "Just kick him a good one in the head and he'll turn ye loose."

With his permission granted, (the owner's, not the dog's) I balance myself with one arm on the hood of my truck and plant the tip of my shoe squarely and forcibly under the dog's chin. He turns me loose. The man chases the two dogs back under the porch and commands them to stay there. They do, but their vigilant eyes continue to watch us from out of the darkness, unblinking and stoic.

Papaw gets out again, and walks over to the man. He says, "Hello, neighbor."

The man returns the greeting, and the two introduce themselves.

"What are ye gittin on yore old car, thar?" Papaw asks, not looking at the car, not seeming too anxious, playing it cool.

"I'z wontin to git about six hunderd fer it." The man says. "I've got about three too many cars, and I need to git rid of at least on of 'em."

"Hmm." Papaw says, rubbing his chin. "Mind if we take a look at her?"

"Hep yoreselves." The man says, handing us the keys, "Look at her all ye wont. We don't charge fer lookin around here."

Papaw circles the car, tapping his walking stick on the dirt, not knowing what he is looking for, but looking for it with the zeal of a dreamy-eyed prospector. He opens the driver's side door. It creaks loudly and bends against the frame, warped. He peers inside at the interior. The seats are ripped and the ceiling hangs down in shreds of tan confetti. He turns and hands me the keys. He tells me to get in.

The air inside the car is pregnant with melancholy, the stale conglomeration of time and vacancy. The seat creaks loudly from the conscription of my weight, but welcoming, the

song of a war bride upon feeling the strong embrace of her lover after years of fretful and lonely woe. The man squats in the shadow of the open door beside me. He peers into the car, watching me, for what, I do not know. He tells me, "Now, this car ain't been started in about a year."

Papaw comes around behind the car and gets in beside me. I put the key in the ignition. It slides in as if it had never left. I place my foot on the brake and start to turn the key.

"Give her a little gas before you start her." The man says.

I press down on the accelerator slightly, and turn the key. The starter whines in an epileptic fit, and the carburetor chokes and sputters, coughing out wads of air and gasoline. The engine turns over twice, and I turn the key back to off. I give it a little more gas, and try again. The starter whines once more, quickly, in anticipation, as one's heart would reach for a loved one long before the fingers. And the carburetor again, coughing and dying and resurrecting and the engine turning over and over. More gas, the engine flirts with me, like a scorned lover, and then more gas. I pump the pedal furiously.

"Don't flood it." Papaw says.

But I do not hear him. There are few things that I know how to do in life, but starting his cars for him is one, which has afforded me much practice.

"Here, lemme give it a try." The man says.

But I cannot hear him either. I am listening to the car now. I am hearing its sorrow, its reluctance to live, and then, talking back to it. I goad it to life gently, like a patient suitor, and the worn, wearied engine sings again, like a siren. The entire front end of the car shakes as the motor idles. I rev the engine, and the car lurches against the parked transmission. A filthy plume of sooty black smoke pours out of the exhaust pipe and ascends toward the heavens like Cain's offering. There is a myriad of sounds from underneath the hood, the rattling of metallic teeth, the obscene spasms of the carburetor flirting with exhaustion. The car makes sad sounds as it idles, like a deaf soprano, singing in discord. In its head hearing the sound it was meant to make, but polluting the air with its foul saturnalias.

The man smiles at me. "Runs just like a Singer Sewing Machine, don't she?"

I mutter something about it running like a rock. I check the various knobs and buttons on the dashboard. These are the things that do not work: The gas gauge, the radio, the heater, the windshield wipers, the interior light, the headlights, the signal lights, the hazard lights, and the cigarette lighter. This is the thing that does work: The horn.

We pull out onto the highway slowly. The engine flirts with death. Papaw says, "Open her up. We'll blow the soot out of her." I push the accelerator almost all the way down, and the car responds instantly. It was meant to run like this. The engine grows steadier the faster we go. Papaw says, "I bleeve this is one fine machine." He reaches to roll the window down, so that he can smoke, and the handle comes off in his hand. He looks at me. "Gerald can fix that." He says. "How 'bout rollin yore winder down to let some of this smoke out."

We cross the French Broad River, and I really open the car up. If the speedometer worked, it would probably have registered one hundred miles per hour. Beneath us, the river lays gently, with a stream of swirling mist above it. Some boats are cutting through it. Hardcore fishermen. The swimmers and skiers and pleasure boaters are all hibernating. I can see their huddled forms in the boat, fighting off the bitter wind, shivering, but going to their fishing holes with determinacy. We cross the bridge. Papaw smokes. I think about fishing.

Going fishing. It was a big deal then, when I was eight years old. Getting up early in the morning, before the sun, like you know something it doesn't. Like you were going to surprise it. Getting all your things ready. Going through your tackle box the night before. Organizing. Trying to decide what you are going to need and what you will not. But taking it all. It was all precious. Checking your rod and reel, testing the line, tying the hook and squeezing the sinkers down on the line. Going out at dusk the night before, finding your own bait. Turning over cinder blocks and logs, prying nightcrawlers up out of the covetous earth. Getting it all ready and going to bed. Not being able to

sleep. Getting up the next morning, drinking coffee. The one time you were allowed to. A tap on the shoulder.

"Are you ready?"

"I'm ready."

"Let's go."

We grabbed our gear and stepped out into the morning's darkness. My uncle lighting a cigarette and tossing his gear into the boat. Me, tossing mine in behind him. We climbed into the truck, which was darker than the moonlight-washed lawn. Darker than the world around us. He turned on the switch, and little lights along the dashboard came to life in the darkness, like tiny neon fairies. My uncle put his coffee cup in a plastic cup holder along the door, and tossed his cigarette out the window. He exhaled in the darkness and the smoke burned my nostrils, but it was all part of fishing. The smell of hot coffee, cigarette smoke, bait and beef jerky. He pulled the gearshift into reverse, and the old truck lurched backward. We had only gone a couple of feet when I heard the screen door close and saw her come down the front porch steps and out into the driveway. She had all of her stuff ready. Her pole, her own tackle box. She even had on a little hat that had a picture of a large mouth bass flailing on it. Her hair was tucked into it, to hide her shame of being a girl. She was all ready to go.

My uncle grinned and stopped the truck. "Well, lookie coming there!"

"Hold on." I said, and got out. I walked up to her forcefully. She stopped. She knew what I was going to say. I had said it before.

"Go back inside."

She looked at me like a little puppy dog. She always did. Her sad eyes staring up at me and driving me into nothingness. A little frown, pulling her face down and me with it.

"I want to go." She said. She was six years old then.

"You can't Tammie." I said, taking her pole from her hand. It stayed there where I had robbed it, as if it refused to believe it had happened.

"Why not?"

"Because it's just the guys this time." I said. "You can go next time."

"That's not fair." She said, pouting. Trying to remain strong. Trying to cry without really starting to cry. Trying to not be a girl in my presence. "I never get to go." She reached for her pole and I swept it behind my back.

"Don't start that." I said.

She frowned harder, and now she was really mad.

"Momma said I could go this time."

"I don't care." I said. "You're not going with us."

"But she said I could."

"And I said you can't. You wouldn't have fun anyway. Why don't you go back to sleep? You can watch cartoons when you wake up."

"I don't want to watch cartoons!" She said, almost shouting. "I want to go fishing!"

I rolled my eyes. She saw it, and started crying. For real this time.

"Why don't you go play with your dolls?"

"I DON'T WANT TO PLAY WITH DOLLS! I WANT TO GO WITH YOU!"

"Well, you can't" I said, tossing her fishing pole into the dark yard.

She dropped her little tackle box on the driveway and folded her arms. She was crying hard now, and staring up at me, tears throwing moonlight back up at the sky.

"Don't cry. We'll do something when I get back.

She said something under her breath, beneath the sobs that I didn't understand.

"I promise."

She turned her back on me and ran into the house.

"You wouldn't have fun anyway." I repeated, to the empty darkness.

I wanted her to go with us. I really did. I didn't care that she was a girl. But there was a multitude of ancient edicts and immutable decrees that were pressed down upon me from ages past. I lived under these rules just like everyone else. Even those

I didn't understand. We obeyed them without question. One of those prescripts was that girls do not go fishing with boys. But it wasn't just that. There was another reason that I never told anybody. She usually caught more fish than I did.

"Pull in up here at this little store and I'll go in and git us a couple 'a dopes and then we'll turn around and take this car back." Papaw says, tossing his cigarette out the window.

We pull into the parking lot of a little country store. It sits off the shoulder like a neglected artifact. There are two gas pumps in front of it. One of the pumps has a cardboard sign with the words, *DON'T WORK* scribbled on it.

"That's good advice." I say, but he doesn't get it.

We park along the side of the building, and start to go in. There is an old man sitting in front of the store, in a rocking chair. He is whittling and whistling like a living Norman Rockwell painting. "What do ye say thar, boys?" He asks us.

"How are you?" Papaw says.

"Doin alright." The man says, shaving off a long sliver of wood.

"Ain't it too cold to be outside?"

The old man laughs. "It ain't never too cold to loaf." He goes back to whistling.

We enter the store. There is not much light. It is not like when you enter a convenience store, where you are pummeled with brilliant light, and whites and reds. This is more like entering into someone's house. The light hides and moves around of its own volition. It knows its place in the darkness. The place smells like bread and produce and cardboard. It is a soft smell. A middle-aged man leans heavily on the counter, watching us because there is nothing else to see. There are shelves along two of the walls, and three rows in the middle. The far wall has a couple of horizontal coolers, with glass sliding. They are filled with ice-cold sodas. Beside the coolers, there is a small space set aside for loafing. Five chairs and five men. They are all old and dressed like farmers. They laugh absently now and then, and talk about the way things used to be. Always about the way things used to be. They live lives that were over years ago. Eyes

always looking backward. Always to the past, where things made sense. That place so far removed from the disillusionment of the present. These are the faces of the defeated.

The door opens. A little bell rings on top of the door. I hadn't noticed it when we entered. A young man comes in, older than me. He looks like he is around twenty. He walks up to the counter. "Hello, Dan." He says to the man behind it.

"Howdy, Tommy. What are you doin here? I thought you'z 'sposed to be at work."

Tommy sighs harshly. "Ain't got no way to git thar."

"Whurs yore car at?" The man behind the counters asks.

Tommy leans against the front of the counter. "Oh, I let my sister borry it, and she let that ole boy she's seein drive it, and he run it off in the ditch."

"That's too bad. It git hurt much?"

Tommy swirls his fingers through a bowl of Tootsie Rolls and closes his eyes in disgust. "Broke two tie rods and warped the axle. Busted the front tires and punched a great big hole in the radiator." He sighs again.

"Reckon ye kin git it fixed?"

"Probably, but it'd cost a lot more than that car's worth. Even if I did git it fixed, it'd probably just tear up a week or two down the road. That car was wore out, anyhow."

They are both silent for a moment. I look at Papaw, who is standing beside me, opening a Coca-Cola bottle on the opener in the side of the cooler. The man behind the counter finally says, "What are you gonna do, Tommy?"

Tommy looks disgusted. "I don't know. I have already missed two days of work on account of that old car. I called my boss and told him that I'd try to git in to work if I could, but I couldn't promise him nothin. He didn't sound too happy. Probably because he's the one that's gonna have to warsh dishes 'till I can make it in to work."

Papaw slides over to the two of them. "Say, yore needin ye a car?"

Tommy looks at him. "I could shore use one. You ain't got an extra one in yore pocket, do ye?"

Papaw laughs. "Well, no, but I got one outside there."

Tommy's eyes widen. "You do?"

"Shore do."

"How much you wontin for it?"

Papaw looks pensive. He strokes his chin, then he rubs his shin with his walking stick. "I need to get eight hunderd dollars out of it."

Tommy's looked disheartened. "I don't know if I got that much money or not."

"That's alright." Papaw says, starting to turn away. "If I can't get that fer it, I'll just keep it for myself."

"Hold on a minute." Tommy protested. "I might be able to work somethin out. I've got kin around here."

"Alright then, let me pay for these dopes and we'll go out thar and look at her."

Papaw pays the man behind the counter for our two drinks, and then he and Tommy exit. I stay inside, not wanting to be in the way. This is his work.

They come back a few minutes later. The man behind the counter looks at them, trying to guess what has just transpired. Papaw comes over to me and Tommy goes to the man. We talk where they can't hear us, they talk where we can't hear them.

"What's goin on?" I whisper to Papaw.

"He's tryin to get some money. He thinks that man thar will cash a check for five hunderd dollars. He says he knows him perty good. He'll pay us that, and then give us the rest when we bring him the title. His momma's house is just down the road. He said she'll give him the rest of the money."

I look at him. "What if that man won't take five hundred for his car?"

Papaw just looks at me and smiles. Like he knows something I don't.

Tommy brings us the money, tells us where his mother's house is located and we leave for the house of the man who owns the car we are selling.

The man is still waiting on the porch as we pull into his driveway. When he sees us, he steps down and approaches. "I

didn't know if you fellers was comin back or not. Y'all must like that car perty good."

Papaw gets out, scratches his head, and walks around the car again. "Well, I'll tell ye, it's alright, but that ain't no six hunderd dollar car. I might go four on it, and I'd be doin ye a favor."

"Hmpf!" The man grunts. "I'd let it rust in the junkyard before I'd sell it for four hunderd dollars. That's a six hunderd dollar car if I ever seen one."

"Look at them tars." Papaw says, pointing with his stick. "They all wore out. It'd cost me at least a hunderd dollars just to git new ones on it."

The man laughs. "Well, I ain't payin for new tars. I'll come down half the price of the tars and take five hunderd fifty dollar fer it."

"I'z thinkin more like four hunderd and fifty." Papaw says, coming around the other side of the car.

"I'll eat that car before I'll take that fer it." The man says, and he comes closer, to get the keys from me. I give them to him. He starts walking toward his house. He turns around at the steps. "Five fifty, take it or leave it."

Papaw says, "Four hunderd and fifty dollars cash, and I don't even really need a car. Take it or leave it."

The man takes a step, then stops, and turns. "Five twenty five."

Papaw scratches his head. "I'll go five for it."

The man laughs and starts for the house.

"Lookie here." Papaw says, starting toward him. "I've got five hunderd dollars cash money I'll give you for this car. We'd be gettin rid of it for ye, it ain't doin nothin but sittin around here collecting rust. Five hunderd dollars. That'd be five hunderd dollars more than what you started out with this mornin."

The man laughs. "I ain't givin you my car!"

"Five hunderd dollars is a whole sight better than nothin."

The man thinks about it for a moment. Then shakes his head and starts up the steps.

"Hold on, now." Papaw says, walking closer to him. "I hate to do this, but you seem like a perty good old feller, so I tell you

what I'm gonna do. You see that lawnmower in the back of my grandson's truck?"

The man looks and nods.

"I'll give you five hunderd for the car, and I'll throw that pushmower in to boot. Now, you couldn't hardly beat that with a stick, could ye?"

The man eases down the steps again. He looks closer at the lawnmower. Then he looks closer at papaw. "Let's go have a look at it." He says.

They both go to look at the machine. I hang around the car and watch for the dogs. Especially Jupiter. After a few minutes, the man goes into the house and gets the title to the car. Papaw tells me to unload the lawnmower. The man gives him the title and he pays him the money.

"Say," Papaw says, "You wouldn't care to drive that car up the road to that little store, would ye. We'll follow you and bring you back."

We follow the man in my truck. He drives incredibly slow, even on the straight-aways. We cruise along at thirty miles an hour. A big pick-up truck pulls up behind me. It is a mammoth Chevrolet, suspended up in the air on huge shocks and four-wheeling suspension. It dwarfs my little truck. He is coming up quickly, his loud pipes blaring, and when we approach a series of curves, he gets right up on my bumper. He can't pass me. The lines are solid yellow. He blares on his horn. Papaw throws his hand up to the rear window. "Hidey." He says, happily. The driver of the truck punches the accelerator, and its engine whines louder. He gets closer to my rear bumper and lays on his horn again. Papaw waves. "Wonder who that is?" He asks, looking into the rear view mirror. The horn comes again, longer and louder this time, for the truck is even closer. I don't know how he is keeping from hitting me. Papaw turns around this time, and waves again, trying to see the face of the driver. "That feller must know me from somewhere." He says, turning back around to face the front. We get out of the curves and the solid yellow line turns into segments. The truck comes speeding around us. When it is even with us, I glance up at the passenger side

window and see a hand and a middle finger raised from it. Papaw waves. "See ye later, neighbor." He says. He doesn't know what *the bird* is.

We leave the car at the store. Papaw stays with it, and I take the man back to his house. When I return, Tommy is back, and he and Papaw are finalizing the deal. The title and cash are exchanged, and then the keys. Tommy gets into the car, and it starts right up. It makes a lot of racket, but it starts right up. He pulls out onto the highway. I hear the transmission shift and see a plume of smoke following the car. It rattles and lurches at first, but then it settles into its path and glides down the road. It is not a bad car.

I watch the car disappear from my truck, and then Papaw gets in. He situates himself. Leans his stick against his knee and gets himself out a cigarette. "You ready to go?" He asks.

"I guess." I say, starting the truck. "You got yore money?"

He pats the back of his pants. "Right here in the bank."

"Well," I say, "you better hang on to it. If anybody finds out you've got it, they are liable to knock you in the head and take it from you."

He dances his little jig. Right there in the cab of my truck. It's not quite as flamboyant, but magic, just the same. "I've got my trusty stick here, and a good stout grandson. I reckon I'll be alright."

We drive.

"What about the tractor?" I ask.

"What tractor?"

I leave it at that.

# XII

*And that is how it happened. That is how we started out for Newport* one Saturday morning with ten dollars worth of soda bottles, and returned with three hundred dollars in cash. But this was no new magic for me. This magic had happened many times before. It had happened so many times that the magic seemed almost commonplace. Every ride to Newport had its own separate magic. Every ride to Newport had its own story. And sometimes, when I don't think about them too much, they all converge into one. One trip to Newport that I have been traveling all my life. One magic.

I try to go there sometimes, but the road seems much shorter now. The trip is over too soon, and it is too silent. I try to see the same things, but the things have changed. It is all gone. I am left with images in my mind's eye. Images to sift through and gather and categorize and label, to associate with. The old men, the tractors, the cars, the stories, the laughter. The green hills, the farms, the houses, the way the sky stretched out forever.

And him.

He is gone. He is far away from me, where I never thought he would be. I look for him sometimes, the way I look for the old sign on Hugh Ogle's Barber Shop, the way I look for the old men at the courthouse, the way I look for Clemmie and George. I look for him, but I do not see him. He is off somewhere, maybe, riding to Newport.

# Epilogue

*I reach my hand into my pocket. My fingers fumble for it. It is old. Its* textures ancient. I pull it out. An old, two-bladed Barlow. Its whittled-look brown handles stained with unnamable stains. The tops of the blades corrupted with rust. Dirt is embedded in the grooves and spaces between. I open it. The long blade is worn down in places. It has known wood intimately. It has done its fair share of whittling and screw-driving and prying and cleaning fingernails. It has been used to play "stretch" and sharpened and re-sharpened and traded and sold. It has been carried through wars and fires and weddings and birthdays and hunting and fishing trips. It has led a good, meaningful life. I close it, and place it on the little ledge beneath the names and the dates, and the little dash.

I kneel down beside the bag at my feet. I put my hands inside of it carefully. I pull out ten old soda pop bottles. Their brand names illegible, obscured by dirt and scratches. It had taken me a long while to find them. I had to search far and wide, through many a side road antique shop and old, falling down barns. I had to find the old ones. I had to find ones that had the words: *.10 deposit* on them. I line them up carefully on the little ledge. Then, I laid the old walking stick before it all. The Indians used to bury their dead with the things that they would need on their journey into the next life. Weapons. Tools. Food. Talismans. The Egyptians would bury beloved pets with the dead. The Romans used to bury their generals with their war horses. The Greeks would place coins in their hands to pay the Ferryman of the River Styx. I left an old knife, some bottles and a walking stick. It seemed that was all he needed. His faith, his love, a knife, some bottles and a stick. It seemed enough to me.

What does a man leave behind besides a dash etched in concrete? What remains of his three score and ten years? A personal history. A legacy. Laughter. Love. Wisdom. The saga of a life well-lived. A proverb laid to rest. A history indelibly inscribed in the hearts of those we have loved. Of those we have touched. Our lives bleed over into others and theirs into others. We become part of a greater whole. A universal truth that will live as long as man breathes breath. As long as tales are told around campfires. As long as songs are sung. As long as books are written.

F
LAM
DISCARD

5/9/14
6

| DATE DUE | | |
|---|---|---|
| MAY 28 2014 | | |
| JUN 24 2014 | | |
| JUL 03 2014 | | |
| JUL 17 2014 | | |
| AUG 16 2014 | | |
| SEP 18 2014 | | |
| | | |
| | | |
| | | |
| | | |

CPSIA information can be obtained
at www.ICGtesting.com
Printed in the USA
LVHW011509070822
725376LV00013B/464

9 780826 485618